THE ELECTION OMEN

YOUR VOTE MATTERS

END TIMES ARMOR SERIES

D1502908

THE ELECTION OMEN
YOUR VOTE MATTERS

Published by Drezhn Publishing LLC
PO BOX 67458
Albuquerque, NM 87193-7458

Cover Design by MIBL ART
www.miblart.com

Print Edition - June 2020
Second Edition

ISBN 978-1-947328-40-2

TABLE OF CONTENTS

YOUR VOTE MATTERS

THE ELECTION OMEN

END TIMES ARMOR SERIES

MARSHA KUHNLEY

INTRODUCTION

DEAR READER

I'm excited that you're here. In this book, you're going to see that God has told us a great deal about the future. It's called Bible prophecy. You're going to learn what God has prophesied in regard to governments, leaders, and cultural issues during the last days. This is fate. There are things God has determined will happen at their appointed times. However, there's more to it than that. Your specific choices will have a direct impact on the fate of nations. Yes, you have free will. You may think fate and free will are opposing forces. Yet they are not. For *The Election Omen*, you're going to see that God's fate and your free will actually work together in perfect harmony. It's quite fascinating. Through this journey you're about to embark on, I'm hoping you'll discover how truly important your choices are and that you'll choose to put on your armor and join the fight.

We are in the last days. Those of you who are spiritually attuned to what's happening today are well aware that we are indeed living in the very last of the last days. In this book, you're going to see how Bible prophecy about these days that we're living in is unfolding right before our eyes. I know the thought of the end times can be scary. If you've put your salvation and faith in the nail-pierced hands of Jesus Christ, then you have nothing to worry about. As a believer, you are saved. If you're not confident that you're saved or you don't really know who Jesus is or what he did to save you, then I encourage you to read How To Be Saved in the Appendix.

Let the journey begin!

END TIMES ARMOR

We are in a war. This isn't an ordinary war with typical weapons where land and resources are at stake. No, this is a spiritual war involving demonic rulers. What's at stake is the most precious thing of all: your soul.

The apostle Paul tells us about this war in Ephesians chapter 6:

> Finally, be strong in the Lord and in the strength of his might. Put on the whole armor of God, that you may be able to stand against the wiles of the devil. For our wrestling is not against flesh and blood, but against the principalities, against the powers, against the world's rulers of the darkness of this age, and against the spiritual forces of wickedness in the heavenly places. Therefore put on the whole armor of God, that you may be able to withstand in the evil day, and having done all, to stand. Stand therefore, having the utility belt of truth buckled around your waist, and having put on the breastplate of righteousness, and having fitted your feet with the preparation of the Good News of peace, above all, taking up the shield of faith, with which you will be able to quench all the fiery darts of the evil one. And take the helmet of salvation, and the sword of the Spirit, which is the word of God; with all prayer and requests, praying at all times in the Spirit, and being watchful to this end in all perseverance and requests for all the saints. (Ephesians 6:10-18)

Paul tells us who we are and aren't fighting in this war. We aren't fighting "flesh and blood" means it's not a war against people, since people are made of flesh and blood. This means your unbelieving neighbor who disagrees with you on the key issues today isn't your enemy. This is a war against the wiles or strategies of "the devil." Satan is the devil. That's right. Satan is very real and he's your enemy. You're going to learn more about him in Chapter 8. You need to know that he's the general of the "principalities," "powers," "rulers of the darkness", and the "spiritual forces of wickedness." Please remember that your fellow humans aren't the enemy. We are living in spiritually dark times where many people are imprisoned by Satan and his lies. Your goal should be to rescue them, not attack them.

Since our enemy is spiritual, we must use spiritual means to both protect and defend ourselves. This is our End Times Armor. This armor isn't ordinary armor of leather or chain mail. It's the "armor of God." Let's look at the elements in this armor. The "belt of truth" is God's Word. You need to know your Bible. Have it stored in your heart and close to you, ready to use it like a tool you'd pull out of a utility belt. The "breastplate of righteousness" is you placing your faith in Jesus. He's the one who makes you righteous. Having "fitted your feet" with the gospel means you're able to demonstrate your faith in both words and actions. The "shield of faith" is you knowing and calling on all the promises of God when Satan's attack comes against you. Do not be afraid. Have hope. Your "helmet of salvation" is being fully confident that you have been saved through your faith in Jesus. You are sealed with the Holy Spirit.

I want you to notice that God gave you a weapon as well. He expects you to use it. The "sword of the Spirit" is your weapon. It's the Word of God. When Satan came against Jesus to tempt him in the wilderness, Jesus combated Satan's lies with Scripture (Matthew 4; Luke 4). There is power in the Word of God. Use it.

> For the word of God is living and active, and sharper than any two-edged sword, piercing even to the dividing of soul and spirit, of both joints and marrow, and is able to discern the thoughts and intentions of the heart. (Hebrews 4:12)

After we've put on our armor, Paul tells us we need to pray at all times. We need to be close to God in order to draw strength from him. We get close to God by talking to God and reading his Word.

The last thought I want to leave with you is the expectation God has put on us to take action. There's a purpose for wearing armor. It's to protect us in the battle. That means we're supposed to be engaged in the battle. Look at how many times God used the word or variation of the word *stand* in the first Scripture. I counted four times. It doesn't say put on God's armor and sit and watch what happens. No, it says stand! This means rise up, hold your ground, hold your position, endure, and display courage and strength.

We're living in one of the most exciting times in all of history. Put on your armor and stand with me in this battle!

PART 1

FREE WILL:
IT'S A PRIVILEGE TO VOTE

CHAPTER 1 - YOUR VOTE MATTERS

Those of us living in the United States of America are truly blessed people. God has put us in a land in which we get to actively participate in how we're governed. We have the right to vote. Unfortunately, many people choose not to. In the 2016 presidential election only 70% of US voting-age citizens were registered to vote.[1] Of those people registered only 87% ended up actually voting. To put this into perspective, that's almost 20 million people who were registered and didn't vote.[2] It's almost 70 million citizens who weren't even registered.[3] That's 90 million lost votes!

There are several reasons why people don't vote. It takes effort to register, understand the issues, learn where each candidate stands, and then cast your vote. Some people just don't want to commit the time and energy it takes. Others don't participate because they think their single vote doesn't matter among a sea of other voters. Then there are those who don't want to vote because they don't like what politics has become. They say it's too much mudslinging and all the candidates are just the same, so it doesn't matter anyway. Let's not forget about another group of nonvoters. This is the group who thinks it's sinful to vote. There's something all of these people have in common and it's an ominous sign of the last days.

"To the angel of the assembly in Laodicea write: The Amen, the Faithful and True Witness, the Beginning of God's creation, says these things: I know your works, that you are neither cold nor hot. I wish you were cold or hot. So, because you are lukewarm, and neither hot nor cold, I will vomit you out of my mouth. Because you say, 'I am rich, and have gotten riches, and have need of nothing,' and don't know that you are the wretched one, miserable, poor, blind, and naked; I counsel you to buy from me gold refined by fire, that you may become rich; and white garments, that you may clothe yourself, and that the shame of your nakedness may not be revealed; and eye salve to anoint your eyes, that you may see. As many as I love, I reprove and chasten. Be zealous therefore, and repent." (Revelation 3:14-19)

Indifference. Apathy. It's the sin of the Laodicean church. They were called out for being lukewarm.

There are seven letters to seven different churches in Revelation. The churches represent different periods of time throughout the church age. The church age is the period of time since Jesus was crucified up until the rapture.

The rapture is when God removes everyone who has put their faith in Jesus from earth. Believers will be safely in heaven with Jesus during the coming tribulation period. You can read my book *Rapture 911: What To Do If You're Left Behind* to learn all about it.

The Laodicean letter is the last of the letters to the churches. So, it marks the last period of time in the church age. Do you know what event comes next in Revelation? It's the rapture. The period of time right before the rapture and subsequent tribulation period is marked by a time of spiritual indifference. A time when people just don't care, couldn't be bothered, and aren't convicted of sin. It's a time when Christians don't realize how late we are in the last days. A time when people scoff at Jesus coming because it doesn't matter to them if he does or doesn't. This is a time when people have quit fighting God's battles. They're sitting on the sidelines living it up. Christians aren't trying to win souls anymore. They're just indifferent about it. That's exactly where we find ourselves today, isn't it?

So, what's the cure? The letter ends by telling us to "be zealous." It means have intense feeling, passion, and enthusiasm. It's the opposite of being lukewarm and indifferent. Here are two people in the Bible who were described as zealous: Elijah and the apostle Paul.

> Elijah replied, "I have zealously served the LORD God Almighty." (1 Kings 19:10 NLT)

> He said, "I am indeed a Jew, born in Tarsus of Cilicia, but brought up in this city at the feet of Gamaliel, instructed according to the strict tradition of the law of our fathers, being zealous for God, even as you all are today." (Acts 22:3)

That's who we're supposed to be role modeling in the last days. Elijah and Paul were both on fire for the Lord! We should be too. The spiritual battle is still raging, and we're called to fight. Remember that's why we're equipped with the armor of God and our sword of the

Spirit. One of the ways you can join the fight is by voting. I know that may seem really boring to some of you, but it's of the utmost importance and you're going to learn why you should vote and why your specific vote matters as you continue this chapter. I'm also going to counter the demonic belief that says it's sinful to vote.

Let's start by understanding what it means to vote and what the Bible says about it. The word *vote* means we get to express our opinion by choosing. We get to vote for presidents, judges, school officials, proposals, laws, and taxes to name a few things. We get to choose, elect, support, or endorse whoever or whatever is on the ballot. Some Christians say we shouldn't vote because it's not mentioned in the Bible, that the disciples didn't vote, and that Jesus didn't vote. Well, the word *vote* is actually in the Bible. I found it in the WEBP and NLT, Acts 26:10.

> I also did this in Jerusalem. I both shut up many of the saints in prisons, having received authority from the chief priests; and when they were put to death I gave my vote against them. (Acts 26:10)

Here, we see the apostle Paul voted in favor of killing Jesus's followers. This was of course before he himself became a believer. In this instance he wasn't voting in an election for an official. Instead, he was deciding someone's fate. That's because the word *vote* is about deciding and choosing. There are in fact several examples in the Bible of people choosing leaders. Let's look at some.

> The men of Judah came, and there they anointed David king over the house of Judah. ... David sent messengers to the men of Jabesh Gilead, and said to them.... "Now therefore let your hands be strong, and be valiant; for Saul your lord is dead, and also the house of Judah have anointed me king over them." (2 Samuel 2:4-5, 7)

In the Scripture above, we see the men of Judah selected David to be their king. Some time passes and, in the Scripture below, we read that all the elders of the tribes of Israel selected David to be king over all of Israel.

> Then all Israel gathered themselves to David to Hebron, saying, "Behold,

we are your bone and your flesh. In times past, even when Saul was king, it was you who led out and brought in Israel. Yahweh your God said to you, 'You shall be shepherd of my people Israel, and you shall be prince over my people Israel.'" So all the elders of Israel came to the king to Hebron; and David made a covenant with them in Hebron before Yahweh. They anointed David king over Israel, according to Yahweh's word by Samuel. (1 Chronicles 11:1-3)

I know what some of you are thinking. I thought God picked David to be king, not the people. Didn't the prophet Samuel anoint him as king when King Saul was still reigning? Yes, you're right (1 Samuel 16). God did choose David to be the next leader. Yet, we also know that God lets people have free will. God choosing David was a prophetic act. God knew the people would choose David. God just confirmed their choice of leader in advance.

Let's look at some leaders after David. David's son Absalom was king for a time when the people thought he'd do better than David and they made him king instead. Notice it says of Absalom, "whom we anointed over us." The people picked him.

"Absalom, whom we anointed over us, is dead in battle. Now therefore why don't you speak a word of bringing the king back?" ... He bowed the heart of all the men of Judah, even as one man, so that they sent to the king, saying, "Return, you and all your servants." (2 Samuel 19:10, 14)

Well that didn't last very long. Absalom died in battle and guess what? The people chose David as their leader again. God let the people keep choosing leaders. How about after David's son Solomon's reign?

When all Israel heard that Jeroboam had returned, they sent and called him to the congregation, and made him king over all Israel. There was no one who followed David's house, except for the tribe of Judah only. (1 Kings 12:20)

After Solomon's death, the nation of Israel split. Solomon's son Rehoboam reigned in Judah, while Jeroboam was chosen by the people to lead the rest of Israel. We've just looked at several examples where God clearly let the people choose their leader. There are many examples of this in the Old Testament. In the New Testament there isn't because the people were under the rule of Roman emperors. They didn't get a say in their government during that time period. Just because the apostles lived under different circumstances than you and didn't vote for leaders doesn't mean the act of voting or making a choice is sinful and not permitted by God. It's what you choose or vote for that can be sinful. I know the New Testament authors would have jumped at the chance to vote for leaders. Think of all the times the people tried to force Jesus to be king. Their attempts failed because it wasn't Jesus's time to reign. It wasn't God's will for that time. Jesus had to die for all of us sinners before he could become the physical king on earth.

Does that mean the people who wanted Jesus to be king were being sinful because they were going against God's will? No. Remember when Jesus was riding into Jerusalem on the donkey and the people were cheering?

"Blessed is the King who comes in the name of the Lord!" (Luke 19:38).

The Pharisees tried to get Jesus to rebuke them. Jesus refused and said the rocks would burst out cheering if the people were quiet. You see, God said we should pray for God's will to be done on earth as it is in heaven (Matthew 6:10). We know that Jesus is King of kings. It's not wrong to desire his rulership here. **Your vote matters because it brings Jesus glory.**

Now, I know that some of you still don't see the point in voting because you think you might choose poorly and then actually go against the will of God. So, you've decided you'll just stay out of it. This attitude reminds me of a parable that Jesus spoke. Keep in mind that parables are stories that illustrate how things work in God's kingdom, heaven. Let's see what it says.

Watch therefore, for you don't know the day nor the hour in which the Son of Man is coming. "For it is like a man going into another country, who called his own servants and entrusted his goods to them. To one he gave five talents, to another two, to another one, to each according to his own ability. Then he went on his journey. Immediately he who received the five talents went and traded with them, and made another five talents.

In the same way, he also who got the two gained another two. But he who received the one talent went away and dug in the earth and hid his lord's money. Now after a long time the lord of those servants came, and settled accounts with them. He who received the five talents came and brought another five talents, saying, 'Lord, you delivered to me five talents. Behold, I have gained another five talents in addition to them.' His lord said to him, 'Well done, good and faithful servant. You have been faithful over a few things, I will set you over many things. Enter into the joy of your lord. He also who got the two talents came and said, 'Lord, you delivered to me two talents. Behold, I have gained another two talents in addition to them.' His lord said to him, 'Well done, good and faithful servant. You have been faithful over a few things. I will set you over many things. Enter into the joy of your lord.' He also who had received the one talent came and said, 'Lord, I knew you that you are a hard man, reaping where you didn't sow, and gathering where you didn't scatter. I was afraid, and went away and hid your talent in the earth. Behold, you have what is yours. But his lord answered him, 'You wicked and slothful servant. You knew that I reap where I didn't sow, and gather where I didn't scatter. You ought therefore to have deposited my money with the bankers, and at my coming I should have received back my own with interest. Take away therefore the talent from him and give it to him who has the ten talents. For to everyone who has will be given, and he will have abundance, but from him who doesn't have, even that which he has will be taken away. Throw out the unprofitable servant into the outer darkness, where there will be weeping and gnashing of teeth.'" (Matthew 25:13-30)

Jesus told this story right after he told his followers to be paying attention for his next coming. So, it's especially pertinent today when we know Jesus is coming any minute to rapture his believers. This parable is illustrating some important truths regarding our relationship with Jesus. Jesus is our Lord, he's gone away to heaven, "another country," and he's entrusted his believers, "his own servants," with his goods here on earth. When we see Jesus face to face, he's going to hold us accountable for what we did with the goods he gave us.

Did you read what the last servant did with his lord's money? He buried it because he was afraid to do anything with it. You do not want to be like that wicked lazy servant. The treasure his lord gave him was taken from him and given to another. Then he was cast out. God has given you free will and the gift of voting. He expects you to use what he's given you to bring glory to him. We're all storing up treasure in heaven based on the decisions and actions we take here on earth. Don't lose your treasure. If you're a believer, you are filled with Jesus's Holy Spirit. Don't be afraid to make a decision. He will help you make the right choice. I understand that it's hard to make a choice, especially when it seems like none of the candidates are good, but we're still expected to make one. In subsequent chapters in this book you're going to learn how to vote and pick leaders based on clear direction God gives us in the Bible. Don't be apathetic anymore. **Your vote matters because it impacts your future heavenly treasure.**

Another reason some people have against voting is that it's a worldly system and believers are supposed to be separate from the world. Here's what the Scripture says (Jesus is the one speaking):

> I pray not that you would take them from the world, but that you would keep them from the evil one. They are not of the world, even as I am not of the world. Sanctify them in your truth. Your word is truth. As you sent me into the world, even so I have sent them into the world. (John 17:15-18)

We learn that we are indeed not of this world. That's because believers are of heaven. However, we're not removed from the world. He didn't tell his followers to go home and wait for him to come again and not participate in anything. In fact, Jesus did the opposite and sent them into the world. He's sent all of us believers into the world. He prayed that we would be kept from Satan, "the evil one." We do that by knowing God's Word, which is the truth. Yes, we're supposed to be separate from the world, but at the same time still live in the world. People should be able to tell that you're a follower of Jesus by how you live, talk, and by the things you do and don't do. Here's how Jesus describes it:

> You are the salt of the earth, but if the salt has lost its flavor, with what will it be salted? It is then good for nothing, but to be cast out and trodden under the feet of men. You are the light of the world. A city located on a hill can't be hidden. Neither do you light a lamp and put it under a measuring basket, but on a stand; and it shines to all who are in the house.

> Even so, let your light shine before men, that they may see your good
> works and glorify your Father who is in heaven. (Matthew 5:13-16)

We're supposed to be like salt and like a lamp shining in the dark.
If you choose to shut yourself in and not try to make a difference, it's
like putting a basket over the light that Jesus has filled you with. **Your
vote matters because it shines a light on the darkness.**

Some people go a bit further with the world system and say that
Satan is in control down here on earth. So, they reason that Satan is
controlling all the voting since it's his system. Thus, we shouldn't
participate. I'm going to be honest; this is one hot mess of bad
reasoning and poor interpretation of Scripture. Let's break it down so
you can see for yourself. Recall that Jesus was tempted by Satan in the
wilderness (Matthew 4:8-10). Satan offered Jesus all the kingdoms of
the world if Jesus would worship him. Jesus didn't fall for the
temptation. He rebuked Satan instead and told him to only worship
God. They reason that Satan could only offer Jesus all the kingdoms
because he's the god down here and the one who's really in charge.

> Satan, who is the god of this world, has blinded the minds of those who
> don't believe. (2 Corinthians 4:4 NLT)

When God created Adam and Eve, he gave them dominion over the
earth. When they sinned, they forfeited it to Satan. So, yes, Satan is the
"god of this world." Notice that god is spelled with a little g. That's of
utmost importance. Satan is still accountable to God, with a capital G.
Satan has to get permission from God. See for yourself:

> Now on the day when God's sons came to present themselves before
> Yahweh, Satan also came among them. Yahweh said to Satan, "Where have
> you come from?" Then Satan answered Yahweh, and said, "From going
> back and forth in the earth, and from walking up and down in it." Yahweh
> said to Satan, "Have you considered my servant, Job? For there is no one
> like him in the earth, a blameless and an upright man, one who fears God,
> and turns away from evil." Then Satan answered Yahweh, and said, "Does
> Job fear God for nothing? Haven't you made a hedge around him, and
> around his house, and around all that he has, on every side? You have
> blessed the work of his hands, and his substance is increased in the land.

> But stretch out your hand now, and touch all that he has, and he will renounce you to your face." Yahweh said to Satan, "Behold, all that he has is in your power. Only on himself don't stretch out your hand." (Job 1:6-12)

Satan only has the power to do what God allows him to do. God is the one in control of his entire creation, including Satan. So why did Satan tell Jesus he could give him all the kingdoms if he's not really the one in charge? God gave Satan the authority and allowed him to tempt Jesus with this. Satan wanted Jesus to bypass the cross. Satan hates you and didn't want Jesus to save you. Since Jesus was tempted with rulership, that means Jesus must have wanted to take all the kingdoms. Of course he did! In fact, it's the sole reason he left heaven and came to earth. To redeem all of us sinners. Yet he didn't. It's because Jesus couldn't redeem mankind and all the kingdoms until he died for us first. If Jesus had yielded to that temptation, we would all be dead in sin still. While we have to contend with Satan's influence on the world, Satan is only the god of people who don't believe.

> Let every soul be in subjection to the higher authorities, for there is no authority except from God, and those who exist are ordained by God. Therefore he who resists the authority withstands the ordinance of God; and those who withstand will receive to themselves judgment. ... Therefore give everyone what you owe: if you owe taxes, pay taxes; if customs, then customs; if respect, then respect; if honor, then honor. (Romans 13:1-2, 7)

The apostle Paul explains to us in the Scripture above that God is the one in control of leaders and governments. It also says we should give what we owe. And what do you owe your government? Your vote. Your participation. We live in a country in which our government needs citizens to participate in selecting leaders. If none of the Christians voted think of what would happen.

This is what's at the heart of the demonic lies telling you not to vote. If none of the Christians voted, who would rise to power? The Bible gives us the answer. It's the Antichrist! The Antichrist rises to power after the rapture (Revelation 13). Right after all the believers have been removed from the earth. Satan doesn't want you to vote because he indwells the Antichrist. He wants to usher in hell on earth so that he can be worshiped. Satan is the one behind the Laodicean church and this attitude of indifference today. He knows your vote is valuable and that's why he doesn't want you to use it. There's still time to push back against evil and help people come to know Jesus. **Your vote matters because it's one of your weapons in the war against Satan.**

Let's continue examining reasons why Christians don't vote. Some claim we shouldn't vote because we're not supposed to sow discord (Proverbs 6:19) or cause divisions (Romans 16:17) and they say voting does exactly that. Well, those Scriptures are speaking of people who have an evil intent to cause strife and division among fellow believers by spreading lies. These are people who teach things that are contrary to God's Word for their own personal gain. Those Scriptures aren't about how voting causes division. God's Word is sharper than a two-edged sword and it pierces the soul (Hebrews 4:12). Yet, God commands us to preach the gospel knowing it's going to produce hatred toward us (John 15:18-20). People are going to disagree with you because of your faith in Jesus. That's not the same thing as causing strife among Christians.

Another reason some people don't vote is because they don't want to help someone be exalted. After all Jesus did say people who "exalt themselves will be humbled" (Luke 14:11). It's not a sin to desire a leadership role. The apostle Paul reveals to us in the Scripture below that governments is a gift.

> God has set some in the assembly: first apostles, second prophets, third teachers, then miracle workers, then gifts of healings, helps, governments, and various kinds of languages. (1 Corinthians 12:28)

Other Bible translations use the words *administration* and *leadership*. It's the act of governing or leading. That's a gift from God. God doesn't give people gifts that are sinful. In another Scripture, Paul tells us that desiring to be an elder in the church is a good thing (1 Timothy 3:1). So, desiring a leadership role in government isn't a bad thing. This requires a better understanding of the word *exalt*. It's about the heart and intent of the person. It's someone who wants the glory. The sin is pride. Someone who wants to be a leader so they can be on TV and get praise from mankind is being prideful. Remember this was Satan's first sin. He wanted to exalt himself above God because he wanted to be worshiped (Isaiah 14). We're supposed to be humble, be a servant, and seek to bring glory to Jesus. This is one of the things you must consider when choosing a candidate. Who is the person really going to serve—you or themselves?

Now, let's discuss believers who don't vote because they believe the battle isn't ours to fight. They say we're ambassadors of heaven (2 Corinthians 5:20) and ambassadors don't involve themselves in foreign battles. It's true, that people who have put their faith in Jesus are indeed ambassadors of heaven. But you have dual citizenship. You're a citizen of earth and a citizen of heaven. When you became a believer, you didn't lose your earthly citizenship. God gave Adam and Eve dominion over the earth after he created them. Your future eternal home is earth. After the millennial period when Jesus reigns on earth for 1,000 years, God is going to make a new earth for the believers to live on (Revelation 20:7-21:1).

> Let your Kingdom come. Let your will be done on earth as it is in heaven.
> (Matthew 6:10)

When Jesus taught the disciples how to pray, he told them to pray that God's will would be done on earth just like it is in heaven. That means your heavenly citizenship trumps your earthly citizenship. That you should be actively using your earthly citizenship to bring the values and culture of heaven to earth. When you make choices here on earth you're acting as a representative of heaven. So, make choices that God would agree with.

The other reason some say the battle isn't ours to fight is because the angels are fighting the spiritual battle for us. There are several instances in the Bible where we indeed see angels fighting battles. We learn in Revelation 12 that there was a war in heaven amongst the angels and that Satan and his army of angels were thrown down to earth. When an angel came to Daniel to answer his prayer and tell him about the end times (Daniel 10), he told Daniel he was held up by another angel and that Michael came to help him. We also know an angel protected Daniel in the lion's den (Daniel 6). That an angel protected Shadrach, Meshach, and Abednego when they were thrown into Nebuchadnezzar's furnace (Daniel 3). You may also remember an impressive display of angelic intervention with Elisha at Dotham (2

Kings 6). That's when Elisha's servant was worried because they were surrounded by the Aramean army. Elisha asked God to let his servant see what he saw. That's when the servant saw the area filled with God's holy angels with chariots of fire. Let's not forget the New Testament. Both Paul and Peter had angelic encounters. Peter was rescued from prison (Acts 12) and Paul was saved in a shipwreck (Acts 27), both by angels.

Did you notice what each of the examples involving people have in common? The angels helped the people in the midst of the battle. They didn't push the person aside and fight the battle for them.

> Are they not all ministering spirits sent forth to minister for those who will inherit salvation? (Hebrews 1:14 NKJV)

That's because angels are ministering spirits and they minister to us. *Minister* means to give aid. We're the ones who inherit salvation and will rule and reign with Jesus in the future. They are here to help us, not do the job for us. In fact, Jesus solidified this fact on the night of his arrest in the garden of Gethsemane.

> Behold, one of those who were with Jesus stretched out his hand and drew his sword, and struck the servant of the high priest, and cut off his ear. Then Jesus said to him, "Put your sword back into its place, for all those who take the sword will die by the sword. Or do you think that I couldn't ask my Father, and he would even now send me more than twelve legions of angels? How then would the Scriptures be fulfilled that it must be so?" (Matthew 26:51-54)

Jesus could have asked God to send angels to fight the battle for him. But he didn't because prophecy must be fulfilled. It's the same for us. The angels can't fight the battles for us because we're each playing a part in how the Scriptures unfold. Fast forward to how Satan's story ends:

> I saw an angel coming down out of heaven, having the key of the abyss and a great chain in his hand. He seized the dragon, the old serpent, who is the devil and Satan, who deceives the whole inhabited earth, and bound him for a thousand years. (Revelation 20:1-2)

It only takes one angel to lock Satan up for 1,000 years. That's right, just one. If God let the angels fight the battle, the war would already be over. It would have been over long ago. It's still raging because God had a plan to create you. He wanted you to come to know Jesus so you could live with him in heaven forever. He created you and gave you a voice because he wants to hear it. **Your vote matters because what you say and do matters to God.**

Let's consider another reason some Christians don't vote. They say Jesus didn't participate in politics, government, or vote during his first coming so they shouldn't either. For someone they claim didn't participate in such things he certainly stirred up a lot of emotions and created division. The rulers wanted him dead because of it. Consider Jesus's encounter with the money changers at the temple (John 2; Mark 11). He turned over their tables and made a whip to drive them out of the temple. The religious leaders challenged his authority to do this but were afraid of him. So, they plotted to kill him. Can you imagine if someone did that today? Jesus took an active role in fighting wickedness and corruption. He wanted to make his home a better place. He was setting an example for us. Throughout Jesus's ministry he spoke publicly against the religious leaders and their laws that burdened the people. Just read any of the gospel books (Matthew, Mark, Luke, John) to see for yourself.

One day the religious leaders asked Jesus if they should pay taxes to Caesar. Jesus didn't ignore them. He rebuked them and then told them what to do: "Give therefore to Caesar the things that are Caesar's, and to God the things that are God's" (Matthew 22:20). If Jesus didn't care about politics and government, he wouldn't have answered them.

Here's another thing I want you to think about regarding Jesus. We know that God is in control and puts all leaders in their position (Romans 13:1). We also know that Jesus is God in the flesh (Colossians 2:9). So that means Jesus put all of the leaders in their position during his first coming. Jesus put Caesar in power. Jesus put Herod and Pilate in power. Jesus put all the religious leaders, including the chief priest, in authority. Jesus also picked every single one of his disciples. When Jesus picks people, he's voting. He's choosing them. He orchestrated everything exactly the way it needed to be during his first coming. Jesus is most certainly involved in politics. After all he's the King of kings (1 Timothy 6:15). **Your vote matters because politics is**

important to Jesus.

There are two people in the Bible who stand out as examples for how we should be living in these last days. They are examples of how we should live in this sinful world and participate in it yet remain separate and usable by God. They are Daniel and King David. Let's look at Daniel first. He was taken captive from Jerusalem and became a servant of King Nebuchadnezzar and the rulers who followed him in Babylon: King Belshazzar, King Darius, and King Cyrus. God put Daniel in the service of the kings. Did Daniel keep quiet, do everything the kings said, and stay out of government affairs? No, he certainly didn't. God gave Daniel the ability to interpret dreams. So, he spoke to the kings and conveyed God's messages to them. He was so trusted that the kings consulted him in matters requiring wisdom and he was promoted to a position of high power. Daniel used his position to influence the kings. We should do the same. We should use what we can to influence our government. Voting is one of the tools of influence.

Everyone in the government knew Daniel worshiped God. When his jealous coworkers convinced King Darius to force everyone to worship the king, what did Daniel do? He refused and continued to worship God publicly for all to see. You know, Daniel didn't have to do that publicly. He could have worshiped in secret and perhaps no one would have noticed. But he didn't do that. You see, that's the example for us. God forcibly put Daniel into a government role, but he didn't force Daniel to be courageous and stand against evil. We're not supposed to cower away, not participate, or act like a Laodicean. So, Daniel got thrown into a lion's den. And you might too for standing up for something. But God sent an angel to help him in the midst of that battle and shut the lion's mouth. Do you know what happened as a result of Daniel's courage? King Darius realized God was the true God because he protected Daniel. He commanded everyone to worship God. Just think of how many people might come to know God and be saved because you had the courage to participate in this spiritual battle we're in. **Your vote matters because souls are at stake.**

I think King David is the best example for living in the end times. There are some parallels between David and us believers. You see, David was anointed king by the prophet Samuel years before he actually became the king (1 Samuel 16:12-13). We talked about this earlier. It was a prophetic act by God. If you think about it, the same thing applies to us. As soon as we put our faith in Jesus, the Holy Spirit fills us up and we're guaranteed all of God's promises for believers (Ephesians 1:14). One of those promises is that we're heirs with Jesus (Romans 8:17, Revelation 20:4). You are going to be a ruler in Jesus's future government on earth. Just like King David, you've been anointed before you can start your reign as well.

This means we should look at King David in the time between his anointing and when he actually became king and see what he did. This will help us see what we should be doing while we wait for Jesus to come. So, what did David do? He served the king. It was King Saul. He started out as his musician and played the harp to comfort him. Then he rose through the ranks when King Saul discovered he was a warrior. After he slew Goliath, he became a leader in King Saul's army. Here's what King Saul had to say of David:

> For Yahweh will certainly make my lord a sure house, because my lord fights Yahweh's battles. Evil will not be found in you all your days. Though men may rise up to pursue you and to seek your soul, yet the soul of my lord will be bound in the bundle of life with Yahweh your God. He will sling out the souls of your enemies as from a sling's pocket. (1 Samuel 25:28-29)

David fought God's battles. In fact, it's when David wasn't fighting God's battles that David got into trouble. You see, it was war time, and David was supposed to be out fighting, but he chose to sit around at home instead. That's when he sinned with Bathsheba (2 Samuel 11). It's the same for us. If we're being lazy and not fighting God's battles, that's when temptation will come knocking. Engaging in God's fight keeps us focused and busy. There's no room for sinful behavior to enter.

The apostle Paul reiterated this truth for us in his letters to Timothy:

> I commit this instruction to you, my child Timothy, according to the prophecies which were given to you before, that by them you may wage the good warfare. (1 Timothy 1:18)

> You therefore must endure hardship as a good soldier of Christ Jesus. No soldier on duty entangles himself in the affairs of life, that he may please

him who enrolled him as a soldier. (2 Timothy 2:3-4)

He encouraged Timothy to "wage the good warfare" and be a "good soldier of Christ Jesus." That's what I'm encouraging you to do today as well. Decide today who you are going to serve - Jesus or Satan.

He who is not with me is against me. (Matthew 12:30)

Jesus spoke those words himself. You see, there isn't any neutral territory with God. If you're acting like a spectator instead of a soldier, then you're working against Jesus. Shake off the sin of the Laodicean church and rise up, put on your armor of God, and get your sword of God's Spirit ready. In these last days before Jesus returns to rapture the believers and before his second coming, we must take a stand against evil. In the Bible, God's warriors conquered evil rulers on the battlefield. Today, we're blessed with the ability to conquer evil rulers with our vote. **Your vote matters because you stand with Jesus.**

CHAPTER 2 – SATAN WANTS TO STEAL YOUR VOTE

Even though we have the right to vote, there's a lot of people who don't. It reminds me of a parable Jesus told about a farmer scattering seeds (Matthew 13). Recall that some of the farmer's seeds fell on a path and the birds came by and ate them. Jesus said this was like Satan stealing God's Word so it couldn't be planted. This establishes that Satan is a thief. Satan has a goal to steal anything from you that he can in order to prevent you from bringing glory to God. One of those things he's often successful at stealing is your voice. Your vote is your voice. He knows it, so he's after it. I'm going to show you how he's stealing it.

Only 53% of the citizen voting-age population voted in the November 2018 midterm elections.[1] Over the last 40 years that percentage has trended relatively flat, in the upper 40s. During presidential elections, as you might expect, more people turn out. In the 2016 election 61% of the citizen voting-age population voted.[2] Yet, that still means during important national elections 40-50% of eligible voters aren't voting. According to a Pew Research Center survey, 25% of respondents who didn't vote in 2016 didn't vote because they didn't like the candidates or the issues and 15% didn't believe their vote made a difference.[3] There you have it. We're living in a culture of apathy. If those people had shown up to vote, the voter turnout in 2016 could have been 77% instead of 61%.[4] That's a big difference.

Here's something your enemy, Satan, doesn't want you to know. Christians who have put their faith in Jesus Christ, made a huge impact in the 2016 national election. The Barna Group research company classifies voters based on their faith affiliation. Believers (evangelical and non-evangelical) accounted for 30% of voters in the 2016 election, agnostic/atheist (skeptics) were 21%, other faiths 5%, and the biggest percentage went to what they call Notional Christians at 43% of voters. A Notional Christian is someone who says they're a Christian but hasn't accepted Jesus as their savior.

This data reveals an opportunity. Notional Christians. I see this as a group of people on the fence with their faith since they identify as a Christian but haven't committed yet. Their vote was essentially split in

2016 between Trump (49%) and Clinton (47%).[5] Perhaps that's you. I want to encourage you to get to know God and Jesus better. Find a good Bible believing and preaching church in your area and start attending regularly. The best way to know how to vote is to be filled with the Holy Spirit. He guides us and teaches us all things. Perhaps this is how you would describe a friend or family member of yours. I encourage you to invite them to your church. Get them a copy of this book so that they can better understand the spiritual war we're in and how important their voice is in this war.

George Barna from Barna Group research had this to say about the 2016 election:[6]

> "Voters who considered themselves to be Christian were more likely to vote for Trump than Clinton. Those who were not associated with the Christian faith were overwhelmingly behind Clinton. Each of the three Christian segments – evangelicals, non-evangelical born agains, and notional Christians – went with Trump. Both of the non-Christian segments – those associated with other faiths as well as the skeptics – were in Clinton's camp.
>
> "There has been no discussion about the fact that the skeptic vote really kept Hillary Clinton in the race. The 33-point margin she retained with that one-fifth slice of the voting population was her primary faith base. The size of the skeptic population continues to grow while the born again community continues to shrink. That is a trend that will be a major challenge for conservative and Republican candidates in the future."

In the 2016 election, only 61% of voters actually voted. That's the same percentage of believers who turned out as well.[7] So almost 40% chose not to vote and instead let someone else's opinion represent them. You just read above that the population of atheists and agnostics is growing. That's who represents you when you choose not to vote. This is how Satan is playing the thief. When Christians don't show up at the polls, atheists are there to fill the gap. Those are people who don't even believe that God exists. **Don't let Satan steal your vote!** Just think of the difference believers could make if everyone joined the battle.

We are in the midst of a spiritual war. It's important to understand what people who don't believe in God or Jesus are supporting. It's a key indicator that Satan is likely a supporter of it himself. Because remember, you're either for Jesus or against him. As you read above, the non-Christian segments voted for Clinton in 2016. It was an overwhelming majority of them, 71% of people with other faiths and 60% of agnostic/atheists.[8] They aligned with the Democratic Party. This is important because people who haven't placed their faith in Jesus are clearly drawn to the things the Democratic Party is promoting, promising, and actively working to achieve. We must understand what those things are. As believers, Jesus calls us to shine a light on and expose the darkness. Before you can shine your light, you must choose to participate and not hide your light.

In the subsequent chapters, we're going to explore the key issues of today and get an understanding of both sides: those who support it and those who are against it. We're going to identify the darkness and shine a light on it. Then we're going to evaluate each issue with a biblical prophetic lens and see what the Election Omen foretells. Get ready to use your voice and vote!

CHAPTER 3 - CELEBRATE YOUR RIGHT

We're celebrating some huge milestones regarding the right to vote this year—2020. Did you know that the right to vote and details on who was eligible to vote wasn't included in the constitution when the US was founded? The founding fathers left it up to the states to decide who could vote. As you could imagine only the privileged were allowed to vote. The states determined men who owned land could vote, except for New Jersey which let women property owners vote until 1807. At the turn of the 19th century most states removed property ownership requirements and only gave white men voting rights.[1]

It wasn't until after the Civil War that citizenship and voting rights were guaranteed at the national level. The 14th amendment to the constitution in 1868 stated that men who were at least 21 years of age were citizens. Many states continued to deny black men the right to vote even though they were American citizens at this time. That's where the 15th amendment comes in. It was ratified in 1870 and states the right of citizens to vote can't be denied on account of race, color, or prior condition of servitude (aka former slaves). This year, America is celebrating the 150th year anniversary of granting black and other minority male citizens the right to vote.[2]

It's estimated that at least 620,000 soldiers died in the Civil War. Black Americans made up 10 percent of the 2 million strong Union army at the end of the war, and 40,000 of them died during the war.[3] They fought for a basic human right: the right to be a citizen and receive all the entitlements of citizenship.

How happy do you think these men were 150 years ago when they could finally participate in the government? Be grateful for what they sacrificed and achieved for the American people. Don't "spit in their faces" so to speak and lightly regard their accomplishment. Demonstrate your gratitude by exercising your right to vote.

Unfortunately, their struggle didn't end there. Many states continued to make it nearly impossible for black and minority men to vote because they instituted poll taxes and literacy tests. Fast forward 95 years to 1965. That's when Dr. Martin Luther King Jr. and the thousands who joined him affected change. They marched from Selma, Alabama to the state capital building in Montgomery as a protest to bring attention to their plight and to register to vote. Three marches took place in March of that year. The first of which is referred to as "Bloody Sunday" because the protesters were beaten. Three people died during the marches, two at the hands of the KKK.[4]

Here's how Dr. King concluded the marches:

> "Let us march on ballot boxes until we send to our city councils, state legislatures, and the US Congress, men who will not fear to do justly, love mercy, and walk humbly with thy God."[5]

That's the reason we vote. That's the reason people have willingly sacrificed for this right. Dr. King recognized the spiritual war we're in. As the end of the current age draws near, now more than ever we must vote.

The marches resulted in passage of the Voting Rights Act of 1965. It took an incredible 95 years to end the battle the Civil War started. The Act prohibited literacy tests and enforced the voting rights guaranteed in the 14th and 15th amendments through appointed federal examiners that registered people to vote in areas with a history of discrimination. States could no longer have any voting law that resulted in discrimination against racial or language minorities.[6] Prior to this legislation, it's estimated 23% of black Americans were registered to vote. Just a few years later in 1969, 61% were registered.[7]

President Lyndon B. Johnson was a key supporter of the Voting Rights Act. He addressed Congress and asked them to support it. Here's an excerpt from his moving, landmark speech:

> "This was the first nation in the history of the world to be founded with a purpose. The great phrases of that purpose still sound in every American heart, North and South: 'All men are created equal'—'government by consent of the governed'—'give me liberty or give me death.' ... Our fathers believed that if this noble view of the rights of man was to flourish, it must be rooted in democracy. The most basic right of all was the right to choose your own leaders. The history of this country, in large measure, is the history of the expansion of that right to all of our people. Many of the issues of civil rights are very complex

and most difficult. But about this there can and should be no argument. Every American citizen must have an equal right to vote. There is no reason which can excuse the denial of that right. There is no duty which weighs more heavily on us than the duty we have to ensure that right."[8]

President Johnson believed that ensuring every American citizen is able to vote is our ultimate duty. Let that sink in for a minute. It's a very strong statement and it carries with it a heavy responsibility. You have a responsibility to vote because voting is the foundation of democracy. If you choose to shirk your responsibility, you're eating away at what makes America great.

The 15th amendment isn't the only voting legislation we're celebrating in 2020. Let's talk about Susan B. Anthony. I hope you know who she is. If she were still alive, she'd be 200 years old this year. She was a women's rights activist who was prominent in the 19th century. Much like Dr. Martin Luther King Jr., she had a dream that she fought hard to achieve—a woman's right to vote. The first women's rights convention in the US was held in 1848 and the right to vote was a topic discussed. Early women's rights leaders believed suffrage was the most effective means in which to change an unjust system.[9] In 1872 Anthony and several other women were arrested after they voted in the presidential election.[10] After 30 years of persuading the public and the government, in 1878 California Republican Senator Aaron A. Sargent introduced the 19th amendment on her behalf. It didn't pass. Over the years it was defeated in Congress 4 times by a Democratic Party controlled Congress.[11]

In 1917, the tide began to change. Unfortunately, Anthony wasn't alive to see it. Women who were protesting outside the White House began getting arrested. Many protesters were beaten. Some were jailed or sent to workhouses where they remained for months at a time. Some of the women imprisoned went on a hunger strike to protest their treatment. They were forcefully fed raw eggs through a feeding tube to prevent them from dying while imprisoned.[12] These women who desired to be treated like true citizens of this great country and vote were instead treated like the worst of criminals.

Disgusted by the treatment of the protesting women, President Woodrow Wilson pressured Congress to take action on the 19th amendment. Here's an excerpt from his address to Congress:

> "Are we alone to ask and take the utmost that our women can give—service and sacrifice of every kind—and still say we do not see what title that gives them to stand by our sides in the guidance of the affairs of their nation and ours? We have made partners of the women in this war; shall we admit them only to a partnership of suffering and sacrifice and toil and not to a partnership of privilege and right? ... We shall need them in our vision of affairs, as we have never needed them before, the sympathy and insight and clear moral instinct of the women of the world. ... We shall need their moral sense to preserve what is right and fine and worthy in our system of life as well as to discover just what it is that ought to be purified and reformed. Without their counsellings we shall be only half wise."[13]

In 1918, when Republicans gained control of the House and Senate, it finally passed. The amendment was worded exactly the same as the first one proposed in 1878. In 1920, 8 million women voted in a presidential election for the first time.[14]

This year, come November presidential election time, remember what Susan B. Anthony and the other suffragettes endured to secure a woman's right to vote, your mother's right to vote, your wife's right to vote, your sister's right to vote, and perhaps your own right to vote. Celebrate their legacy by voting.

CHAPTER 4 – DON'T BE DECEIVED: ELECTORAL COLLEGE VS POPULAR VOTE

There's a lot of talk these days about changing the presidential election to a popular vote. After all, that seems like it'd be a better democratic process and more fair, right? Wrong! There's a reason every single Democratic candidate running for president is in favor of this. I already mentioned in a prior chapter that people who don't want anything to do with God are drawn to that party. That means Satan is behind the things they support. Something is afoot with this whole popular vote business, and I'm going to expose it for you.

The US is not a pure democracy. We're a democratic constitutional republic. There's a big difference between the two. In a pure democracy, the majority always rules, and minorities have little to no say. Democracies easily give birth to tyrants and dictators. In the US, we have representatives that are democratically elected where the rules of the government and rights of the people are established in a constitution.

The constitution of the US details how the president, vice president, and members of Congress are chosen. We have a House of Representatives and a Senate because they represent two different groups.

The House of Representatives is just like it sounds. The members represent the population of each state. They serve a two year term. So, the entire House is elected every two years. Each representative is chosen based on a popular vote of registered voters in their state. The candidate with the most votes in the state election wins. The constitution establishes the number of seats in the House. It's currently set at 435. Each ten year Census is what determines how many seats each state gets out of that 435.[1] Every state gets at least one representative. The bigger states will obviously have more representatives than the smaller states. My state of New Mexico has three representatives while California has the most with 53. That also means the bigger more urban states have more influence in the House. That's because the House was established to represent the people.

The Senate is quite a bit different from the House. Senators represent the states. They serve a six year term, and one-third of them are elected every two years. Each state gets two senators. So, every single state has an equal vote, equal influence, and equal say. We are the United States after all. Each state is unique in its culture, its natural resources, its jobs, and its challenges. It's important for each state to have a voice in government and foreign affairs. Now, it used to be that senators were chosen by their state legislatures.[2] The 17th amendment, ratified in 1913, changed it so that senators are elected by a popular vote just like representatives in the House.[3]

Here's where we get to the Electoral College. The constitution gives each state their number of electors. It's equal to their number of senators plus their number of representatives. Using my example from earlier, New Mexico has 5 electors (2 senators plus 3 representatives), and California has 55 electors (2 senators plus 53 representatives). The constitution lets each state determine their electors however they see fit. Your state's electors are not your actual senators and representatives. They are a separate group of people chosen specifically for the task of voting for the president and vice president. That's it. They are expected to vote for the candidates of the party that selected them. The constitution also lets each state decide how their electoral votes are awarded to the presidential candidates. Most states, 48 of them, use a winner-take-all system. That means whoever wins the popular vote in the state gets all the electoral votes. Maine and Nebraska are the exceptions. They use a district system in which electoral votes are allocated based on who won the popular vote in each congressional district.[4] Let's see an example of how this works.

California has 55 electors, so each political party would select 55 people that pledge to vote for the president and vice president candidates chosen by their party. Come national election day, let's say the Democratic Party president and vice president candidates win the popular vote in California. Since this is a winner-take-all state, that means the 55 electors the Democratic Party chose get to cast their vote for president and vice president. The electors represent the people, so they're expected to confirm their state's choice of candidate. All 55 electoral votes would go to the Democratic Party president and vice president candidates.

This same thing happens in every other state. Electoral votes are awarded to the winner of the state's popular vote. With this method each state gets a say in who is elected president.

In the 2016 election, Trump won the popular vote in 30 states.[5] That's 60% of the US voting for him. Here's how a writer for the National Review put it:

> "Do we want a president who wins by running up the score in one or two states, or do we want a president who wins by garnering narrower victories in a wide array of states? Clinton won New York and California. Trump won Texas. And Florida. And North Carolina, Ohio, Michigan, Wisconsin, Pennsylvania, and even one electoral vote in Maine. He won the Electoral College by assembling a more politically and geographically diverse group of states than Clinton did. In our system, winning the Electoral College confers legitimacy because such a victory exemplifies the reality the Electoral College was created to ground in our political order: that the United States is a federal union of semi-sovereign states."[6]

So, what would a national presidential election look like if we ditched the Electoral College and went with a national popular vote? Well, it would eliminate almost every state's influence in selecting the president. The 4 biggest states have 30% of the registered voters in America (California, Texas, Florida, New York). It only takes 10 states to get to 50% of the registered voters.[7] 10 states. That's all it would take for a candidate to win the presidency. They'd only have to garner support from people in the most populous states. That's only 20% of America people! Do you really want to elect a president that the majority of states oppose? What kind of United States would that be? It wouldn't be united at all. Ah! Now we've gotten to the truth of this.

Let's look at the 2016 election and the popular vote a bit closer. Clinton won the national popular vote by 2.8 million people. She got 48% of the vote compared to Trump at 46%. But did you know that Clinton got 4.3 million more votes than Trump in California? If you remove the biggest state from the national popular vote equation suddenly the picture changes a lot. Excluding California, Trump won the national popular vote by 1.4 million votes.[8] That's how much one large state can impact a national election. This is why the founding fathers liked the Electoral College so much. It's because it prevents a candidate who is only popular at a regional level from dominating a national election.

This is why the Democrats are pushing for a national popular vote. They want California and New York to rule the US. That's what this is all about. They want to force their policies on the rest of the states. We are not a country run by one or two states. We cannot let the big states bully all the others into voting like them. We must remember we are a country run by 50 states that each get a say in the government. We do not let the majority enslave the minority here. Do not let Satan steal your vote! Do not let Satan divide this country!

Here's how a writer for The Mental Recession explains it:

> The Electoral College is a system that prevents areas with massive populations – such as the liberal cesspools of New York and California – from exclusively deciding who leads the rest of the country. It gives voice to sparsely populated areas in middle America and levels out those from densely populated coastal elite locales.
>
> New York is a microcosm of this – Governor Andrew Cuomo wins election every cycle because he captures areas such as Long Island, New York City, and areas in Buffalo, while the majority of the state overwhelmingly rejects him. These areas control what happens in the entire state, much to the detriment of upstate New York.[9]

If you don't believe the big liberal states want to steal your vote, here's something truly nefarious that's happening under your nose that you need to know about. It's called the National Popular Vote initiative.[10] Since the constitution established the Electoral College and it'll take an amendment to the constitution to alter that, this nonprofit group is going a different route, bypassing the very foundation our government is built upon. They're using an interstate compact among states where states agree to tell their electors to vote for the candidate who won the national popular vote instead of the candidate who won their state's popular vote. They're stealing a state's vote! Unbelievable, I know. Yet, they've already convinced 15 states to join this unholy alliance. No surprise California and New York have signed up. I'm quite torqued that my state of New Mexico has as well. Think your state is too smart for this? Think again. Arizona and Oklahoma, it's already passed in one of your legislative chambers. The fact this isn't going to the voters in each state says a lot as well. They're being sly about it for a reason. How would you like your state's choice of president to not count? I don't think we have to worry too much about this though. This alliance doesn't go into effect unless they get a majority of the states to sign up. And it seems to me this clearly violates Article I, Section 10 of the constitution which prohibits states from entering into alliances.[11] I doubt this will hold up in the courts if they manage to convince enough states to give away their votes. Consider this another piece of evidence that highlights how Satan is behind this national popular vote business.

There's something else we must take into account when looking at the popular vote historically. In liberal states like California where they have an overwhelming majority of Democrat voters, how many Republicans do you think turned out to vote in the national election? I bet many of them stayed home knowing their vote wasn't going to sway their state's choice. We have to be careful about using a number, like historical popular vote, in a way it's not meant to be used. If the rules were changed and we elected a president based on national popular vote it would have a radical impact on voter turnout.

Now, speaking of voter turnout, there's another topic we must discuss that's grabbing headlines, and it has a big impact on elections. It's voter ID. The constitution states that American citizens aged 18 and over have the right to vote. When you register to vote how do they know you're eligible to vote? The National Mail Voter Registration Form asks if you're a citizen and when your birth date is, but do they check?[12] There's an ID Number field you're supposed to fill out that has state specific instructions. For California you just list your driver's license number. Hum. Guess who can get a driver's license in California? Pretty much anyone, including illegal aliens—people who aren't citizens. You also don't have to be 18 to get a driver's license. So how does a state like California know that you're eligible to register to vote? That's the point. They don't.

The national registration form clearly states that if you're registering to vote for the first time that you must show proof of identification when you show up to vote for the first time. So, how does that work in states that don't have voter ID laws, like California and

New Mexico? Hum, indeed. There are 16 states that don't have a voter ID law.[13] Opponents to voter ID claim it's a burden for people to show proof of ID. I'm really not buying that argument. We have to show ID to carry out normal activities here: opening a bank account, getting a job, buying alcohol, and traveling via plane to name a few. Yet it's a burden to show it when voting? Come on!

Well, perhaps it's not a big deal. That's what the Democrats are saying after all, that there isn't any fraud in voting. Do you believe that? Judicial Watch has an election integrity project that's shining a light on this. Check out these statements of the Judicial Watch findings by a reporter with the National Review:

> At least 3.5 million more people are on U.S. election rolls than are eligible to vote.
>
> My tabulation of Judicial Watch's state-by-state results yielded 462 counties where the registration rate exceeded 100 percent.
>
> All told, California is a veritable haunted house, teeming with 1,736,556 ghost voters.
>
> President Donald J. Trump's supporters might be intrigued to learn that Hillary Clinton's margins of victory in Colorado (136,386) and New Hampshire (2,736) were lower than the numbers of ghost voters in those states. Clinton's fans should know that Trump won Michigan (10,704) and North Carolina (173,315) by fewer ballots than ghost voters in those states.[14]

Judicial Watch is also suing North Carolina for failing to clean up its voter registration data. They state North Carolina data reveals that they have nearly 1 million inactive voters on its rolls. In just 19 North Carolina counties, 20% of the registrations are inactive. The national median state inactive rate is only 9.6%.[15]

Wow! They found 3.5 million people are registered who shouldn't be. Here's another interesting story. A recent Breitbart article indicates that data from the U.S. Election Assistance Commission and other sources show that 42.4 million ballots were mailed to registered voters in the 2018 election. Of those, 10.5 million went missing! That's almost a quarter of the ballots. Los Angeles County accounted for 1.4 million of those missing mail-in ballots.[16]

With the coronavirus outbreak, the Democrats are pushing for mail-in voting without any identification requirements or witness signatures on the ballots. Despite what they say, they aren't pushing this for wholesome reasons. Why would they be willing to hold up relief bills to include this? President Trump has rightly criticized this and pointed out that voting by mail is ripe for fraud. Common sense tells you there are many opportunities for fraud to occur with a mailed-in ballot. The Democrats know this too. They have an evil intent behind pushing this scheme.

Here are just a few ways fraud can occur via the mail. Someone can vote more than once by requesting absentee ballots in multiple states, or by voting by mail and in person. Ballot harvesting is the biggie. This is when someone hand delivers your ballot and waits for you to fill it out, or they conveniently pick up your ballot for you, or they hand you a ballot already filled out and request your signature. Don't ever sign a ballot that's already filled in. Anytime there's a person between you and your ballot being counted there's a potential for something nefarious to happen. Who's to say that person is really going to take your ballot and make sure it's counted? They could throw it away if they know or think you voted for the candidate they don't want to win. Who's to say the person who opens your ballot is going to make sure it's counted? How do you know your ballot even got delivered? It could go missing! Unless you vote in person at the machine or you feed your paper ballot into the machine, there's no way to know for sure that you actually had a say in the election.

I already pointed out above that we've had a problem with mailed ballots going missing in the prior national elections. If states mail ballots out to everyone who's registered, there will be millions of ballots sent out that shouldn't be because the voter rolls aren't clean. Do you think someone who receives a ballot for a dead relative or someone who lived at their residence previously but moved away will be tempted to fill it out? Would a corrupt election official fill it out for their preferred candidate? Unfortunately, it happens. The Heritage Foundation recently shared over 1,000 examples of voter fraud across the US. Many of the examples they shared were absentee ballot fraud.[17]

Nothing to see here, move along.... That's what Satan wants you to do, to think it's no big deal when in reality it's a huge deal. This voter fraud most certainly impacted the national popular vote in 2016. Just think of how this is also impacting smaller local elections where a few votes make all the difference. We must push for in person voting until there's a secure way to vote by mail. We need a national voter ID law to combat non-citizens from voting. Until we have that, Satan will continue stealing votes.

Would you like to know about another way Satan is stealing your vote? It seems pretty innocuous on the surface. It's that we don't have a citizenship question on the Census. I mentioned earlier that the ten year Census is what determines how many seats each state gets in the House of Representatives. Now, why do you think all the Democrats are opposed to asking this simple question on the Census? It's because non-citizens fill out the Census. Here's the shocking truth about this as spoken by a reporter with Breitbart:

> "Research by the Center for Immigration Studies' Steven Camarota and Karen Zeigler finds that annual illegal and legal immigration to the U.S. will redistribute political power in the form of 26 House seats away from a number of red states and towards massively populated blue states like California and New York.
>
> "California, by 2020, is set to gain 11 congressional seats solely due to the fact that noncitizens, rather than just American citizens, are counted in congressional apportionment.
>
> "As Breitbart News has chronicled for years, the counting of only American citizens to divide up congressional districts and Electoral College votes would shift power away from the affluent, metropolitan coastal cities of the U.S. and towards middle America."[18]

So, there you have the truth. California and New York are enticing immigrants to their states by promising them all sorts of free stuff because they're hoping to steal votes away from middle America. It's imperative that we know how many non-citizens are in each state. The national election is on the line.

With the 2020 national election coming up, be mindful of Satan trying to steal your vote. If someone comes to your door and hands you a ballot to fill out, don't do it! If you must vote absentee, make sure you mail it or drop it off yourself. Don't give your ballot to anyone. Satan could easily throw those away or alter them. Don't sign a ballot someone else has already filled out. If you need assistance filling out a ballot, make sure the person fills it out exactly the way you tell them to. Vote in person if you can.

Remember that we're in a war. Your vote is a weapon in that war. Use it!

> You are all children of light and children of the day. We don't belong to the night, nor to darkness, so then let's not sleep, as the rest do, but let's watch and be sober. ... But since we belong to the day, let's be sober, putting on the breastplate of faith and love, and for a helmet, the hope of salvation. (1 Thessalonians 5:5-6, 8)

PART 2

FATE:
GOD HAS A PLAN

CHAPTER 5 - GOD DETERMINES GOVERNMENTS

In prior chapters, we looked at how we should be using the free will God has given us to be active participants in government while we're waiting for Jesus to return. In these next few chapters, we're going to explore God's plan or fate. The Bible tells us that God is clearly the one in control:

> For I alone am God! I am God, and there is none like me. Only I can tell
> you the future before it even happens. Everything I plan will come to pass.
> (Isaiah 46:9-10 NLT)

This concept of fate vs free will can be a difficult one to grasp for sure. God knows all things—past, present, and future. Because he knows what's going to happen in the future, he can reveal it to us in the past. That's prophecy, predestination, or fate. However, you have free will. You know this because you make choices all the time. You can choose to follow God or not. You can choose to sin or not. It's just that God has planned and therefore knows all the consequences of each choice and he also knows what you're going to choose. To give an overly simplistic example, think of one of those books you read as a kid where you get to pick your own adventure. You know, where you decide what the character does in a situation and then flip to the corresponding next page. In that example, God is like the author and you are like the reader. God wrote the story with every choice, adventure, and outcome accounted for and you get to choose which path you take. If you have the Holy Spirit living inside of you then God is working within you so that you'll want to do things that please him and bring him glory (Philippians 2:13). That's the sweet spot where your choices align with God's will.

We're living during a time that often seems scary. We're told we're killing the planet and that we must start colonizing Mars. We see mass shootings, wars, epidemics, and natural disasters on the news. It can seem like it's out of control. But it's not. God is in control. He has a plan. Government and leaders in the government are part of his plan.

Do you know who created the first government? God did. He created the angels before he created us humans and he made some of them leaders over others. Of course, God was supreme as their maker. That's a government. It's when one or many have authority and influence over others. Satan was one of those leaders in heaven before he sinned and got kicked out (Ezekiel 28:14; Revelation 12:9). We also read in the Bible about one of the archangels, Michael, who is a leader of an army of angels (Revelation 12:7; Daniel 10:3). When God created the first humans, Adam and Eve, he made it clear he was their maker and they were accountable to him. They were in his garden, he gave them dominion over it and the animals, and he gave them one rule to follow (Genesis 2). In God's first governments he was the direct authority. They were theocracies.

Throughout time, the types of government we've had on earth have changed to fulfill God's purposes. Government began as a theocracy in the garden with Adam and Eve. After they sinned and got banished from the garden, God remained their authority. He didn't formally put any rulers into place on earth for quite some time. God was still their ruler. Would they continue to strive to follow him in their fallen sinful state? Well, you know what happened. Eventually, no one was following God anymore except for Noah. Because the world was full of wickedness and violence and people only thought about evil, God flooded the earth (Genesis 6-8). In this period, the people chose to worship sin and evil. We know the father of that behavior is Satan (John 8:44). God was their authority, but they chose to worship Satan instead of God.

Right after the flood, God still didn't formally put any rulers into place on earth. He was still testing mankind to see what they would choose to do. Would they follow God or not? He commanded Noah and his sons to go forth and fill the earth. That's not what happened though. Instead, mankind gathered in one place and built the huge tower of Babel that reached into the heavens (Genesis 11). The people went up instead of spreading out. They were trying to make a name for themselves. They wanted to live in the heavens with God. They wanted to be like God. This time, people chose to worship themselves instead of God.

After this, God set apart a people group, a nation, which would be an example government for the rest of the world. It's Israel (Isaiah 49;

1 Corinthians 10). God's promises for Israel began with Abraham (Genesis 12). Abraham worshiped God. After several generations, Abraham's descendants became captives. They were all slaves of the Egyptian Pharaoh. They sold everything they had, including themselves, to Pharaoh so they wouldn't starve. They didn't trust God to provide for them. So, they put their faith in a foreign god, an idol.

As you may recall, the Pharaohs treated them harshly. This is when God formally chose a leader for the people. God already knew what people did when they didn't have a leader. Instead of following God, they sought other leaders. They had already worshiped sin, Satan, themselves, and now an idol. Now it was time to see what people would do when they had an intermediary leader chosen for them by God. He chose Moses.

> Yahweh said, "...Come now therefore, and I will send you to Pharaoh, that you may bring my people, the children of Israel, out of Egypt." Moses said to God, "Who am I, that I should go to Pharaoh, and that I should bring the children of Israel out of Egypt?" He said, "Certainly I will be with you." (Exodus 3:7, 10-12)

Once Moses led the people out of bondage, God established a formal government for them (Exodus 18; Numbers 11:16-17). God let Moses select leaders to put in charge of ten, fifty, one hundred, and one thousand people. Those leaders handled disputes and issues that arose. They went to Moses with things that required his help and God's ruling. All the while, Moses continued to be the people's representative before God. God was even physically present with the people during this time. He appeared to the them as a pillar of cloud during the day and a pillar of fire at night (Exodus 13:21). This government was still a theocracy because God was the clear authority. The people also had representatives that were filled with God's Spirit to guide them.

So why did God decide to create a government for the people? We get some understanding from Moses. When he was near death, he asked God to appoint a new leader so the people wouldn't be like sheep without a shepherd.

> Moses spoke to Yahweh, saying, "Let Yahweh, the God of the spirits of all flesh, appoint a man over the congregation, who may go out before them,

and who may come in before them, and who may lead them out, and who
may bring them in, that the congregation of Yahweh may not be as sheep
which have no shepherd." (Numbers 27:15-17)

Domestic sheep without a shepherd can't protect themselves, find
good pasture, find water, or get out of trouble. They need a shepherd.
Prior to Moses, the people didn't have a shepherd. Once the people
entered the promised land, God's pillar didn't go before them anymore.
God created the government to be shepherds for the people.

Paul the apostle explains that a government is also a servant of
God. It's meant to help people do good and not evil because a
government honors those who do right and punishes those who do evil.

Let every soul be in subjection to the higher authorities, for there is no
authority except from God, and those who exist are ordained by God. ...
For rulers are not a terror to the good work, but to the evil. Do you desire
to have no fear of the authority? Do that which is good, and you will have
praise from the authority, for he is a servant of God to you for good. But
if you do that which is evil, be afraid, for he doesn't bear the sword in vain;
for he is a servant of God, an avenger for wrath to him who does evil.
(Romans 13:1, 3-4)

I know some of you think government is inherently evil. That's not
how God sees it. He instituted it for our benefit. During the time of
Moses and Joshua, the people worshiped and followed God because
they had a godly government.

Now, after Moses and Joshua died, God didn't appoint a new leader
over all of Israel. Remember, they had elders who were filled with the
Spirit who should have been leading their own groups of people.
Unfortunately, they didn't. The next generation didn't know God or
any of the miracles he had done for Israel (Judges 2:10). The
government and its leaders failed to do their job. They weren't good
shepherds. So, the people went right back to what they had done in the
past. They worshiped the gods of all the people groups around them.
Without a godly government, the people quickly went astray.

So, God raised up people called judges in the Bible. Gideon,
Samson, and Samuel are some examples. God gave the people
shepherds when they cried out to him for help. The judges delivered

the people from their sin and captivity and turned them back to worshiping God. But it got to a point where the people no longer wanted judges. They wanted a king.

> Then all the elders of Israel gathered themselves together and came to Samuel to Ramah. They said to him, "Behold, you are old, and your sons don't walk in your ways. Now make us a king to judge us like all the nations." But the thing displeased Samuel when they said, "Give us a king to judge us." Samuel prayed to Yahweh. Yahweh said to Samuel, "Listen to the voice of the people in all that they tell you; for they have not rejected you, but they have rejected me as the king over them. According to all the works which they have done since the day that I brought them up out of Egypt even to this day, in that they have forsaken me and served other gods, so they also do to you. Now therefore, listen to their voice. However, you shall protest solemnly to them, and shall show them the way of the king who will reign over them." (1 Samuel 8:4-9)

The people wanted to be like all the other nations around them who had kings. When Samuel discussed the people's request with God, "Yahweh," God told him not to take it personally. The people were rejecting God as their king, not Samuel as their judge. It's what the people had always done, reject God. God warned the people what would happen, but he still let the people have what they asked for. Here, we see God give them a new type of government. While this appears to be something the people demanded of God and he acquiesced, it was actually prophesied long before this happened. Let's see what Moses told all the people right before they entered the promised land.

> When you have come to the land which Yahweh your God gives you, and possess it and dwell in it, and say, "I will set a king over me, like all the nations that are around me," you shall surely set him whom Yahweh your God chooses as king over yourselves. (Deuteronomy 17:14-15)

God knew the people would turn from him and demand a king. It was fate. Yet our free will works in perfect harmony with God's plan and prophecies. God gave the people what they asked for and chose Saul as their first king (1 Samuel 9-10).

After King Saul, God continued to place kings over his people. They had kings right up until they were taken captive in Babylon. When the Israelites were allowed to return to their land, they were still governed by the kings in Babylon. When we fast forward to the New Testament, we see the Roman Empire is the new government and Caesar is the king. It's the same type of government we all live under today. We call our kings by different names—president, prime minister, chancellor, chairman, supreme leader—but it's still the same if you think about it. Sure, the details regarding how leaders are chosen and the type of power they have vary across nations. But it's still one ruler over many people. Just like in the first government God created which had people under Moses in positions of authority, it's the same today. We all live under some type of king on earth.

This is the last type of government we'll see before the rapture—kings. It's also the last type of government before eternity starts. Jesus is the King of kings after all, and he will physically rule as king on earth during the millennial period. We're going to explore this in detail in Part 7 when we look at future fulfillments of the Election Omen.

I hope you learned that God chooses governments all while honoring our free will. In the next chapter, we're going to explore God's plan in choosing leaders.

CHAPTER 6 – GOD DETERMINES LEADERS

I'd like you to recall an example I shared in the prior chapter with the pick your own adventure book. God, as the author, has filled the story with leaders who do good and leaders who do evil. Sometimes in the story, you, as the reader, get to pick which leader to follow, but other times events and circumstances make someone a leader. Even though you may try to orchestrate a certain outcome with your choices, it doesn't always play out like you envisioned. That's because a good story has twists, challenges, and unexpected heroes. It's exactly like this in real life too.

Many people get anxious about elections because they so desperately want the candidate they've voted for to win. After the 2016 national election, I saw my doctor for my annual visit. She asked me if I was upset, anxious, or depressed about the election results because she'd seen a high number of patients who exhibited those traits and required medication to help them cope. That made me sad because it illustrated a lack of faith. Whatever happens that puts a leader into authority, remember that God is the author. He's planned every outcome and knows how the story ends. Focus on doing your part in the story. Participate and make good choices. Keep turning the page. If you've put your faith in Jesus, then you have no reason to be anxious. Your eternal future is secure.

Let's look at some examples from the Bible that help us understand God's role as the author of the story. In this Scripture, the prophet Daniel reveals that God both establishes and removes kings:

> Daniel answered, "Blessed be the name of God forever and ever; for wisdom and might are his. He changes the times and the seasons. He removes kings and sets up kings. (Daniel 2:20-21)

Paul the apostle tells us all authority comes from God:

> Let every soul be in subjection to the higher authorities, for there is no authority except from God, and those who exist are ordained by God. (Romans 13:1)

It also reveals something else that's interesting. He said every soul is subject to higher authority. That means the leader that God put into power is subject to God too. He or she is accountable for their actions just like you and me are. That's why Paul said leaders need to take the gift of leadership that God bestowed on them seriously (Romans 12:8). God expects a leader to be a good shepherd. They will answer for it if they aren't.

That's right, God puts both good and bad leaders into power. I know some of you may think God only puts good leaders into power and that sinful people are the ones who put evil leaders into power. No, that's not the case. All leaders have free will. They can choose to obey God or chase after sin. They also both serve a purpose.

Some of you may be thinking of Hosea 8:4 to counter the points I just made about God picking leaders. Let's have a look at it:

> They have set up kings, but not by me. They have made princes, and I didn't approve. Of their silver and their gold they have made themselves idols, that they may be cut off. (Hosea 8:4)

If you just read the first Scripture above it seems like the people somehow thwarted God's plan and picked a leader he didn't ordain. Almost like they were able to write a character into God's own story. When we keep reading, we see what this is really about. Their idols. They made themselves kings and princes that God didn't approve of out of gold and silver. They created false gods they could worship.

Let's read about a real human king that God picked. God chose King David to be king over all of Israel. We regard David as a good king, yet we know that David wasn't perfect by any means. He committed adultery with Bathsheba, got her pregnant, and had her husband killed in battle to cover it up (2 Samuel 11-12). We also know that David was accountable to God for that sinful behavior because God took the son that resulted from that sin. David still ended up in God's hall of faith (Hebrews 11:32), his next son with Bathsheba, Solomon, built the first temple, and it's through David's descendants that Jesus was born. God still picked David even though he knew all those bad choices he would make.

> Now therefore tell my servant David this: 'Yahweh of Armies says, "I took

you from the sheep pen, from following the sheep, to be prince over my people, over Israel." (2 Samuel 7:8)

Perhaps you're wondering why God chose David. It's because David had a heart like God's (1 Samuel 13:14). In a subsequent chapter we're going to look at the qualities that make a good leader. This is one of them. Even though God picked David, we read in Chapter 1 that the people chose him (2 Samuel 2:4). So, which is it? Who picked David— God or the people? Both did.

Let's look at another leader God picked—Nebuchadnezzar. You likely know him as the evil ruler of Babylon who conquered Israel and took them into captivity. Yes, God picked the bad guy.

> Jeremiah the prophet spoke to all the people of Judah, and to all the inhabitants of Jerusalem: ... "Yet you have not listened to me," says Yahweh, "that you may provoke me to anger with the work of your hands to your own hurt." Therefore Yahweh of Armies says: "Because you have not heard my words, behold, I will send and take all the families of the north," says Yahweh, "and I will send to Nebuchadnezzar the king of Babylon, my servant, and will bring them against this land, and against its inhabitants, and against all these nations around. ... "It will happen, when seventy years are accomplished, that I will punish the king of Babylon and that nation," says Yahweh, "for their iniquity." (Jeremiah 25:2, 7-9, 12)

God referred to Nebuchadnezzar as his "servant." God used him and his army to discipline Israel because they kept sinning by worshiping false gods. This isn't a leader the people of Israel chose per se because they certainly didn't elect him. But their choices resulted in him being their leader. So, in a sense, they did pick him. We also read above that God promised to hold Nebuchadnezzar accountable for his own sins too. Let's see what happened:

> All this came on the king Nebuchadnezzar. ... The king spoke and said, "Is not this great Babylon, which I have built for the royal dwelling place by the might of my power and for the glory of my majesty?" While the word was in the king's mouth, a voice came from the sky, saying, "O king Nebuchadnezzar, to you it is spoken: 'The kingdom has departed from

you.'" ... This was fulfilled the same hour on Nebuchadnezzar. He was driven from men and ate grass like oxen; and his body was wet with the dew of the sky until his hair had grown like eagles' feathers, and his nails like birds' claws. At the end of the days I, Nebuchadnezzar, lifted up my eyes to heaven, and my understanding returned to me; and I blessed the Most High, and I praised and honored him who lives forever, for his dominion is an everlasting dominion, and his kingdom from generation to generation. (Daniel 4:28, 30-31, 33-34)

Nebuchadnezzar was prideful and thought he had built Babylon by his own strength. After God humbled him, we learn that Nebuchadnezzar praised God. You see, that was God's ultimate reason for disciplining both Israel and Nebuchadnezzar. It's so they would come to know him and put their faith in him. God uses all types of people and leaders to bring about his will. The prophet Isaiah received this message from God that reiterates this important truth for us:

Yahweh says to his anointed, to Cyrus, whose right hand I have held to subdue nations before him and strip kings of their armor, to open the doors before him, and the gates shall not be shut: "I will go before you and make the rough places smooth. I will break the doors of bronze in pieces and cut apart the bars of iron. I will give you the treasures of darkness and hidden riches of secret places, that you may know that it is I, Yahweh, who calls you by your name, even the God of Israel. ... I have given you a title, though you have not known me. I am Yahweh, and there is no one else. Besides me, there is no God. I will strengthen you, though you have not known me, that they may know from the rising of the sun, and from the west, that there is no one besides me. I am Yahweh, and there is no one else. ... I have raised him up in righteousness, and I will make all his ways straight. He shall build my city, and he shall let my exiles go free, not for price nor reward," says Yahweh of Armies. (Isaiah 45:1-6, 13)

Cyrus was one of Nebuchadnezzar's successors. He was one of the kings over Babylon while the Israelites were in captivity there. God called him his "anointed." That means he was divinely chosen by God. We also learn that even though Cyrus didn't know God, that God held his hand. God was with him. I hope that brings you comfort like it does me. God is with the leaders he picks. So why did God pick an unbeliever like Cyrus to lead the people? He told us: "that you may know that it is I" and "that they may know...I am Yahweh." God picked Cyrus so he could reveal himself to Cyrus and the people of Israel. It's the same reason he picked Nebuchadnezzar. We should look at all of our leaders through this lens. How is God using the leader to reveal himself?

Now that we understand that God picks leaders, good and bad ones, to reveal himself to us, let's look at other ways God uses leaders. Peter tells us they are sent for our good because they honor those who do right and they punish those who do wrong (1 Peter 2:13-14). We learn in Judges 17:6 that when the people didn't have a leader that each person did whatever seemed right to them. This tells us that leaders help guide us in doing what's right. However, since all leaders are sinners, it means they could guide us down the wrong path too. In that case, God uses the leader to give us the opportunity to choose good or evil, to choose if we'll serve God above all else (Acts 5:29; Joshua 24:15).

God uses leaders the world considers foolish to shame people who think they are wise. He picks people to lead who seem powerless in order to shame the powerful. Both the foolish and the powerless are used to show the world that what they consider important isn't. They both put an end to people boasting about their own strength (1 Corinthians 1:27-28). Consider Moses and all of the disciples that Jesus picked. Moses was 80 years old when God chose him, and he wasn't a good speaker. The disciples, whom God entrusted to lead the early church and spread the gospel, were mostly fishermen. How about King David? He was a shepherd and yet God chose him to display his power among the people (Isaiah 55:4).

Since we're all accountable to God as our maker, he's also our judge. So, he sends leaders like Nebuchadnezzar and the Assyrian king to discipline sin and wickedness (Jeremiah 25, Isaiah 10). When God allows a leader to discipline the people, there's always a limit he places on them. Jesus himself told us that when the Antichrist is in power there will be greater oppression at that time than there ever has been or will be. But God chose to shorten the days for the sake of people who put their faith in him during that time (Mark 13:19-20). Any evil ruler, even if they are inhabited by Satan or another fallen angel, are also under Jesus's authority. Not in the future. They are right now.

> Jesus Christ, who is at the right hand of God, having gone into heaven, angels and authorities and powers being made subject to him. (1 Peter 3:21-22)

That means, just like he did with Job, Satan still has to get permission from Jesus before he can test anyone (Job 1). If God allows it, remember that God is in control and that it's for your benefit. God is using that ruler and the difficult time to help you know him and bring you closer to him. Don't lose hope. God also uses leaders like Moses, Cyrus, and Gideon to rescue people from oppression (Exodus 3; Isaiah 45; Judges 6). We know how this story ends—Jesus is coming (Revelation 22)!

You may think that because God is choosing the leaders that there's no reason for you to vote. That's not the case. If you're still struggling with why you should vote, I encourage you to reread Chapter 1 and remember all the reasons your vote truly matters to God. Also remember the pick your own adventure book example. You're like the reader. The pages of the book won't turn themselves. You have to make a choice and flip to the next page. In this Laodicean culture we're in, there's enormous pressure to sit on the sidelines and not do anything. That's exactly what Satan hopes you'll do too. It'd be like letting someone else make the choice in the story and turn the page. But then it wouldn't be your adventure anymore, would it? Satan will most certainly take control of your part if you let him. Don't forfeit your choice and the path the story takes to Satan.

Now, let's consider who Jesus and Satan would vote for.

PART 3

WHO WOULD JESUS AND SATAN VOTE FOR?

CHAPTER 7 - JESUS WOULD VOTE FOR...

Before we can consider who Jesus would vote for, we need to have a clear understanding of who Jesus is. So, let's begin there. Jesus is God in the flesh.

> Have this in your mind, which was also in Christ Jesus, who, existing in the form of God, didn't consider equality with God a thing to be grasped, but emptied himself, taking the form of a servant, being made in the likeness of men. And being found in human form, he humbled himself, becoming obedient to the point of death, yes, the death of the cross. Therefore God also highly exalted him, and gave to him the name which is above every name, that at the name of Jesus every knee should bow, of those in heaven, those on earth, and those under the earth, and that every tongue should confess that Jesus Christ is Lord, to the glory of God the Father. (Philippians 2:5-11)

He left heaven and became a man so he could die for you. He died for everyone. He did it because we're sinners and we need a savior in order to live with him in heaven. That's because heaven is only for perfect and holy people. Remember Adam and Eve got kicked out of the garden once they sinned (Genesis 3). They couldn't remain there in their sinful state. We don't have the power to make ourselves perfect and holy. Only God can do it. Jesus loves us so much that he was willingly tortured and crucified to save us. All we have to do to be considered perfect and righteous is believe (Ephesians 2:8-9).

Since Jesus is God, that means he has all the qualities of God. What do you think is God's best quality? I think it's love. It's a key theme in the entire Bible. It's the reason God created us, because it gave him pleasure to do so. He created us even though he knew we would sin against him. He loves us unconditionally. It's one of the reasons he chooses rulers like Nebuchadnezzar to discipline us when we've strayed from him. God's discipline originates from love. Love is also the reason Jesus died for us. In fact, that's how God showed us that he loves us. He willingly died for us (Romans 5:8). If you think about it, love is also the reason sin exists. If sin didn't exist, how would you know that God loves you? It's because of sin that God was able to display his sacrificial love for us.

This is the most important attribute we should keep in mind when regarding how Jesus would vote—love. We need to understand that it's not our kind of love though. We place conditions on love because we usually expect love in return. We also withhold love from people we despise. That's not how Jesus loves. His love is perfect, unconditional, and sacrificial. From the Amplified Bible, here's how the apostle Paul describes love:

> Love endures with patience and serenity, love is kind and thoughtful, and is not jealous or envious; love does not brag and is not proud or arrogant. It is not rude; it is not self-seeking, it is not provoked [nor overly sensitive and easily angered]; it does not take into account a wrong endured. It does not rejoice at injustice, but rejoices with the truth [when right and truth prevail]. Love bears all things [regardless of what comes], believes all things [looking for the best in each one], hopes all things [remaining steadfast during difficult times], endures all things [without weakening]. (1 Corinthians 13:4-7 AMP)

By measuring each candidate and each issue against this biblical definition of love, we can get insight into how Jesus would vote. We often associate love with the heart. You know what, Jesus does too. Let's consider King David. Do you remember how God described him in the Bible and why God picked him?

> Yahweh has sought for himself a man after his own heart, and Yahweh has appointed him to be prince over his people. (1 Samuel 13:14)

> He raised up David to be their king, to whom he also testified, 'I have found David the son of Jesse, a man after my heart, who will do all my will.' (Acts 13:22)

God chose David because of his heart. It wasn't because David's heart was perfect. Only Jesus is perfect. In fact, David ended up committing some serious sins when he was king: adultery and murder. Yet God picked him anyway knowing those sins were in his future. **Jesus would vote for the person with a heart like his.** So then what does it mean to have a heart after God's?

> I will give them one heart, and I will put a new spirit within them. I will
> take the stony heart out of their flesh, and will give them a heart of flesh,
> that they may walk in my statutes, and keep my ordinances, and do them.
> They will be my people, and I will be their God. (Ezekiel 11:19-20)

This Scripture describes two kinds of hearts. A "stony heart" and a "heart of flesh." The "heart of flesh" comes with "a new spirit" that God provides. This results in obedience to God. When someone places their faith in Jesus, they're filled with his Holy Spirit (Ephesians 1:13-14). That's the "new spirit" that's required for a "heart of flesh." When a person believes that Jesus is the Son of God, that he died for their sins, that he didn't stay dead, and that he's alive and reigning in heaven, they get a perfect heart. King David describes it for us here in a conversation he had with his son, Solomon:

> You, Solomon my son, know the God of your father, and serve him with a
> perfect heart and with a willing mind; for Yahweh searches all hearts, and
> understands all the imaginations of the thoughts. If you seek him, he will
> be found by you; but if you forsake him, he will cast you off forever. (1
> Chronicles 28:9)

A perfect heart requires a willing mind. That's because this type of person will desire to do Jesus's will. We know David sought after God with all his heart. He wanted to please God by doing God's will (2 Chronicles 7:17). In fact, that's even why Jesus came, to do God's will. Earlier in this chapter, we read that Jesus was obedient to God to the point of death. Has the candidate you want to vote for put their faith in Jesus and do they desire to do his will? **Jesus would vote for the person with a perfect heart.**

I know what you're thinking. How are we supposed to vote if it doesn't seem like any of the candidates have put their faith in Jesus? That's an omen in and of itself that we'll get to later in this book. First, you need to know that Jesus wants everyone to be saved. He wants everyone to come to know him and put their faith in him (2 Peter 3:9). **Jesus will always pick a leader who will draw people to God.** Israel's sin cycle that's clearly seen in the Old Testament illustrates this. The people had a godly leader like King David. When he died, they started drifting away from God. Eventually they forgot about all the miracles God did for them. The rulers and the people started worshiping idols and the evil rulers started oppressing them. That's when the people finally turned back to God. God rescued them, the people repented, and the cycle started over. The key takeaway here is if the people continued to have a leader like King David, they wouldn't have drifted away from God to begin with. We should always vote for the person who's as closely aligned with God's own heart as possible. So, let's continue examining more qualities that God looks for in a person's heart.

The heart of a servant comes up frequently in the Bible. A *servant* is a person who performs the duties of a master. King David had this type of heart (1 Kings 14:8). He willingly fought God's battles. It's also referred to as an obedient heart in which it was used to describe King Josiah (2 Kings 23:25). He obeyed all the laws of Moses and followed God with all his heart. There's also a fear of God that's associated with servant hearts (Deuteronomy 5:29, 10:12). That's when we express wonder, awe, and respect toward God. Those feelings toward God lead to worship, prayer, and spending time reading the Bible.

Digging deeper, there's also a concern for others and for the needy when you have a heart like a servant. The prophet Elisha is a great example of this. He felt compassion for people and acted to help them. He helped a poor widow provide for herself. He helped a woman whose son died by earnestly praying for him. God heard his prayers and brought him back to life. He also fed the needy during a famine (2 Kings 4). Servants take action and get things done. They willingly work for the Lord.

Of course, Jesus displayed what it truly means to be a servant by dying for our sins. However, he also gave a hands-on lesson regarding this to his disciples. It was the night before his crucifixion, and they had all just finished the Passover meal. That's when the disciples started arguing amongst themselves about which of them would be the greatest. Here's what Jesus told them:

> He said to them, "The kings of the nations lord it over them, and those who have authority over them are called 'benefactors.' But not so with you. Rather, the one who is greater among you, let him become as the younger, and one who is governing, as one who serves. For who is greater, one who sits at the table, or one who serves? Isn't it he who sits at the table? But I am among you as one who serves. (Luke 22:25-27)

To be great requires serving. Then Jesus proceeded to wash each of the disciple's feet while they all sat at the table. He was the greatest in the room and yet he performed what they considered the lowest, demeaning task. He was showing them that being a servant leader doesn't repel people from you. It does the opposite. It draws people to you and creates respect and love. When considering a candidate, look at how they serve others and what they're willing to do for the people. See how they treat the hard working citizens of the country. What do they do when a natural disaster strikes? Are they out there helping and comforting the people or not? **Jesus would vote for the person with the heart of a servant.**

Another type of heart to consider when deciding upon a candidate is the generous heart. After Moses led the Israelites out of Egyptian slavery, he took an offering for God's tabernacle. He asked that those with "generous hearts" present their gifts to the Lord (Exodus 35:5). We learn that all of the people were eager to help, and they gave freely to God. There's a key truth there. People who are givers are ultimately giving to God (Proverbs 19:17). It demonstrates their love. Generosity also requires sacrifice. We must give something up in order to give it to someone else. God gave us the most generous gift he could. His name is Jesus and he sacrificed himself because he loves us.

Boaz was a wealthy landowner with a giving heart. He let the poor work behind his harvesters and gather grain from his field. He even had his men pull out bundles and purposely drop them for Ruth, a woman working in his field. What's more is that he let the women work in his field throughout the entire harvest. He was generous every day and willingly sacrificed from his own wealth (Ruth 2). What about the candidate you're considering? Look at what they spend their time and money on. Is it themselves or others? How do they measure up when compared to Boaz? **Jesus would vote for the person with a generous heart.**

Now, let's consider another heart. As a new young ruler, King Solomon asked God for some help:

> "Give your servant therefore an understanding heart to judge your people, that I may discern between good and evil; for who is able to judge this great people of yours?" This request pleased the Lord, that Solomon had asked this thing. God said to him, "Because you have asked this thing, and

have not asked for yourself long life, nor have you asked for riches for yourself, nor have you asked for the life of your enemies, but have asked for yourself understanding to discern justice, behold, I have done according to your word. Behold, I have given you a wise and understanding heart, so that there has been no one like you before you, and after you none will arise like you." (1 Kings 3:9-12)

He asked God for an "understanding heart" otherwise known as wisdom and wow, did he get it. The Bible says he had knowledge as vast as the sand that is on the seashore (1 Kings 4:29). Even the queen of Sheba traveled to speak with him and get her questions answered (1 Kings 10:1). Did you notice why Solomon asked for wisdom? It's because he wanted to be able to judge God's people fairly. He needed to be able to discern the truth and recognize right from wrong. God was so impressed with Solomon's request that he gave him abundant wealth in addition to wisdom. That demonstrates how valuable this trait is. The candidate you vote for should be wise as well. Does the person have the education and experience that'll enable their success in the leadership role? Do they value truth and hold others accountable to doing what's right? **Jesus would vote for the person with a wise and understanding heart.**

Speaking of judging people fairly, there's another heart that goes hand in hand with Solomon's wise heart. It's the incorruptible heart. In the Bible, it's called a heart that's full of integrity or uprightness (1 Chronicles 29:17). This heart describes someone who has strong moral convictions. They strive to do the right thing and behave as an ambassador of Jesus. They don't get pleasure from doing things that are sinful or by indulging in things they shouldn't, like alcohol (Proverbs 31:4-5). They certainly wouldn't take a bribe (Proverbs 29:4). In fact, they despise corruption.

There's a king in the Bible who had a heart like this. In the early years of King Asa's reign, he abhorred idol worship and tore down the altars and shrines of false gods in every single one of Judah's towns (2 Chronicles 14). He repaired the altar the people built to worship God and he got the people to renew their covenant with the Lord. His grandmother didn't get special treatment either:

King Asa even deposed his grandmother Maacah from her position as

> queen mother because she had made an obscene Asherah pole. He cut
> down her obscene pole, broke it up, and burned it in the Kidron Valley. (2
> Chronicles 15:16 NLT)

Not only did King Asa cut down and burn his grandmother's idol, but he also removed her from his court. He took away her position of authority over the people because she misguided them. People with incorruptible hearts are cleaners. King Asa cleaned up Judah by removing the corruption and reestablishing righteousness. How about the candidate you'd like to vote for? Do they have strong moral convictions and a desire to wipe out wickedness like King Asa? **Jesus would vote for the person with the heart full of integrity.**

A word comes to mind when I think of people like King Asa. It's zealous. People who passionately pursue something are zealous. The apostle Paul is probably the best example of this in the Bible. Before he knew Jesus, he was so passionate about his faith in the law that he persecuted people who followed Jesus (Acts 22:3-4; Galatians 1:13-14). He was a terrorist. Ah! But you know what happened to him while he was traveling to Damascus to round up some believers. That's right, he met Jesus. And it changed his heart.

> No, a true Jew is one whose heart is right with God. And true circumcision
> is not merely obeying the letter of the law; rather, it is a change of heart
> produced by God's Spirit. And a person with a changed heart seeks praise
> from God, not from people. (Romans 2:29 NLT)

Paul described his changed heart as being produced by God's Holy Spirit. After Jesus confronted him and he believed, he realized he was a sinner. In fact, he described himself as the worst sinner (1 Timothy 1:12-16). He repented and turned away from his wicked ways. His zeal didn't disappear. It was just re-purposed. With his changed heart, Jesus would use him to advance the gospel. As one of the early church leaders, he had a profound impact on the world. And he continues to today because a good portion of the New Testament was written by him.

We often get hung up on finding a candidate who's perfect, who's never sinned, and who's never been on the wrong side of an issue. Jesus doesn't look at that. This is what he looks for:

The sacrifices of God are a broken spirit. O God, you will not despise a broken and contrite heart. (Psalm 51:17)

It doesn't matter what sinful things someone did in their past. What matters is what their heart is like today. Has the candidate you're considering turned from their prior sinful ways? Are they still fighting against God or are they now fighting for the things that God would fight for? **Jesus would vote for the person with a repentant heart.**

Another characteristic of someone who has turned from their prior sinful ways is humility. They have the ability to reflect on their actions and change course when presented with a better way. They aren't proud, haughty, or stuck-up. In fact, they are the very opposite. They have a humble heart (Psalm 131:1). Do you know who the Bible says is the most humble person? It's Moses (Numbers 12:3). When he described humility to the Israelites, he told them it was a test from God to prove their character, to see if they would obey (Deuteronomy 8). One of the roots of a humble heart is the ability to listen and receive advice.

One of the Egyptian Pharaohs mentioned in the Bible did exactly that. He listened to a godly man named Joseph. Do you remember the story? Pharaoh had a nightmare about sickly scrawny cows eating fat healthy cows and knew it was a bad omen. Pharaoh sought advice from his wise men who remembered Joseph could interpret dreams. Joseph consulted God and told Pharaoh that his dream was about the future. They would have seven years of prosperity followed by seven years of famine. He told Pharaoh they should collect grain during the good years so that they'd have it during the dry years. Now, Pharaoh could have responded in a number of ways to what Joseph said. I think many rulers today would flat out laugh at someone like Joseph who professed to talk with God and speak the future. They'd completely dismiss what he said. Not only that, but many rulers wouldn't have sought advice to begin with. They'd boast in their ability to figure everything out. That's not what Pharaoh did though. This king of Egypt listened to a man he didn't even know. He knew there was wisdom in his words. Pharaoh not only chose to heed Joseph's warning and advice, but he appointed Joseph to supervise it all. This Pharaoh's humble heart ended up saving his people. When looking at a candidate to vote for, consider their ability to seek counsel from others who are wise.

King Hezekiah is another good example. The Bible says he was faithful and trusted in God, so he was successful in all that he did.

> Hezekiah didn't reciprocate appropriate to the benefit done for him, because his heart was lifted up. Therefore there was wrath on him, Judah, and Jerusalem. However, Hezekiah humbled himself for the pride of his heart, both he and the inhabitants of Jerusalem, so that Yahweh's wrath didn't come on them in the days of Hezekiah. Hezekiah had exceedingly great riches and honor. He provided himself with treasuries for silver, for gold, for precious stones, for spices, for shields, and for all kinds of valuable vessels.... Moreover he provided for himself cities, and possessions of flocks and herds in abundance; for God had given him abundant possessions. ... However, concerning the ambassadors of the princes of Babylon, who sent to him to inquire of the wonder that was done in the land, God left him to test him, that he might know all that was in his heart. (2 Chronicles 32:25-27, 29, 31)

Here we read that Hezekiah was very wealthy and when the Babylonian princes asked him about it, instead of attributing his success to God, he attributed it to himself. Uh oh! He could have been a powerful witness for God. But he had a prideful heart. So, God afflicted him with a sickness that made him realize his error. He told God he was sorry for what he'd done (Isaiah 38). He humbled himself because he knew his success was from God. This is another important characteristic of a heart full of humility. They know their success can't be attributed solely to themselves. They're able to recognize the help they've received along their journey. Is the candidate you're considering boasting about themselves or what others have done for them?

Hezekiah displayed another type of heart we're going to examine in more detail shortly. In his humility he also had a thankful heart. In fact, he was thankful for the sickness that God inflicted on him because it was for his own good (Isaiah 38). I don't know about you, but I don't usually thank God for my misery. So, I'm impressed. I think God was impressed too. When God promised to restore Hezekiah's health, Hezekiah asked for a sign. God moved the shadow on the sundial backward ten steps (Isaiah 38:8). God turned back time for him! That should tell us how much Hezekiah's heart meant to God. Does your candidate look for the good and give thanks in the midst of difficult times? **Jesus would vote for the person with a humble heart.**

Let's continue looking at the thankful heart. This type of heart is full of emotions. It goes hand in hand with joy and praise. The apostle Paul describes it for us here:

> And let the peace of God rule in your hearts, to which also you were called in one body, and be thankful. Let the word of Christ dwell in you richly; in all wisdom teaching and admonishing one another with psalms, hymns, and spiritual songs, singing with grace in your heart to the Lord. (Colossians 3:15-16)

"With grace in your heart" means with thanksgiving. When God has done something good and wonderful in your life, you might think to thank him. Doing so might lead to you telling God how good he is and then, before you know it, you've got a joyful tune in your head and heart. That's because a thankful heart produces a rejoicing heart. Now, how many of you have considered thanking God before something wonderful happened?

King Jehoshaphat is an expert on a thankful heart. Several nations declared war against King Jehoshaphat, and it terrified him. He fasted and prayed to God for guidance, along with all his people. God answered their prayers and told them not to be afraid. He instructed them to march out against their enemy, take their positions, stand still, and watch (2 Chronicles 20). Let's read what happened next:

> As they went out, Jehoshaphat stood and said, "Listen to me, Judah and you inhabitants of Jerusalem! Believe in Yahweh your God, so you will be established! Believe his prophets, so you will prosper." When he had taken counsel with the people, he appointed those who were to sing to Yahweh and give praise in holy array as they go out before the army, and say, "Give thanks to Yahweh, for his loving kindness endures forever." When they began to sing and to praise, Yahweh set ambushers against the children of Ammon, Moab, and Mount Seir, who had come against Judah; and they were struck. ... When Judah came to the place overlooking the wilderness, they looked at the multitude; and behold, they were dead bodies fallen to the earth, and there were none who escaped. ... They took plunder for three days, it was so much. On the fourth day, they assembled themselves in Beracah Valley, for there they blessed Yahweh. Therefore

the name of that place was called "Beracah Valley" to this day. (2 Chronicles 20:20-22, 24-26)

You see, King Jehoshaphat knew the secret to a thankful heart. He appointed singers to go before the army and give thanks to God. They were thankful and rejoicing before the battle even started. He knew that a thankful heart didn't depend on their circumstance. How many of us have that kind of faith? As soon as their song of thankfulness departed their lips, God wiped out their enemy. They reaped the benefit and praised God so much that day that they renamed the valley "Beracah," which means Blessing. Their thankfulness produced rejoicing which led to blessing. Does the person you're considering voting for thank God and others for everything they've done for them? How about their attitude? Are they joyful?

I want to point out something else that's required before you can have a thankful heart. Paul mentioned it in the Scripture we looked at above (Colossians 3:15). It's the peace of God. He says it must rule in our hearts for us to be thankful. King Jehoshaphat was at peace. He knew his prayer had been answered and he believed and trusted that God would deliver him and his people. It's this same peace that we get when we place our faith in Jesus (Philippians 4:7). Does your candidate seem at ease and full of faith or are they anxious and fearful about the future? **Jesus would vote for the person with a happy, thankful heart.**

So far, we've looked at nine different kinds of hearts that represent the type of people Jesus would vote for. The last one we're going to discuss is the pure heart. Once again, Paul reveals the truth about a type of heart:

> The purpose of my instruction is that all believers would be filled with love that comes from a pure heart, a clear conscience, and genuine faith. (1 Timothy 1:5 NLT)

The pure heart is one that's filled with love. We started our journey through hearts of the Bible because Jesus is love and he chose King David because he had a heart like his. We also looked at how the apostle Paul described love (1 Corinthians 13:4-7). We're going to finish off by considering another quality of a pure heart filled with love.

It's "boldness," which means confidence and courage.

> We know and have believed the love which God has for us. God is love, and he who remains in love remains in God, and God remains in him. In this, love has been made perfect among us, that we may have boldness in the day of judgment, because as he is, even so we are in this world. There is no fear in love; but perfect love casts out fear, because fear has punishment. He who fears is not made perfect in love. We love him, because he first loved us. (1 John 4:16-19)

People who have a pure heart do brave things. I want you to consider Queen Esther. King Xerxes chose her as his wife not because she was brave or smart or had any other quality of a leader, but because she was beautiful. Even though Xerxes chose her, we must remember that God is in control of the story and chose her first. You see, God knew that one of King Xerxes' advisors would plot to kill the Jewish people. Esther was Jewish. When she became aware of the impending doom of her peoples, she had a difficult choice to make. Would she approach the king and petition him on behalf of her people? I know we don't typically think of having a conversation with someone as difficult, but in this case her life was at stake. That's because they had a law that if you approached the king when you weren't invited and the king refused to see you, then you were punished by death. Esther's life was on the line, but so were the lives of the people she cared about. Which did she value more—hers or theirs?

There's another secret to having a pure heart. It's sacrifice. You can guess what she did. Esther was willing to sacrifice her life to petition the king. Her bravery ended up saving her people. You can read all about her story in the biblical book of Esther. Esther had enormous faith in God and because of that she acted boldly. Esther had a heart like Jesus. One that was full of love for God and her people.

Consider the candidate you'd like to vote for. Have they done brave and bold things? What have they sacrificed because they love and serve the people? **Jesus would vote for the person with a love filled pure heart.**

> Love and faithfulness keep the king safe. His throne is sustained by love.
> (Proverbs 20:28)

CHAPTER 8 – SATAN WOULD VOTE FOR...

In similar fashion to the prior chapter, we're going to start our understanding of who Satan would vote for by first learning who Satan is and what his goals are. Satan is not imaginary, he isn't red with horns, he doesn't have a pitchfork, he isn't the ruler of hell, and he's not the brother of Jesus. Satan is a fallen angel, otherwise known as a demon. He's called fallen because he "fell" from heaven when God kicked him out. He was created by God and given the name Lucifer.

Most people view Satan as some horrendous looking beast. That couldn't be further from the truth. Satan is a beautiful angel and he ruled over angels in heaven as a "cherub who covers." He served God very closely prior to his rebellion. The prophet Ezekiel tells us about Lucifer here:

> You were in Eden, the garden of God. Every precious stone adorned you: ruby, topaz, emerald, chrysolite, onyx, jasper, sapphire, turquoise, and beryl. Gold work of tambourines and of pipes was in you. They were prepared in the day that you were created. You were the anointed cherub who covers. Then I set you up on the holy mountain of God. You have walked up and down in the middle of the stones of fire. You were perfect in your ways from the day that you were created, until unrighteousness was found in you. By the abundance of your commerce, your insides were filled with violence, and you have sinned. Therefore I have cast you as profane out of God's mountain. I have destroyed you, covering cherub, from the middle of the stones of fire. Your heart was lifted up because of your beauty. You have corrupted your wisdom by reason of your splendor. I have cast you to the ground. (Ezekiel 28:13-17)

So, what happened? His "heart was lifted up" means his downfall was the sin of pride. He was also "unrighteous," "filled with violence," "profane," "corrupted," and loved "splendor." That's why God cast him out of heaven. God is perfect and holy and nothing corrupt can be in his presence. That's why we, as sinners, need Jesus and his righteousness to cover us so we can live in the presence of God.

The prophet Isaiah describes the sin that infected Lucifer, which means the "shining one," in this Scripture:

> How you have fallen from heaven, shining one, son of the dawn! How you
> are cut down to the ground, who laid the nations low! You said in your
> heart, "I will ascend into heaven! I will exalt my throne above the stars of
> God! I will sit on the mountain of assembly, in the far north! I will ascend
> above the heights of the clouds! I will make myself like the Most High!"
> Yet you shall be brought down to Sheol, to the depths of the pit. (Isaiah
> 14:12-15)

Did you notice that his sinful downfall started with his heart? He used "I will" five times. The last one sums it up. He wanted to be "like the Most High" means he wanted to be God. In his book *Angels*, Billy Graham states: "Underneath Satan's pride lurked the deadliest of all sins, the sin of covetousness. He wanted what did not belong to him. Virtually every war ever fought began because of covetousness."[1] That's how Satan's war began as well. Once his heart was corrupted, he launched a rebellion against God and convinced a third of the angels to join him (Revelation 12:3-9). God cast him out of heaven to the earth with the other fallen angels. Ever since, he's been wreaking havoc on the earth and afflicting mankind.

We know Lucifer as Satan. He goes by many names in the Bible that reveal his true nature including: god of this world (2 Corinthians 4:4), adversary (1 Peter 5:8), serpent (Genesis 3), devil (Matthew 4), dragon (Revelation 20:2), accuser (Revelation 12:10), father of lies (John 8:44), murderer (John 8:44), deceiver (Revelation 12:9), and a false angel of the light (2 Corinthians 11:14).

You can surmise pretty easily that Satan hates God. Because of that, Satan also hates everything that God loves. You know that God loves you. Thus, Satan hates you. You need to understand that his goal is to keep you from knowing God or Jesus, to keep you from understanding how to get saved, and to prevent you from living in heaven for eternity. He desires to keep people blind to the truth. That way they'll be condemned to the same fate as him, an eternity separated from God and spent in hell. Did you know that hell was created by God specifically for the fallen angels (Matthew 25:41)? It's not meant for you. Heaven is.

When we continue reading Isaiah 14, we learn more about Satan's intentions. His spirit is seen in the behavior of the king of Babylon. He aims to make nations weak, shake the earth and kingdoms through war, make the world a wilderness with disease and plagues, destroy cities, oppress people, rule people with anger, and keep the Israelites imprisoned. Here's how Jesus summed up Satan's motives:

> The thief only comes to steal, kill, and destroy. I came that they may have life, and may have it abundantly. (John 10:10)

"Steal, kill, and destroy." The one word I used to describe Jesus is *love*. Satan's word is the exact opposite. Does the candidate you're interested in supporting display love or hate for the people? **The most important attribute to keep in mind regarding how Satan would vote is hate.** Both of these emotions originate in the heart. Remember from the prior chapter that once a person places their faith in Jesus, he gives them the Holy Spirit and a new heart. A heart just like his. Well, if you don't have a Jesus filled heart that means you have a Satan filled heart.

> You used to live in sin, just like the rest of the world, obeying the devil-- the commander of the powers in the unseen world. He is the spirit at work in the hearts of those who refuse to obey God. (Ephesians 2:2 NLT)

People who aren't obeying Jesus are living in sin and obeying the devil. You know that the "devil" is Satan and the apostle Paul tells us in the verse above that Satan is the spirit working in the hearts of people who obey him. Since that's anyone who hasn't placed their faith in Jesus, that's most of the world! Since Jesus has the perfect heart that means Satan has the opposite, a wicked heart. This is how Jesus described the wicked and evil heart:

> For out of the heart come evil thoughts, murders, adulteries, sexual sins, thefts, false testimony, and blasphemies. (Matthew 15:19)

A ruler who displays those qualities is a ruler that Satan is backing. Let's consider King Solomon. We looked at him in the last chapter as a ruler Jesus would vote for because he had a wise heart. Unfortunately, he was also a ruler Satan was backing. Remember that Satan desires to destroy. He didn't want to see the Israelites get all the blessings God promised to them if the people continued to obey him like they did under King David. Satan is fueled by hatred. So, Satan turned King Solomon's heart. Let's see how he did it:

> Now king Solomon loved many foreign women ... of the nations concerning which Yahweh said to the children of Israel, "You shall not go among them, neither shall they come among you, for surely they will turn away your heart after their gods." Solomon joined to these in love. He had seven hundred wives, princesses, and three hundred concubines. His wives turned his heart away. ... For Solomon went after Ashtoreth the goddess of the Sidonians, and after Milcom the abomination of the Ammonites. Solomon did that which was evil in Yahweh's sight, and didn't go fully after Yahweh, as David his father did. Then Solomon built a high place for Chemosh the abomination of Moab, on the mountain that is before Jerusalem, and for Molech the abomination of the children of Ammon. ... Yahweh was angry with Solomon, because his heart was turned away from Yahweh, the God of Israel, who had appeared to him twice, and had commanded him concerning this thing, that he should not go after other gods; but he didn't keep that which Yahweh commanded. (1 Kings 11:1-3, 5-7, 9-10)

Here we see that King Solomon clearly had a problem with lust. That's one of the sexual sins that's a hallmark of a wicked heart. Lots of foreign women turned his heart. He wanted to please all his wives more than God. So, he built places to worship all their foreign gods and participated in that worship with them. It's sad to see that the great King Solomon ended his journey by being called a ruler who did evil in God's sight.

Take a look at the candidate you're considering voting for. Do they support or commit the acts that comprise a wicked heart? Do they tell the truth? Do they say blasphemous things about God? Since Jesus would vote for a person with a perfect heart, **Satan would vote for the person with a heart like his—a wicked heart.**

Satan accomplished something far greater here than just getting King Solomon to sin. The kingdom of Israel was split in two afterward. The unified nation was no more. There's the destroy that Satan is after. We know he stole Solomon's heart from God, but he also stole the hearts of all the people (1 Kings 11:33). They were all worshiping the foreign gods. Since they worshiped sin, death would be their fate

(James 1:14-15; Romans 6:23). They would die in their sins, unsaved. Satan accomplished all the goals of his wicked heart: steal, destroy, and kill. This has been Satan's tactic throughout history. Get the ruler to sin, then the people will sin, and then they'll all turn away from God. It's a cycle clearly seen in the Old Testament.

How about the person you'd like to vote for? Do they pull people away from God or draw people to him? What legislation do they support regarding prayer in schools and elective Bible classes in public schools? Since Jesus would vote for the leader who will draw people to God, **Satan will always vote for the leader who will turn people away from God.**

Let's look at another type of heart that indicates Satan supports the leader. It's the selfish heart. This heart has the qualities of bitter jealousy, selfish ambition, boasting, lying, confusion, and every evil deed. Yikes!

> If you have bitter jealousy and selfish ambition in your heart, don't boast and don't lie against the truth. This wisdom is not that which comes down from above, but is earthly, sensual, and demonic. For where jealousy and selfish ambition are, there is confusion and every evil deed. (James 3:14-16)

This is not the kind of heart you want to have. A selfish person is someone who is only concerned about themselves. They will seek to benefit themselves at any cost and with complete disregard for others. King Jeroboam had a selfish heart. He succeeded King Solomon as ruler over ten of the twelve tribes of Israel (1 Kings 11:35). He created golden calves for the people to worship and he made anyone a priest who wanted to be one, including himself. He did that because he didn't want the people traveling to Jerusalem to worship at the temple. He was afraid the people would like King Rehoboam better than him and then they'd want to kill him (1 Kings 12). So, he turned the people away from God toward worshiping false gods all because he was jealous of King Rehoboam and he selfishly wanted to remain king. He was also envious of the tribe of Levi. They were the appointed priests who worshiped in the temple. He wanted to be special just like them. So, he violated God's law just so he could be a priest too. King Jeroboam didn't have the interests of his people in his heart. He only cared about himself.

Now, consider the candidate you'd like to see elected. Do they want to serve themselves or serve the people? During their time in office have they done what they promised, or did they lie to you just so they could get elected and flip sides? Since Jesus would vote for the person with the heart of a servant, **Satan would vote for the person with a selfish heart.**

Selfishness goes hand in hand with greed. *Greed* is a selfish or excessive desire for more. In these verses, "heart's cravings" is a greedy lust:

> In arrogance, the wicked hunt down the weak. They are caught in the schemes that they devise. For the wicked boasts of his heart's cravings. He blesses the greedy and condemns Yahweh. (Psalm 10:2-3)

It's ironic that King Jeroboam was jealous of King Rehoboam because they were actually very similar. King Rehoboam succeeded King Solomon and ruled over the people of Israel who lived in Judah. All of the elders of all the people in Israel told him that King Solomon imposed a heavy tax burden on them and asked him to lighten it. The people said they'd all serve him as king over all of Israel if he did. Well, I'm sure you can guess that he didn't. He sought the counsel of his father's advisors, but he had no intention of listening to them. The advisors told him to be a servant to the people. That's what Jesus would have said too. But he dismissed their advice and instead listened to his friends who told him to add an even heavier burden on the people since they complained (1 Kings 12). King Rehoboam was bitter and greedy. He desired wealth for himself above the welfare of the people.

Is your candidate like King Rehoboam? Examine their taxation plan and determine if it's a heavy burden. Since Jesus would vote for the person with a generous heart, **Satan would vote for the person with a greedy heart.**

There's an important characteristic of King Rehoboam that led to his sin. He didn't listen. He didn't listen to the people. He didn't listen to his advisors. He only wanted to listen if the person told him what he desired to hear. As you can imagine, he didn't listen to God either, as evidenced in the verse below:

> He did that which was evil, because he didn't set his heart to seek Yahweh.

(2 Chronicles 12:14)

He had a rebellious disobedient heart too. If you think about it, any heart that doesn't belong to Jesus is rebellious and disobedient. There's a traitorous prince in the Bible that usurped the throne, temporarily, from his father, the king, because he had a rebellious heart. That's right, it's Absalom, King David's son. Absalom was jealous of his father, so he schemed to win the hearts of the people. He went to the city gate early in the morning and told anyone who had a case to bring before King David that there wasn't any judge to hear them. However, if he was their king, he would hear them and give them justice. Absalom was a liar. When one of Absalom's brothers slept with his sister, he had him killed. Absalom was a murderer. When Absalom rose up against his father and took over as king in Jerusalem, he listened to bad advice because he liked what the advisor told him. He didn't realize the advisor was helping King David. Absalom wasn't able to discern the truth. So, he slept with all of his father's concubines on top of the palace for all to see. Then he and his army pursued King David so they could kill him. Absalom certainly had a rebellious heart.

Is your candidate a rebel like Absalom? Have they been involved in trying to overthrow an elected official? Do they think they're smarter than our nation's founding fathers and desire to fundamentally change our democracy? Since Jesus would vote for the person with a wise and understanding heart, **Satan would vote for the person with a disobedient rebellious heart.**

Absalom didn't just have a rebellious heart. He also had a heart that was dishonest and crooked. In this verse, "perverse in heart" means corrupt:

> Those who are perverse in heart are an abomination to Yahweh. (Proverbs 11:20)

A person with a corrupt heart doesn't have moral convictions. They have an "anything goes" spirit. The apostle Paul encountered a couple rulers who were like this. They were the governors of Judea, Felix and his successor Festus. The Jewish high council brought charges against Paul because he believed in Jesus and because they didn't like him preaching the gospel. They wanted him killed. His case was taken to the governor, Felix, to decide. Paul was kept in prison for two years while Felix deliberated. Two years!

> Meanwhile, he also hoped that money would be given to him by Paul, that he might release him. Therefore also he sent for him more often and talked with him. But when two years were fulfilled, Felix was succeeded by Porcius Festus, and desiring to gain favor with the Jews, Felix left Paul in bonds. (Acts 24:26-27)

Felix was looking out for himself, not Paul. He wanted a bribe and he wanted the Jews to like him. He was certainly a corrupt judge who wasn't interested in doing what was right, fair, or just. When Festus became governor, he had the exact same qualities. Since he wanted to please the Jews, the ones who brought charges against Paul, he wanted to hear Paul's case too, but this time in hostile Jerusalem (Acts 25:9). Paul was rescued from Jerusalem by Commander Lysias because the Jews had plotted to kill him. Festus didn't have any regard for Paul either. He was just as crooked as Felix and only wanted what was best for himself.

Consider your candidate in light of these two governors. Do they have strong moral convictions, or are they more like Felix and Festus and are willing to look the other way because they have no moral absolutes? Do they only bend to the wishes of large donors or large corporations because it lines their pockets? Since Jesus would vote for the person with a heart full of integrity, **Satan would vote for the person with a corrupt heart.**

Since Felix and Festus thought more of themselves than others, they were also prideful. That's the next type of heart Satan would support. The prophet Daniel dealt with a proud king. He succeeded Nebuchadnezzar as king of Babylon—King Belshazzar. Some scholars believe Belshazzar was Nebuchadnezzar's grandson, while others believe "son" in the Scripture below is used in a more general sense to denote they occupied the same office.[2]

Now, you may remember from Chapter 6 that King Nebuchadnezzar had a pride problem. His "heart was lifted up" as the Scripture below indicates. So, God drove him from the city, and he became like an animal and ate grass like an ox for years. When he came to his senses, he praised God and humbled himself. Tell me, if you knew someone who had the same thing happen to them, would you remember it? I know you would. Not only that but you'd remember their testimony from that ordeal. It's not everyday someone behaves like a cow for years! Well, King Belshazzar chose not to remember or learn anything from King Nebuchadnezzar. He decided it'd be a good idea to take the gold vessels and cups that were taken from the temple in Jerusalem and drink wine from them with his wives and concubines, all while worshiping false gods of gold and silver. That's when a hand appeared out of thin air and wrote a message to him on the wall. He called the prophet Daniel to interpret it for him:

> To you, king, the Most High God gave Nebuchadnezzar your father the kingdom, and greatness, and glory, and majesty. ... But when his heart was lifted up, and his spirit was hardened so that he dealt proudly, he was deposed from his kingly throne.... He was driven from the sons of men, and his heart was made like the animals', and his dwelling was with the wild donkeys. He was fed with grass like oxen, and his body was wet with the dew of the sky, until he knew that the Most High God rules in the kingdom of men, and that he sets up over it whomever he will. You, his son, Belshazzar, have not humbled your heart, though you knew all this, but have lifted up yourself against the Lord of heaven; and they have brought the vessels of his house before you, and you and your lords, your wives, and your concubines, have drunk wine from them. You have praised the gods of silver and gold, of bronze, iron, wood, and stone, which don't see, or hear, or know; and you have not glorified the God in whose hand your breath is, and whose are all your ways. ... This is the writing that was inscribed: ... MENE: God has counted your kingdom, and brought it to an end. TEKEL: you are weighed in the balances, and are found wanting. PERES: your kingdom is divided, and given to the Medes and Persians. (Daniel 5:18, 20-23, 25-28)

Here we learn that King Belshazzar indeed knew everything that happened to the prior king. But he chose to disregard it all. He didn't believe in God. Instead, he worshiped false gods while mocking and profaning God at the same time by drinking from cups that were dedicated for use in God's temple. He thought a whole lot more of himself than he should have. He didn't have any fear or respect for God.

Is the candidate you'd like to support prideful like King Belshazzar? Do they understand and respect the wishes of the people they represent? Do they surround themselves with wise advisors or are they too arrogant for that? Since Jesus would vote for the person with a humble heart, **Satan would vote for the person with the proud heart.**

Did you notice in the verses above that Nebuchadnezzar's "spirit was hardened" in pride? When we think of things that are hard, we think of stone, brick, and materials that are unmovable and unbreakable. A heart can be hard as well. It's a heart that's stubborn and unwilling to change. Which ruler do you think had the hardest heart in the Bible? I think it was Pharaoh, the one Moses dealt with. I counted 18 references to his hard heart in the book of Exodus.

> When Pharaoh saw that the rain and the hail and the thunders had ceased, he sinned yet more, and hardened his heart, he and his servants. The heart of Pharaoh was hardened, and he didn't let the children of Israel go, just as Yahweh had spoken through Moses. (Exodus 9:34-35)

You know the story of Moses rescuing the Israelites from slavery under the Egyptian Pharaoh (Exodus 7-14). God sent ten plagues against Pharaoh and his people. The signs proved God was to be exalted, not Pharaoh, and that the Israelites were God's people, not Pharaoh's. Even with all of those miraculous signs Pharaoh refused to believe. He didn't want to. He didn't want to let the Israelites go. He didn't want to admit that he himself wasn't a god. What he wanted was to have his way and keep on sinning.

Is the candidate you're considering stubborn like Pharaoh? Despite overwhelming signs and evidence of something, do they refuse to believe? Have they been confronted with a sin or mistake and refuse to own up to it and change their ways? Since Jesus would vote for the person with a repentant heart, **Satan would vote for the person with a hard heart.**

Do you know what Pharaoh did after he finally let the Israelites go? He turned against them and chased after them with his army (Exodus 14). He was so angry that his hard heart exploded in a fit of rage. He was now bent on killing all of them. This is what becomes of the hardest of hearts. They hate, just like Satan does. Hate manifested is murder.

> Anyone who hates another brother or sister is really a murderer at heart. And you know that murderers don't have eternal life within them. (1 John 3:15 NLT)

Consider the candidate you're supporting. What do they do when they don't get their way? Do they accept defeat and carry on or do they get angry, vengeful, and scheme to get even? Since Jesus would vote for the person with a pure heart, **Satan would vote for the person with a murderous heart.**

So far, we've looked at nine different wicked hearts that are just like Satan's. The last heart we're going to look at filled the leaders of the Israelites after they left Egyptian slavery and were traveling with God to the promised land. It's the ungrateful heart.

> Because you didn't serve Yahweh your God with joyfulness and with gladness of heart, by reason of the abundance of all things. (Deuteronomy 28:47)

Korah, Dathan, Abiram, and 250 other leaders rebelled against Moses (Exodus 16). They started out by complaining that Moses was their leader. Then they complained that Moses took them out of Egypt, where they had milk and honey, just so they could die in the desert. They also complained that Moses hadn't yet given them new land with fields and vineyards like he promised. Moses informed them that they weren't complaining about him, but about God. As you can imagine, God wasn't happy about it. These Israelite leaders forgot how horrible their lives were as slaves in Egypt. They cried out to God for help, and they witnessed God's deliverance firsthand. They saw all of the mighty miracles he performed in Egypt, they saw him part the Red Sea, they saw him rain manna from heaven for them to eat every day, and they saw him create rivers of water from rocks in the desert. Yet, they weren't grateful for what God had done for them. Instead, they complained about what God hadn't done for them yet. They should have been filled with joy. But they were thankless grumblers.

Does the candidate you support constantly complain instead of looking for the good? Do they clap or sit in silence when there's reason to celebrate the good things God has done? Since Jesus would vote for the person with a happy, thankful heart, **Satan would vote for the**

person with the sour ungrateful heart.

Dear children, don't let anyone deceive you about this: When people do what is right, it shows that they are righteous, even as Christ is righteous. But when people keep on sinning, it shows that they belong to the devil, who has been sinning since the beginning. But the Son of God came to destroy the works of the devil. Those who have been born into God's family do not make a practice of sinning, because God's life is in them. So they can't keep on sinning, because they are children of God. So now we can tell who are children of God and who are children of the devil. Anyone who does not live righteously and does not love other believers does not belong to God. (1 John 3:7-10 NLT)

CHAPTER 9 – GOD'S GUIDANCE FOR CHOOSING LEADERS

In addition to considering the heart of a person, another good way we can gain wisdom about selecting leaders is by studying what the Bible says about leadership. There are two sections of Scripture that we're going to examine. One regarding how to select a king and one with instructions for selecting an elder of the church. Both examples will shed some light on the qualities we should look for when selecting a leader.

When the Israelites were about to enter the promised land, Moses gave them instructions about selecting a king if that's what they later decided to do. Here's the advice he gave them:

> You shall surely set him whom Yahweh your God chooses as king over yourselves. You shall set as king over you one from among your brothers. You may not put a foreigner over you, who is not your brother. Only he shall not multiply horses to himself, nor cause the people to return to Egypt, to the end that he may multiply horses; because Yahweh has said to you, "You shall not go back that way again." He shall not multiply wives to himself, that his heart not turn away. He shall not greatly multiply to himself silver and gold. It shall be, when he sits on the throne of his kingdom, that he shall write himself a copy of this law in a book, out of that which is before the Levitical priests. It shall be with him, and he shall read from it all the days of his life, that he may learn to fear Yahweh his God, to keep all the words of this law and these statutes, to do them; that his heart not be lifted up above his brothers, and that he not turn away from the commandment to the right hand, or to the left, to the end that he may prolong his days in his kingdom, he and his children, in the middle of Israel. (Deuteronomy 17:15-20)

First, it says they should pick a king that "God chooses." We're meant to pray about selecting a leader and ask God for guidance. Next, we see the king should be a fellow Israelite and not a foreigner. That's because a foreigner wouldn't know God nor would he obey God's commands. So a foreign king would put them at risk of falling away from the Lord. It's the same with us. The founding fathers of the US determined the president should be a natural born citizen for similar reasons. A foreigner wouldn't know the American culture and values like someone born and raised here. Loyalty matters. Jesus would choose leaders who have a relationship with him and who don't worship false gods.

Next, Moses tells us the king shouldn't "multiply horses to himself" and, more specifically, because God didn't want them returning to Egypt to buy those horses. I know this one seems a bit odd and really specific. There are a couple things here to understand. Multiplying horses means he has a lot more than he needs. Horses were used in war and having too many of them would make the king trust in his own strength instead of God's. That's the sin of the pride of life (1 John 2:16). Jesus would choose a leader who trusts in him for strength. Now, this isn't saying the king shouldn't have an army and be able to protect and defend the nation. Moses didn't say the king shouldn't have any horses. It's the act of multiplying them or having more than enough that's the issue. When considering our leaders, we should be mindful of if they're gathering more items for the government than what's needed. Jesus would choose a leader who calls on God for help.

The second thing we must also remember is that when the Israelites were in Egypt that they worshiped the same false gods the Egyptians did. God delivered them from that, and he didn't want them returning to be tempted again. Today, we shouldn't pick a leader who wants to return the nation to prior bondage or prior sins. A leader shouldn't undo progress God has made. An example for the US would be a candidate who desires to return to a pre-Civil War America when there was segregation and slavery. God delivered us from that. Jesus would choose a leader who follows God, not one who fights against him.

Then Moses says the leader shouldn't "multiply wives to himself" because they will turn his heart away from God. Moses knew a future king would be tempted to marry women from surrounding nations in order to form alliances. Well, we know the surrounding nations worshiped false gods. So those women would bring their false gods and customs with them into any marriage. We also know that God wants leaders to trust in him and not rely on other nations for help or strength. This is the sin of lust of the flesh (1 John 2:16) that would turn the leader away from God and toward seeking pleasure. They wouldn't be serving God and the people anymore. Instead, the king would want to please all of his wives. Today this isn't about leaders having had multiple wives because they've been married and divorced. This is about choosing leaders who aren't involved in sexual sins or a party type lifestyle that would distract them from their purpose. Jesus would choose a leader who is aligned with him and trusts in him.

Next, Moses said the king must not multiply "silver and gold" to himself. Before the people chose Saul as their first king, God warned them the king would tax them (1 Samuel 8). This isn't about leaders who are wealthy and who gained their wealth appropriately. We shouldn't choose leaders that will burden people unnecessarily with taxes just so they can get rich. This is the sin of lust of the eyes (1 John 2:16). Jesus would vote for a leader who wouldn't oppress people financially.

The last part of the Scriptures above tells us the king should write and read God's Word every single day. It's so his heart wouldn't be filled with pride, making him seem better than the people he serves, and turn him away from God. Remember that Jesus would vote for a person with a humble heart. We should elect a leader who makes God's Word a priority in their life as evidenced by them reading it, knowing it, and studying it.

Today, we live in a nation where the church is very much separated from the government. But that's not how it was for the first government God established for the Israelites after he rescued them from Egyptian slavery. Remember while God was clearly their authority, Moses was the spiritual leader and political leader that God placed over the people. Then Moses picked elders from each tribe to share the leadership burden. God's perfect government is a theocracy with Jesus as the ruler. So, it's important for us to understand what qualities Jesus looks for in church leaders. We should look for these same qualities in our political and civic leaders too.

The apostle Paul charged Timothy with appointing church elders in each city he visited. These are the instructions and qualities he told Timothy to look for when choosing one of these leaders for the people:

> Appoint elders in every city, as I directed you— if anyone is blameless, the
> husband of one wife, having children who believe, who are not accused of

loose or unruly behavior. For the overseer must be blameless, as God's steward, not self-pleasing, not easily angered, not given to wine, not violent, not greedy for dishonest gain; but given to hospitality, a lover of good, sober minded, fair, holy, self-controlled, holding to the faithful word which is according to the teaching, that he may be able to exhort in the sound doctrine, and to convict those who contradict him. For there are also many unruly men, vain talkers and deceivers ... whose mouths must be stopped. (Titus 1:5-11)

The elder should be someone who believes in the "faithful word" the disciples taught. As such, he should be able to help others grow in their faith and speak up against people who teach things that contradict God's Word. The elder should have self-discipline and self-control, being considered blameless," "sober minded," "holy," and "not violent." This same type of discipline should be seen in the leader's family life as well. That's because if someone struggles to lead a small family how can they possibly be good at leading a church or nation full of families? If the leader is leading their family, it'll be evidenced by children who behave and who believe. A good elder teaches their children God's Word. The leader should also be content. That manifests by them having one wife and not being greedy. Lastly, they should demonstrate care for others by being hospitable.

We can apply all of these qualities to leaders we're electing. The leader should definitely be self-disciplined and have a family life that reflects that. They should have strong convictions and be comfortable speaking out against those who challenge what they believe. We most certainly want a leader who's a good steward, isn't greedy, and doesn't desire to profit from the people. Leaders should be servants and as such they should have a deep love for the people they serve and want to be pleasant and receptive to them. Let the apostle Paul's guidelines for choosing an elder help you choose a godly leader.

Now that you've got a solid understanding of how God determines leaders and who Jesus would vote for, let's examine why Jesus put certain modern day leaders into power.

PART 4

FATE + FREE WILL: THE OMEN

CHAPTER 10 - THE ELECTION OMEN

In the prior chapters, we looked at how God has given us free will while at the same time orchestrating all things. I likened it to a pick your own adventure book in which God is the author who wrote the story and all the outcomes, and we're the reader choosing the path the story takes. This is the chapter where our free will and God's predetermination come to a head. You see, God has already written the outcome for human government. Every day that passes we move closer and closer to the one world government under rulership of the Antichrist. Jesus Christ, God in the flesh, will rule for eternity after defeating the Antichrist. While we're progressing toward this outcome each day, it's not a straightforward linear progression where you take a step forward each day. Instead, we're progressing in a cyclical fashion. A cycle is simply a period of time in which a sequence of events transpires. You're going to see that during each cycle we either progress toward the final human government, hold our ground, or actually take a step away from the Antichrist government. What's more interesting is that as we examine these cycles, a pattern emerges that we can apply to today. Get ready because the election omen will be revealed.

Let's start our journey by discussing the cycles. If you've read the books of 1 and 2 Kings in the Bible, you'll be familiar with Israel's sin cycle. The people started out with a godly leader and by worshiping God. Then they got a ruler who drew them away from God and they started worshiping false gods. Then the evil ungodly ruler oppressed the people until they finally sought God for help. God delivered them by giving them another godly leader. Then the cycle repeated.

King David is the gold standard for good kings. He followed and obeyed God with all of his heart (1 Kings 14:8). He had a heart like God (Acts 13:22). When he was ruler, the people did not advance toward evil or the Antichrist government. However, that quickly changed with the next rulers. Thus, the cycle begins.

Once David died, his son Solomon became king. Solomon started out doing good but crashed and burned. He did evil because he married a lot of foreign wives, built altars for his wives' false gods, worshiped those false gods, and ultimately turned the people away from God (1

Kings 11). The people took a step toward Satan and his Antichrist government. When King Solomon died, God split the nation of Israel in two—Judah and Israel.

Israel never had a godly ruler after the split. All of its rulers did evil in God's eyes. All they did was take steps toward Satan until they were captured by the Assyrians. Judah on the other hand is where we clearly see cycles and a pattern.

King Solomon's son Rehoboam became king of Judah and he did more evil than King Solomon (1 Kings 14:22). So here we see the people took yet another step toward Satan. After Rehoboam died, his son Abijam was king and he did the same kind of evil (1 Kings 15:3). The people held their ground. They didn't advance toward Satan. The next ruler of Judah was King Asa, Abijam's son. Now he did good in God's eyes. In fact, God compares him to King David (1 Kings 15:11). So here we see the cycle complete. The cycle started with good King David and progressed to a King Rehoboam type of evil with King Abijam before God delivered the people and gave them another godly ruler, King Asa. In that cycle, the people took a couple steps toward Satan.

Let's look at this next cycle that starts with King Asa. The cycle started when the people took a step toward God and away from Satan. After Asa died, his son Jehoshaphat became king and he did good like his father. However, God tells us he didn't remove the pagan shrines (1 Kings 22:43). So, let's say the people took a tiny step toward Satan. The next king was Jehoram, Jehoshaphat's son. He committed evil like Israel's King Ahab did (1 Kings 8:18). That's a whole new level of evil. Of all the evil kings in the Bible, Ahab is the most wicked (1 Kings 16:29-33). He's the polar opposite of King David. Just like God compares good kings to King David, he compares evil kings to King Ahab. Here, we see the people took a leap toward Satan and the final human government during King Jehoram's reign. The cycle continued to progress with Jehoram's son King Ahaziah who did the same kind of evil as Ahab (2 Kings 8:27). It's not until we get to King Joash, Ahaziah's son, that we see a godly ruler again. Now, he wasn't compared to King David because he didn't destroy all the altars of the foreign gods (2 Kings 12:2-3). The people only took a small step back toward God this time.

When we continue to examine the cycles, let's see what emerges. Cycle 1 begins with King David (godly gold standard) and ends with

King Abijam (evil like King Rehoboam). Cycle 2 begins with King Asa (like godly King David) and ends with King Ahaziah (like the most wicked King Ahab). Cycle 3 begins with King Joash (good, but not like King David) and it ends with King Ahaz (evil like King Ahab, 2 Kings 16:2-3). Cycle 4 starts with King Hezekiah (good like King David, 2 Kings 18:3) and finishes with King Amon (evil like King Ahab, 2 Kings 21:20-22). Cycle 5 kicks off with King Josiah (good like King David, 2 Kings 22:2) and terminates with King Zedekiah (evil like Ahab, 2 Kings 24:19). That's the last of the cycles. It's during King Zedekiah's reign that the people of Judah were taken captive to Babylon.

Did you notice a pattern? The people started with the gold standard of godly rulers with King David. As they moved away from God and toward Satan, the rulers became more wicked until they couldn't get any more wicked than King Ahab. Once they got to that level of evil, they always returned to it after the godly king. What's more is that cycle 4 and 5 illustrate the rulership of polar opposites. The people had the most wicked rulers and then a ruler who was like King David. And here lies a key truth in the election omen. Keep in mind that an omen is a prophecy, warning, or sign of a future event. **A nation will advance in wickedness until it reaches the polar opposite of God.**

> They abandoned Yahweh, the God of their fathers, who brought them out of the land of Egypt, and followed other gods, of the gods of the peoples who were around them, and bowed themselves down to them; and they provoked Yahweh to anger. ... Yahweh raised up judges, who saved them out of the hand of those who plundered them. Yet they didn't listen to their judges; for they prostituted themselves to other gods, and bowed themselves down to them. They quickly turned away from the way in which their fathers walked, obeying Yahweh's commandments. They didn't do so. ... But when the judge was dead, they turned back, and dealt more corruptly than their fathers in following other gods to serve them and to bow down to them. They didn't cease what they were doing, or give up their stubborn ways. (Judges 2:12, 16-17, 19)

As the verses above show us, this same pattern was evident during Israel's time of judges. After Moses and Joshua died, the people turned away from God. God sent judges to save them and turn them back, but they always "dealt more corruptly than their fathers." They continued to sin more and more each time they turned away. You may be wondering why the cycles didn't keep going. Why didn't God send the people another godly ruler after King Zedekiah? Let's see what God told the prophet, Jeremiah:

> Yahweh said to me, "Proclaim all these words in the cities of Judah, and in the streets of Jerusalem, saying, 'Hear the words of this covenant, and do them. For I earnestly protested to your fathers in the day that I brought them up out of the land of Egypt, even to this day, rising early and protesting, saying, "Obey my voice." Yet they didn't obey, nor turn their ear, but everyone walked in the stubbornness of their evil heart. Therefore I brought on them all the words of this covenant, which I commanded them to do, but they didn't do them.'" (Jeremiah 11:6-8)

God gave them a prophet who warned them what would happen if they didn't follow God. Jeremiah warned the people that judgment was coming. He even told them Nebuchadnezzar was going to invade. As the Scripture above says, they refused to listen. They had evil stubborn hearts. That's a heart like Satan. The people had reached the point of no return. God didn't give them a godly king because the people didn't want one. They didn't want to repent and turn back to God. That's why God sent a foreign ruler, King Nebuchadnezzar, to take them into captivity. Thus, another piece of the election omen is revealed. **When a nation turns completely away from God and reaches the point of no return it will bring judgment upon itself.**

> "Everyone who passes by it will be astonished and say, 'Why has Yahweh done this to this land and to this house?' They shall answer, 'Because they abandoned Yahweh, the God of their fathers, who brought them out of the land of Egypt, and took other gods, worshiped them, and served them. Therefore he has brought all this evil on them.'" (2 Chronicles 7:21-22)

The Scripture above shows us that God warned the people about his judgment when King Solomon reigned. Yet, the judgment isn't entirely bad for the people. Wicked and oppressive rulers have a way of sparking revival. That's because people who are oppressed think back on their past when they had it better and they remember God. God knew they would remember him and cry out to him for help during their oppression in Babylon. You may recall from a prior chapter that King Nebuchadnezzar ended up turning to God as well (Daniel 4). So, we see that God ultimately used this calamity for good. That's another truth in the election omen. **A nation under an oppressive ruler will remember God and seek him once again.**

> The Egyptians mistreated us, afflicted us, and imposed hard labor on us. Then we cried to Yahweh, the God of our fathers. Yahweh heard our voice, and saw our affliction, our toil, and our oppression. Yahweh brought us out of Egypt with a mighty hand, with an outstretched arm, with great terror, with signs, and with wonders. (Deuteronomy 26:6-8)

I also want you to notice that Jeremiah was told to remind the people of the "covenant." They were supposed to be obeying it and they weren't. This is referring to the covenant God gave the Israelites through Moses. God had rescued the people from Egyptian captivity, and they were getting ready to enter the promised land (Deuteronomy 28-30). It's a prophecy that describes the blessings they'd get if they obeyed God and the curses they'd get if they didn't. The blessings that are promised include abundant crops and livestock, God conquering their enemies, prosperity, many children, and them lending to nations instead of borrowing. Their nation would be awed. Now, if they didn't obey, they'd get the curses which include frustration with everything they did, diseases, scorching heat and drought, no rain, locusts, defeat by their enemies, panic, oppression, and exile. Their nation would be ridiculed.

So, what did the covenant entail? What were they supposed to be doing?

> Behold, I have set before you today life and prosperity, and death and evil. For I command you today to love Yahweh your God, to walk in his ways and to keep his commandments, his statutes, and his ordinances, that you may live and multiply, and that Yahweh your God may bless you in the land where you go in to possess it. But if your heart turns away, and you will not hear, but are drawn away and worship other gods, and serve them, I declare to you today that you will surely perish. ... I call heaven and earth to witness against you today that I have set before you life and

death, the blessing and the curse. Therefore choose life, that you may live, you and your descendants, to love Yahweh your God, to obey his voice, and to cling to him; for he is your life, and the length of your days, that you may dwell in the land which Yahweh swore to your fathers, to Abraham, to Isaac, and to Jacob, to give them. (Deuteronomy 30:15-20)

It's simple. They were supposed to love God. When you love someone with all your heart you naturally want to do things that please them. If we love God, we'll desire to obey him. The more we love God, the more our heart becomes like God's heart.

So, the people got to a point that they no longer loved God. They didn't want anything to do with him. So, God gave them exactly what they wanted. He gave them a foreign ruler who didn't know God, Nebuchadnezzar. There's a key truth here that further reveals the election omen. **God gives a nation the ruler they desire.**

Yes, they knew God, but they wouldn't worship him as God or even give him thanks. And they began to think up foolish ideas of what God was like. As a result, their minds became dark and confused. ... And instead of worshiping the glorious, ever-living God, they worshiped idols made to look like mere people and birds and animals and reptiles. So God abandoned them to do whatever shameful things their hearts desired. (Romans 1:21, 23-24)

If the majority of people in a nation want to follow God, they'll get a godly ruler. However, if they don't, then of course the opposite will happen. You must remember that we all have free will. We live in a country in which we get to exercise our free will and elect leaders. God honors the choices we make with the free will that he gives us. He then uses our free will to accomplish his purposes. He knows the outcome and consequences of the choices we make.

The ruler of a nation reflects the collective attitudes and beliefs of the nation. What's more is that the leader is a key instrument in determining the future course of a nation. Remember that if Satan can get the ruler to sin, the people will follow. Just think of all the kings in the Bible who built idols for the people to worship. Even Aaron created a golden calf for the people to worship while Moses was on the mountain with God. Aaron created the calf because the people asked him to (Exodus 32). You know, he could have said no. But he didn't because he had the same attitude the people did. This is also clear from the cycles we looked at earlier because as the cycles progressed the rulers continued to get more and more evil until they reached the King Ahab level of wickedness. That's why it's so important for us to vote for leaders who have hearts that Jesus can get inside and act through. Otherwise, Satan will fill their heart instead.

Now let's apply what we've learned to today. Do you think we're following this biblical pattern? First, let's start by considering if the US has any tie to the Mosaic Covenant and the blessings and curses. What's really fascinating is not only is there a connection, but it's been there since the very beginning of our nation! Our very first president, George Washington, spoke these words during his inauguration speech in 1789:

> "...it would be peculiarly improper to omit in this first official Act, my fervent supplications to that Almighty Being who rules over the Universe, who presides in the Councils of Nations, and whose providential aids can supply every human defect, that his benediction may consecrate to the liberties and happiness of the People of the United States, a Government instituted by themselves for these essential purposes: and may enable every instrument employed in its administration to execute with success, the functions allotted to his charge. In tendering this homage to the Great Author of every public and private good I assure myself that it expresses your sentiments not less than my own; nor those of my fellow-citizens at large, less than either. No People can be bound to acknowledge and adore the invisible hand, which conducts the Affairs of men more than the People of the United States. Every step, by which they have advanced to the character of an independent nation, seems to have been distinguished by some token of providential agency.
>
> "Since we ought to be no less persuaded that the propitious smiles of Heaven, can never be expected on a nation that disregards the eternal rules of order and right, which Heaven itself has ordained: And since the preservation of the sacred fire of liberty, and the destiny of the Republican model of

Government, are justly considered as deeply, perhaps as finally staked, on the experiment entrusted to the hands of the American people."[1]

In his first official act, Washington made a fervent supplication, that's a heartfelt prayer, to God. He asked God to consecrate the government in its purpose to provide liberties and happiness to the people of the United States. *Consecrate* means to make sacred or set apart to worship God. Hum, that's what God's chosen people, the Israelites, are—set apart to worship God. Washington further states that his homage or respect for God expresses the people's sentiments as well. So now this entire prayer applies to all the people and the nation. Then he confirms the covenant, just like Moses did before they entered the promised land, when he said we can't expect the blessings or "smiles of Heaven" if we disregard God's eternal rules.

So, what are God's eternal rules? It's the Ten Commandments (Exodus 20). But Washington and the people of his time had the New Testament which sums up God's rules nicely. In fact, this particular Scripture is spoken by Jesus himself:

> One of the scribes ... asked him, "Which commandment is the greatest of all?" Jesus answered, "The greatest is, 'Hear, Israel, the Lord our God, the Lord is one: you shall love the Lord your God with all your heart, and with all your soul, and with all your mind, and with all your strength.' This is the first commandment. The second is like this, 'You shall love your neighbor as yourself.' There is no other commandment greater than these." (Mark 12:28-31)

"Love the Lord your God with all your heart." That's what God requires of us. You see, if we love God, we'll naturally love the things God loves, including our neighbor. This is the exact same command that God gave the people of Israel before they entered the promised land (Deuteronomy 30:15-20). This is the command the covenant hinges upon. If the nation loves God, the nation is blessed. If the nation turns from God and abandons their love for him, the nation is cursed.

You know, George Washington and Moses have a lot in common. God used both of them to deliver people from bondage. Moses rescued the Israelites from slavery under Pharaoh and Washington was commander of the Continental Army during the American Revolutionary War against Great Britain. God used both of them to establish and lead a new nation. Moses led Israel and Washington led the US. God was with both leaders and established his covenant with the people through them. Moses proclaimed God's covenant to the people before they entered the promised land. We read above that Washington established God's covenant with America on his inauguration day. We, the people of the US, are indeed tied to the Mosaic Covenant and God's blessings and curses. Because of this, we can apply the cycles we learned about to the US as well.

So, what do the cycles reveal for the US? Where are we in the progression toward the polar opposite rulers and the point of no return? Well, unless you've been living under a rock the last few years, I'm sure you've noticed our country seems more divided today than it has in the past. In particular, we're divided about our politics, government, and our president. It seems like President Donald Trump is the polar opposite of President Barak Obama, doesn't it? The Democratic Party hates Trump so much that they've done everything they can think of to remove him from office. The level of attacks he's received from the Democrats and the media hasn't happened to a president before. In the 2016 presidential election, 79% of Evangelical Christians voted for Trump while 60% of atheists and agnostics voted for Clinton.[2] What if we look at the 2008 presidential election between Obama and McCain? Turns out 88% of Evangelical Christians voted for McCain while 76% of atheists and agnostics voted for Obama.[3] Wow! There is very clearly a spiritual divide among who votes for particular rulers. **The United States has most certainly arrived at the time of polar opposite rulers.**

We're seeing the fulfillment of the election omen and we're already quite far into the cycle of progression. So, have we reached the point of no return? Is God's judgment coming?

There's another cycle and pattern I want to look at with you before we consider how far along we are on God's timetable. I hope all of you reading this are aware that we are indeed living in the end times. It's the period of time before Jesus's second coming. The biggest sign of his soon return is the nation of Israel. God prophesied his people would once again be a nation when Jesus returns (Isaiah 66, Ezekiel 36-37, Joel 3:2). That happened in May of 1948. Israel had ceased being a unified nation after King Solomon's reign. They were taken into Babylonian captivity in 586 BC. Although they returned to their land 70 years later, they were never a nation again until 1948. It's only been 53 years since Jerusalem was restored to the nation of Israel in 1967. Since we're living in the end and I've established that cycles are important, we must look at the very beginning to discover the next pattern.

After God created the earth and Adam and Eve, the population multiplied. Although the people didn't have a ruler, they still followed the truths revealed in the election omen. The people advanced in wickedness until they were as wicked as Satan. In fact, they were so evil that God was sorry he ever made people. That's when the people reached the point of no return and brought judgment upon themselves. God flooded the entire earth and destroyed everyone and everything (Genesis 6-8). God saved the only person who loved him, Noah. Noah chose God while everyone else chose Satan. God gave all of them what they asked for.

In the time between the flood and when God established kings for his people, two events stand out. The first is the tower of Babel. After the flood, God told the people to spread out and fill the earth. They disobeyed and did the opposite when they got together in one city and built a tower that could reach up into the heavens. So, they went up instead of out. It was an act of defiance. They wanted to be like God and live where God lives. They were full of pride and worshiped themselves. That sounds like Satan, doesn't it? Once again, we see the cycle and election omen manifest. The people turned from God, toward Satan, and brought judgment on themselves. God stopped their construction project, gave them all different languages, and made them spread out over the earth (Genesis 11).

The second event is the evil Egyptian ruler, Pharaoh. Just like what happened after King David, the people continued to sin, commit evil, and worship false gods. They reached the point of no return and ended up as slaves of Pharaoh. What's crazy is that they willingly chose to be slaves. They sold all of their possessions and themselves to Pharaoh in exchange for food. They trusted Pharaoh to take care of them instead of God (Genesis 47). Just as the election omen foretells, God gave the people the ruler they wanted—Pharaoh. When they finally cried out to God, he sent Moses to rescue the people from that oppression with all sorts of powerful signs and miracles so they would know God and trust in him (Exodus 7-11).

Let's look at the pattern we see in these events I just described in reverse order. Step 7 is God's deliverance with powerful signs from the evil ruler Pharaoh. Moving backward, Step 6 is life under the evil ruler Pharaoh. Step 5 is when God directly intervened after they built the tower of Babel. Step 4 is when they had a centralized government and built the tower of Babel because they desired to be God. Continuing in reverse, Step 3 is where we get to the time of righteous Noah after the flood. Step 2 is when God destroyed the world with the flood. Lastly, Step 1 is when God created the earth.

Now, let's overlay that pattern above to what the Bible tells us the future holds. It's going to be quite revealing! Since we're living in the end times, the next event the Bible tells us to be expecting is the rapture (1 Thessalonians 4:16-17). It's when Jesus removes the people who've put their faith in him from what's coming on the earth. They'll be safely residing in heaven. This hearkens back to Step 7, God's deliverance from Pharaoh with powerful signs. The rapture will certainly be a powerful deliverance.

After the rapture, the people left behind will live under the rule of the Antichrist (Revelation 13). We're going to learn more about him in a later chapter. For now, you just need to know he'll be the most evil ruler. It'll be like Step 6 when the Israelites lived under evil Pharaoh's rule.

The time period after the rapture and before Jesus's second coming is called the tribulation period because of the great anguish that people will experience (Mark 13:19). That's because God will be directly intervening by sending all sorts of judgments and plagues against the Antichrist and mankind (Revelation 6-19). Many judgments are eerily similar to the plagues God sent against Pharaoh. So, this is like a mix of Step 6 and Step 5 when God directly intervened after they built the tower of Babel and sent judgments against Pharaoh.

Another interesting thing that happens during the tribulation period is that the Antichrist establishes and rules over a centralized world government in which everyone worships him (Revelation 13). He even declares himself God (2 Thessalonians 2:4). The people's worship shows their agreement and devotion to him and the world government. It's like Step 4 when our ancestors got together in one city and built the tower of Babel so they could be like God, isn't it?

Continuing our progression forward we get to Jesus's second coming and his reign upon the earth (Revelation 20). That's like the time right after the flood, when righteous Noah lived on the earth, Step 3.

After Jesus's 1,000 year reign on the earth, God will destroy the earth in a great fire (Revelation 21; 2 Peter 3:5-7). That's very much like Step 2 above when God destroyed the earth the first time with a flood.

Lastly, God will create a new earth and a new heaven, just like in Step 1. Please refer to the table below to see a side by side comparison of what we just learned.

Moses to Creation	Today to Eternity
7. God's deliverance from Pharaoh with powerful signs	1. The rapture, deliverance from tribulation and a powerful sign
6. Evil Pharaoh rules the people	2. Evil Antichrist rules the people
5. God intervenes and judges the people	3. God intervenes with tribulation judgments
4. Tower of Babel and centralized government	4. Antichrist one world government
3. Righteous Noah	5. Jesus's second coming and his 1,000 year reign
2. God's destruction of the earth with the flood	6. God's destruction of the earth with fire
1. God creates the heavens and the earth	7. God creates a new heaven and new earth

This is really intriguing. The pattern reveals that the end of times will play out like the beginning of times, only in reverse order. It's almost as if God is undoing what was done. In a way, he is doing just that. When Adam and Eve sinned, it infected and cursed all of God's creation. The Bible tells us how God plans to redeem us, restore us, and undo the curse of sin (Romans 8). If you want to be included in God's redemption and perhaps even get raptured, all you have to do is put your faith in Jesus.

The key to understanding if the US has reached the point of no return is figuring out how close we are to the Antichrist's reign.

Remember, the election omen foretells that once a nation reaches that point of no return that judgment comes upon it. The Bible tells us what that judgment is that's coming. It's the tribulation period when the Antichrist is the ruler, and there's a centralized one world government.

A distinguishing factor of the Antichrist's reign is the one world government. You know we already have the foundation of that in place today. It's the United Nations. Let's discover when we as a globe decided to start creating our modern day tower of Babel and world government. We have to go way back to 1920. Yes, that's right. It's been 100 years! I find that a bit ominous, don't you? The League of Nations was created right after World War I. The US had an instrumental role in its creation. President Wilson won the Nobel peace prize for his efforts. Even though our country helped create it, we weren't a member of it. The League of Nations ultimately failed in its goal of preventing another world war and it dissolved in 1946 when it transferred all of its assets to the United Nations. As you likely guessed, the United Nations was created in 1945 as a result of World War II. Once again, our nation played a key role in its creation. However, this time the US was one of the founding member nations. The key difference between the United Nations and the one world government is that each country still has national sovereignty today. When the Antichrist reigns, they won't. Of the 195 countries in the world today, 193 are in the United Nations.[4] Wow! I'd say that's a really clear sign that we're close to the Antichrist's global government.

Another indicator we can look at is the rise of Pharaohs, or dictators. The Antichrist will be the ultimate evil dictator. After the people built the tower of Babel, the next key event was their enslavement by Pharaoh. So, let's see if there's any progression toward dictators or if democracy still reigns today.

After World War I, three notable dictators rose to power. Stalin ruled over the Soviet Union, Hitler ruled over Germany, and Mussolini ruled Italy. All of them persecuted people and committed genocide. Millions of people died under these rulers. Hitler even started World War II when he invaded Poland. I think we can all agree that these are notorious bad guys. So, what about after World War II?

After World War II democracy flourished for a period of time. However, we still had dictators. The first dictator who comes to mind is Mao Zedong who ruled China. Like the dictators before him, he also committed mass genocide. It's estimated 40 to 80 million peopled died during his reign.[5] That makes him the most wicked 20th century dictator. Yes, even worse than Hitler.

A non-profit organization, Freedom House, prepares annual reports on freedom across the world. It's a left leaning partisan publication, but it has some valuable insights. They look at trends in the types of governments and rulers. Back in 2000 their report said:

> "The middle of the twentieth century also witnessed the spread of totalitarian communism as an alternative form of government, under which a third of the world's population then lived."[6]

So about 70 years ago, one third of the world had a dictator. That's a lot! So how about now? Here are some statements from their latest report published in 2020:

> "Democracy and pluralism are under assault. ...2019 was the 14th consecutive year of decline in global freedom. ... Ethnic, religious, and other minority groups have borne the brunt of government abuses in both democracies and authoritarian states. ... The unchecked brutality of autocratic regimes and the ethical decay of democratic powers are combining to make the world increasingly hostile to fresh demands for better governance."

Their 2020 report illustrates that 25 of 41 (61%) established democracies suffered overall declines in freedom over the past 14 years.[7]

Uh oh! **For the last fourteen years democracy across the globe has declined.** Let's look at the freedom score they give the top 10 most populous nations so we can see how good or bad things are.[8] These countries account for 57% of the world population.[9] The scale is 0 to 100. With 0 being not free at all, meaning the country has a dictator and 100 being totally free. As you can see in the table, only 3 of the 10 countries are considered free. What's equally disturbing is that for 7 of the countries their freedom score declined from last year. Did you also realize that 2 of the biggest countries on the planet are dictatorships—China and Russia? **The time of evil Pharaohs or dictators is certainly upon us as well.**

Country	2020 Score	Designation	Change from 2019
China	10	Not Free	Declined
India	71	Free	Declined
United States	86	Free	Unchanged
Indonesia	61	Partly Free	Declined
Pakistan	38	Partly Free	Declined
Brazil	75	Free	Unchanged
Nigeria	47	Partly Free	Declined
Bangladesh	39	Partly Free	Declined
Russia	20	Not Free	Unchanged
Mexico	62	Partly Free	Declined

So, what's in store for us? What does the election omen foretell?

The closer we get to the tribulation period, the more we'll start to see the polar opposite rulers the election omen reveals. After all, the very end will feature the Antichrist and Jesus Christ as rulers. The polar opposites have certainly manifested today in the US with Trump versus the Democrats, Republicans versus Democrats, and democracy versus socialism and communism.

The closer we get to the tribulation period, the closer we're going to get to an Antichrist like leader and an Antichrist like global government. **The foundation for the Antichrist's global government is already in place and pretty much every country is on board.** All that's lacking is the Antichrist. The progression we'll continue to see is the decline of democracy. That's because the Antichrist will be a dictator who controls everything. People won't be able to participate in his economy unless they have his mark. He'll have the ultimate government control of the world's production. The Antichrist will be a communist.

The ominous sign for the US is that one of the front runners in the Democratic Party presidential campaign was Bernie Sanders. Sanders just recently, the second week of April 2020, officially dropped out of the race and endorsed Biden. About a week prior, Bernie had just suspended his campaign, hadn't endorsed Biden, and was holding on to his delegates to exert influence at the convention. Do you know what happened? Here's what Sanders said in his announcement endorsing Biden:

> "I have been very pleased that your staff and my staff have been working together over the last several weeks to coming up with a number of task forces that will look at some of the most important issues facing this country." [10]

Here are some things Biden said in response to the endorsement:

> "Bernie, I want to thank you for that. It's a big deal. Your endorsement means a great deal to me. I think people are surprised that we are apart on some issues but we're awfully close on a bunch of others."
>
> "I'm going to need you – not just to win the campaign – but to govern." [11]

So, Sanders is now working with Biden to influence Biden's policies. The result is going to be a co-policy, something that both Bernie and Joe support. Because of this recent development, it's important for us to understand both candidates' views on the issues, which we'll do in each chapter on the issues. We can't lose sight of Sanders. At the least, it appears Biden has plans to include Sanders in his government, should he win. Could Sanders be his vice president pick? Some interesting things could happen this summer.

Like the Antichrist, Sanders is also a communist. That's not a popular or good stance to have amongst people who know history. So, they're telling you he's a democratic socialist. There's no such thing. He's in the same camp as Stalin. With the coronavirus outbreak, we've seen the Democrat Party try to hold relief bills hostage in order to push through some of their socialist and Green New Deal policies. It doesn't matter who gets the Democratic nomination, that party will continue to push socialist and communist measures. What we have shaping up for the 2020 presidential election is a communist leaning party versus a democracy loving capitalist. It's another polar opposite. **Since someone who supports the same type of economic system**

the Antichrist will enforce is quite popular in the United States today, I believe we're not too far from the rapture. Believers, get ready to meet Jesus in the clouds!

This progression we're seeing is happening because of what the election omen foretells. **God will give a nation, the people, the ruler they desire.** When people reject God, they're asking for his polar opposite. That's the Antichrist. That's who's coming. It's going to happen. It's just a matter of time. A life apart from God is a life condemned to hell. Unfortunately, that's exactly what the Antichrist will usher in on earth. The tribulation period will be hell on earth. Most of the people alive during that time will die at his hand or by God's judgments.

There's good news though. We believers are still here! That means the Antichrist can't rise to power yet. We have to get raptured first (2 Thessalonians 2). Until that day happens, we have enormous power and influence and we must use it in this spiritual war. Today more than ever we must stand against evil and the progression toward Satan and away from God. Think of all the people who don't know Jesus yet. People you care about and love. We must hope that God continues to give them time to come to know him. The point of no return will come. But it's not here yet. It's imperative that we all vote for the person with a heart like Jesus's who will stem the tide of evil.

> I looked for someone who might rebuild the wall of righteousness that guards the land. I searched for someone to stand in the gap in the wall so I wouldn't have to destroy the land, but I found no one. (Ezekiel 22:30 NLT)

Jesus is looking for brave people to "rebuild the wall of righteousness" that guards our nation. Today, you have a decision to make. It's the same decision the Israelites had to make before they entered the promised land. It's the choice between life and death, following God or not. Choose to love God with all your heart! Choose to obey him no matter the cost! Choose to stand with him today! Join me and stand in the gap in the wall!

PART 5

KEY ISSUES OF TODAY

CHAPTER 11 – MORALITY AND THE GOVERNMENT'S ROLE

Today, many people think that the government shouldn't dictate morality. That the government should only protect our rights to life, liberty, and the pursuit of happiness. Here's a statement from the 2018 Libertarian Party platform to illustrate this belief:

> "Therefore, we favor the repeal of all laws creating 'crimes' without victims, such as gambling, the use of drugs for medicinal or recreational purposes, and consensual transactions involving sexual services."[1]

Is there really such a thing as a crime without a victim? Well, let's consider that we're all accountable to God and his Word tells us that sin is a crime against him. Every sin is a sin against God. Even King David recognized this when he committed adultery with Bathsheba. David is the author of the Psalm below:

> Have mercy on me, God, according to your loving kindness. ... For I know my transgressions. My sin is constantly before me. Against you, and you only, I have sinned, and done that which is evil in your sight, so you may be proved right when you speak, and justified when you judge. (Psalm 51:1, 3-4)

There are many examples of this recognition that God is who we sin against in the Bible. That's because God is the author of the law. He's the judge. He's who we're accountable to when we violate his law.

Every time we sin, we're also sinning against ourselves. Yes, you really are the victim of the crimes you commit against yourself. That's because we're slaves of whatever we obey. If we follow after sin, then we're slaves to sin. That's terrible, especially if you haven't put your faith in Jesus Christ, because your sin will lead to death and eternal separation from God (Romans 6:23). Slaves of sin get pulled into hell. Does that sound victimless to you?

Now, if you're a believer and you have God's Holy Spirit living inside of you, you must also remember that your body is a temple of the Holy Spirit. When we as believers sin, we're desecrating our temples. So now we're up to three victims: God, the Holy Spirit, and ourselves.

On top of that, what kind of example are you being to the world? We're supposed to be ambassadors for Jesus and live in such a way that others come to know him through us. If we're living a life of sin and behaving just as the world behaves, they're not going to see Jesus through that. That's because sin infects and impacts society. Let's look at an example from the Bible. This is when Joshua and the Israelites were conquering Jericho:

> The city shall be devoted, even it and all that is in it, to Yahweh. ... But as for you, only keep yourselves from what is devoted to destruction, lest when you have devoted it, you take of the devoted thing; so you would make the camp of Israel accursed and trouble it. But all the silver, gold, and vessels of bronze and iron are holy to Yahweh. They shall come into Yahweh's treasury. ... But the children of Israel committed a trespass in the devoted things; for Achan, the son of Carmi, the son of Zabdi, the son of Zerah, of the tribe of Judah, took some of the devoted things. Therefore Yahweh's anger burned against the children of Israel. (Joshua 6:17-19, 7:1)

God told them to dedicate all the treasure in Jericho to God and to destroy everything else, otherwise they would curse the "camp of Israel." Unfortunately, we read that Achan didn't follow directions. He took some of the treasure in Jericho for himself. So, what happened? You'd think God would just call out Achan and deal with the sin Achan committed against God. Nope. When they went to conquer the city of Ai, the Israelite soldiers ended up running from their enemy and 36 of them died. When Joshua asked God what happened, he was told they were defeated because of Achan's sin. God held them all accountable to what Achan had done. Achan and his entire family were then stoned to death as a result of his sin. In this example, we learn that the sin of one person impacted himself, his family, and his entire nation.

Remember that Adam's sin impacted every single one of us. In fact, it brought a curse upon all of creation (Genesis 3; Romans 8:20). So why did God hold the entire nation accountable to Achan's sin? It comes down to the fact that we're supposed to look after each other and hold each other accountable to God's law. When Eve was tempted by Satan in the garden and ate the forbidden fruit, where was Adam? It seems he was right next to her. So why didn't he say something to her? Why did he willingly take the fruit from her and eat it? He could have said, "What are you doing Eve? We're not supposed to eat that." But he didn't. Achan buried all the treasure he took under his tent. I find it difficult to believe no one noticed he took anything and that no one noticed he dug a big hole in his tent. At the very least, I'm sure his family knew what he was doing, but they chose not to confront him or tell Joshua.

There is no such thing as a victimless crime. Any of you who have lived with someone steeped in a "personal" sin, like alcoholism, know that it truly does impact their entire family, their friends, their work colleagues, and anyone they encounter. This reasoning today that we should all mind our own business and look the other way at another's sin is the very heart of the Laodicean church. The heart of apathy and complacency. It's the heart of Satan. Remember that he doesn't want you to care about anyone other than yourself because he has a selfish heart.

So, what are we to do? This is where the government and the law come in. God gave us his law so that we would know what sin is. The law instructs us and guides us. Here's how the apostle Paul explains it:

> I wouldn't have known sin except through the law. For I wouldn't have known coveting unless the law had said, "You shall not covet." (Romans 7:7)

> Why, then, was the law given? It was given alongside the promise to show people their sins. But the law was designed to last only until the coming of the child who was promised. God gave his law through angels to Moses, who was the mediator between God and the people. ... Let me put it another way. The law was our guardian until Christ came; it protected us until we could be made right with God through faith. (Galatians 3:19, 24 NLT)

The law taught Paul what sin was. It's a guardian that protects people until they are made right with God through faith in Jesus. This is why we can't repeal all laws. We must have laws about moral behavior so that people understand what God expects of them. How is a child supposed to know they shouldn't lie if no one tells them not to?

Extrapolating that further, how is a person to know they shouldn't steal if there isn't a law to guide them? This is the problem with repealing moral laws. The Bible tells us we're not supposed to cause another person to sin or stumble (Romans 14:13). We do that by educating people on what is and isn't acceptable to God and then behaving appropriately ourselves as good role models.

You know, there was a time in our history in which we didn't have God's law. It's the vast amount of time between Adam and Moses. Do you recall what happened to society during that time? The Flood! It destroyed everyone except Noah and his family. Everyone else on the planet was wicked and only thought evil things continually (Genesis 6). They didn't have God's law to guide them.

Also consider the time between Joshua and King Saul. Everyone did what was right in their own eyes because they didn't have a ruler or government to keep them on the right track (Judges 17:6).

Think back to Chapter 8 when we considered who Satan would vote for. They were rulers who pulled people away from God. Taking the law away from people would do exactly that. That's not what we're called to do as Christians. When Jesus taught the disciples to pray, here's what he said:

> Let your Kingdom come. Let your will be done on earth as it is in heaven.
> ... Forgive us our debts, as we also forgive our debtors. (Matthew 6:10, 12)

We're supposed to make earth resemble heaven. We're supposed to ask God to forgive us of our "debts" or sins and forgive others who sin against us. So, we should strive to make our earthly laws resemble God's heavenly and holy laws as much as we can. The law helps people recognize their sins and their need for a savior who can forgive them. Godly laws will help people who don't know God come to know him and hopefully be saved.

We must have laws that concern things like marriage, drugs, and abortion because we need laws that reflect God's will for human behavior. When we as believers stop caring about what other people do, we're opening the door for Satan. He will take the opportunity to change the laws to suit his own desire. He doesn't want anyone to know God's truth, so he will favor laws that twist it. We can see Satan's influence today in laws that are completely contrary to God's will.

> Woe to those who call evil good, and good evil; who put darkness for light, and light for darkness; who put bitter for sweet, and sweet for bitter! (Isaiah 5:20)

In the subsequent chapters, we're going to tackle many of the important issues of today with our sword of truth, God's Word. We're going to see what the Bible says about the issue, where the main political parties and candidates stand on the issue, and how your vote regarding the issue will bring about the election omen.

As we go through each of the issues, you need to remember that it's more than the office of the president that matter on these. The president does not have the power to legislate! Congress is the legislative branch of the government which makes new laws, changes existing laws, and allocates the budget. Those are the people who have the power to do things like defund Planned Parenthood. The Senate also has the sole power of confirming presidential appointments, like the president's Cabinet and Supreme Court judges. Thus, it's imperative that you vote for state representatives and state senators who align with your biblical values.

There's also one thing you need to start thinking about. It's your "red line" of issues. It's the figurative line that you won't cross so to speak. There are a considerable number of issues and factors we could take into account when determining who to vote for. You are not going to find a candidate who agrees with you about every single issue. You are not going to find a candidate who always acts and behaves the way you'd like a leader to. If you're looking for the perfect candidate, you'll end up getting frustrated and not voting at all, which is what Satan hopes you'll do in this Laodicean culture. The truth is the perfect candidate doesn't exist. Jesus, God in the flesh, will be the only perfect leader. That's why you need a red line. It's the one or two issues that matter the most to you and that your candidate must agree with you on. You're going to have to compromise on the other issues. I know that's not easy, but it's what's required.

Here's a quote from Richard Land, president of Southern Evangelical Seminary, which illustrates his red line:

> "As Christians, we have the duty to be informed voters and to vote our convictions, not our wallets and narrow self-

interests. Let me be crystal clear about this: If I am presented with the choice of voting for a Jewish woman who is going to protect unborn babies but is also going to raise my taxes by 50 percent, and she is running against a Southern Baptist friend of mine who is going to lower my taxes, appoint me to a government position but is also going to support abortion, I am going to vote for unborn babies and against my wallet every time. Why? Because it is my Christian duty, and because I do not want to have to explain one day to my Lord and Savior at the judgment of believers' works (1 Corinthians 3:11-15) why I thought my wallet was more important than unborn babies!"[2]

CHAPTER 12 - ABORTION

As we examine each issue, it's important that we look at what God's Word says as a whole. That's because when we pull individual Bible verses out of their entire biblical context it becomes easy to weaponize God's Word to support anything a heart desires. We don't want to do that. We must look at the bigger picture. That's where Jesus's and Satan's hearts come into play. We must uncover the attitudes, behaviors, and feelings that make up the heart of each issue.

We're going to start our discussion on the issues with abortion. That's because abortion is one of the most important issues facing us today. It's also one of the issues in my red line. It's the debate between life and choice. People are either pro-life and against abortion, or pro-choice and supportive of it.

One of the main arguments revolves around the definition of when life begins. The reasoning being that the fetus isn't a real life human being until life actually begins. Thus, it's okay to terminate it up until that point. So, when does life begin according to God? If we start with the first human being, Adam, his life began after God made him from the ground and then breathed life into him (Genesis 2:7). So, does this mean life begins when a person first breathes? Thus, making abortion okay up until birth? No, absolutely not! This is a perfect illustration of what happens when you only look at one Scripture and disregard what the whole Bible says about an issue.

Let's keep marching through history. Moses tells us that the life of a body is in its blood (Leviticus 17:11). Next up is King David. He said God knit him together in his mother's womb (Psalm 139:13-16). Not only that, but God also recorded every day of David's life in his book while David was in the womb. It's starting to look like life begins sometime in the womb.

When we get to the New Testament and read about Elizabeth, we discover her baby, John the Baptist, leaped inside her womb when Mary entered the room (Luke 1:39-45). John clearly had some recognition, awareness, emotions, and control of his body. This further supports that life is present inside the womb. However, when we get to Mary, who was pregnant with Jesus, we learn she conceived by the power of God himself, the Holy Spirit (Matthew 1:18-20). Since she was pregnant with God in the flesh, who is the creator of all life (John 1:1-4) and who's always existed (Revelation 1:8), that means Jesus had to be alive at conception too. So, what does that mean for us?

The key truth is revealed in a conversation between God and his prophet Jeremiah. God told him that he knew him before he created him in his mother's womb (Jeremiah 1:4-5). What? God knows us before we're even created!? Yes. I agree that it's difficult to comprehend. The apostle Paul confirmed it when he told believers they were created by God for good works, which God planned out beforehand, so that we would walk in them (Ephesians 2:10).

Life doesn't begin at conception, in the womb, or at birth. In fact, it begins way before any of those. Your life began when God first thought about you.

So now, when we consider God's definition of when life begins, the argument that it's okay to terminate a fetus because its life hasn't started yet just doesn't hold up. Ah, but there's an important truth here. The pro-abortion argument isn't really about when life begins. This has become obvious today with support for partial-birth abortion, abortion up until birth, and letting attempted abortion born-alive babies just die. No, it's not about when life begins at all. It's about control.

So now we've reached the heart of the matter. Who is the creator of a life? Is it a man and a woman? Or is it God? You see, the argument is that the creator has the right to determine the fate of its creation. Therefore, people who are pro-choice believe it's a woman's decision to terminate her pregnancy or give birth because, after all, it's her body and her baby. But is it really?

We just learned that God created every single one of us before we were ever born. Remember the pick your own adventure example I used earlier in the book to explain how our will and God's plan work together seamlessly? God has already written the entire story for humanity. That means he's already written our own individual stories and the stories of those he's thought of but who haven't yet been born as well. Yet, we live during a time in which women who get pregnant have a choice regarding what they want to do with their unborn. Do you know why that is? We have free will. So, God lets us create laws that satisfy our sinful desires. But, it's also a test. God is testing each of our hearts every single day. He wants to know if we love him or not. And how do we show God that we love him? Obedience, that's how (Micah 6:8). God wants us to have a heart like his, just like King David did.

Let's consider the hearts that are in play here. Abortion is the result of a woman choosing her life over the life of her baby. A selfish heart is one who places themselves above someone else. Abortion is the act of destroying a life that God created and stealing a baby's life from them. A hateful, thieving, murderous heart is one who doesn't show love and compassion but instead seeks to destroy. Who do these hearts sound like—Jesus or Satan? Jesus tells us in the Scripture below:

> The thief only comes to steal, kill, and destroy. I came that they may have life, and may have it abundantly. I am the good shepherd. The good shepherd lays down his life for the sheep. (John 10:10-11)

It's the voice of Satan. He's the thief. He wants to steal, kill, and destroy. Do you remember what his primary sin was? Pride. A prideful heart is one who places their own will above God's will. A pro-choice or pro-abortion supporter places a woman's will above God's will.

Jesus doesn't have a heart like any of those, does he? No. Jesus has an obedient heart. Remember that he was obedient to the point of death! You know he expects the same of us. Self-sacrifice is the ultimate act of love. An obedient heart is one who accepts God's will in their life. That means they're willing to sacrifice their will for God's. A pro-life supporter accepts God's will in life. They believe people should sacrifice their plans and desires so a life that God created can live.

Well, some people argue that although God creates life, he doesn't really value it. One example they use is when the Israelites were slaves in Egypt. God's last plague was the death of the firstborn among the Egyptians (Exodus 11-12). Other examples they use are all the wars in the Bible in which God commanded that people should die. On the surface it certainly looks like God doesn't value life. However, that's quite far from the case. The reality is that death is a punishment and a judgment from God. Remember that God wants everyone saved. He doesn't take pleasure in the death of the wicked.

> Tell them, "'As I live,' says the Lord Yahweh, "I have no pleasure in the death of the wicked, but that the wicked turn from his way and live. Turn, turn from your evil ways! For why will you die, house of Israel?"' (Ezekiel 33:11)

God sent Jesus to save everyone. Just because God punishes sin doesn't mean he doesn't value life. God's discipline actually proves that he does value life.

> For whom the Lord loves, he disciplines, and chastises every son whom he receives. (Hebrews 12:6)

If God didn't care, he'd let us do whatever we wanted because sin leads to death. If God didn't care, he'd essentially let us commit spiritual suicide. But God does care!

You must consider how valuable each and every person's life is to God. God in the flesh, Jesus, died to save everyone.

> Knowing that you were redeemed, not with corruptible things like silver or gold, from the useless way of life handed down from your fathers, but with precious blood, as of a lamb without blemish or spot, the blood of Christ. (1 Peter 1:18-19)

In the above Scripture, Peter tells us that each person is more valuable than any kind of property. We were each purchased with the perfect, eternal blood of Jesus. Jesus died for each of you reading this book before you were ever even born. He did that so that you could have eternal life.

Even knowing this truth, some people shockingly say that God supports abortion. There are two Scriptures they use to argue this point. In this first Scripture below, God is speaking with Moses and giving him ordinances that him and the Israelites were supposed to follow:

> If men fight and hurt a pregnant woman so that she gives birth prematurely, and yet no harm follows, he shall be surely fined as much as the woman's husband demands and the judges allow. But if any harm follows, then you must take life for life. (Exodus 21:22-23)

Abortion supporters who claim that God supports them, say God clearly doesn't value a fetus as a life, but instead values it as property. They say that's because the offender is only fined and not killed. Read that Scripture above again. That's not what it says. If the woman gives birth early and no harm follows, the offender is fined. That means the baby wasn't harmed either. Yet, look at what happens if there's any harm, any injury, the punishment is life for life. If that baby was born early as a result of the offense and the baby died, the offender would have been stoned to death.

The other example they use to claim God supports abortion is regarding the jealously offering of a husband who's suspicious his wife is adulterous (Numbers 5). The accused wife was taken to the priest and given bitter holy water to drink. If God found her guilty, he'd shrivel her womb and make her infertile. Now, there's a big difference between what's happening in the Bible and what's happening today with abortion. It's choice. In this biblical example, the woman didn't have a choice. Terminating her ability to get pregnant was God's will and decision. She was cursed as a punishment for her sin. Do you think a curse to make her barren was the result the woman wanted? No! Otherwise, it would have been described as a blessing to her. A curse does not illustrate God's support of a particular behavior. It shows his disgust for it. God does not approve of sexual sins.

Speaking of sexual sins, the last argument we're going to look at that Christians use to support abortion is that believers are no longer bound to God's law and can do whatever they want because God's already forgiven them. This one really makes me sad. As a believer, I want to do everything I can to please Jesus. That means being as obedient as I can be. I have a strong desire to obey and follow his commands. That's because God writes his law on the hearts of his believers (Hebrews 10:16). Paul the apostle tackled this very issue. Here's what he said:

> Shall we sin because we are not under law but under grace? May it never be! Don't you know that when you present yourselves as servants and obey someone, you are the servants of whomever you obey, whether of sin to death, or of obedience to righteousness? But thanks be to God that, whereas you were bondservants of sin, you became obedient from the heart to that form of teaching to which you were delivered. Being made free from sin, you became bondservants of righteousness. (Romans 6:15-18)

People who have put their faith in Jesus are living under grace. Believers used to be slaves to sin, but now we're slaves to righteousness. We do what pleases God, not what offends him. What kind of act results in an unwanted pregnancy? Do you think it's a righteous act in the confines of a God ordained marriage between a husband and a wife? You know very well that's it not. But here's some data to prove it. According to the recent Centers for Disease Control (CDC) report on abortion, 86% of abortions in the US are performed on unmarried women.[1] We can all surmise that the married women getting abortions likely got pregnant in an act of adultery. Sexual sins lead to unwanted pregnancies. Christians shouldn't be committing the sexual sins that lead down the road that ends in abortion. We are meant to honor God with our bodies. He lives inside of us after all (1 Corinthians 6:12-20).

The truth of the matter is illustrated in these verses, likely written by Paul:

> For if we sin willfully after we have received the knowledge of the truth, there remains no more a sacrifice for sins, but a certain fearful expectation of judgment, and a fierceness of fire which will devour the adversaries. (Hebrews 10:26-27)

Someone who continues to willfully live in sin after understanding how to be saved isn't saved. Jesus's sacrifice doesn't cover this person because they don't actually believe. They don't have a heart that Jesus has grabbed a hold of yet. Because they don't have a heart like Jesus, that means they still have a heart like Satan.

Now you should fully understand the abortion debate and which side of the issue you as a Christian should be on. It's pro-life by the way! Let's see where the main political parties and the 2020 presidential candidates stand on this issue.

From the Democratic Party platform:

> "We believe unequivocally...that every woman should have access to ... safe and legal abortion...."
>
> "We will continue to stand up to Republican efforts to defund Planned Parenthood...."
>
> "We believe that safe abortion must be part of ... America's global health programming."[2]

From the Libertarian Party platform:

> "Recognizing that abortion is a sensitive issue and that people can hold good-faith views on all sides, we believe that government should be kept out of the matter, leaving the question to each person for their conscientious consideration."3

From the Green Party platform:

> "It is essential that the option of a safe, legal abortion remains available."
>
> "Under the agency of the United Nations, we demand that our government renew and initiate government funding and support for ... abortion in all countries that request it."4

Every one of those parties—Democrat, Libertarian, and Green—supports laws allowing abortion. Also remember that we addressed the issue of why we need to have moral laws in the prior chapter. So, the Libertarian argument to keep the government out of the matter isn't a biblical one.

Just look at who Planned Parenthood is supporting. From an article titled *Planned Parenthood launches $45M campaign to back Democrats in 2020* on TheHill.com:

> "Planned Parenthood will spend $45 million on the 2020 elections, the nonprofit's biggest electoral expenditure in its history, according to CBS News. ... The money will go toward the presidential election as well as congressional and state House races, according to Planned Parenthood Votes Executive Director Jenny Lawson, who told CBS, 'The stakes have never been higher.'"5

The only major political party that doesn't support abortion is the Republican Party. Here's what their platform states:

> "We assert the sanctity of human life and affirm that the unborn child has a fundamental right to life which cannot be infringed."

"We oppose the use of public funds to perform or promote abortion or to fund organizations, like Planned Parenthood, so long as they provide or refer for elective abortions or sell fetal body parts rather than provide healthcare."

"We strongly oppose infanticide."[6]

How about where the 2020 presidential candidates stand? At this moment, it appears the election will be between President Trump and Joe Biden. As I mentioned in Chapter 10, Sanders ended his campaign, but he's now influencing Biden's policies, and according to Biden will have a future role in his government if he wins. We can't rule out Sanders as a potential vice president nominee. So, we'll look at where President Trump, Biden, and Sanders stand on the issues.

Joe wants to make Roe v. Wade federal law, prevent states from adopting laws that restrict abortion, let Planned Parenthood receive government funding, and rescind the Mexico City Policy (or global gag rule) that prevents taxpayer money from funding abortions globally.[7]

What about Bernie? He was recently asked by MSNBC, "Is there such a thing as a pro-life Democrat in your vision of the party?" His response, "I think when we talk about what a Democrat is, I think being pro-choice is an essential part of that."[8] He supports fully funding Planned Parenthood, opposes efforts to undermine or overturn Roe v. Wade, and would appoint judges who are pro-choice.[9]

Since Bernie is currently serving as a US Senator, would you like to know how he's voted on abortion legislation recently? Back in 2003, he voted against the Partial Birth Abortion Ban Act of 2003. Even Biden voted for that ban.[10] He also voted against the Born-Alive Abortion Survivors Protection Act in 2019.[11] He, Elizabeth Warren, and Amy Klobuchar, who were also running for president, refused to vote on this ban in 2020.[12] Are you familiar with this ban? Here's a quote from an article on Pulpit & Pen:

"Democrats in the state of Colorado have defeated legislation designed to mandate medical treatment of babies who survive botched abortions. Such babies will be placed upon tables and left to die without medical treatment, even though they are outside the womb."[13]

Only three Democrats in the US Senate believe we should save babies who are born alive, even if their mother doesn't want them and didn't mean for them to survive. As I said earlier, the abortion debate has nothing to do with life. It's about playing God.

So that leaves us with President Trump. Here's what he recently said about abortion at the 2020 March for Life:

> "It is my profound honor to be the first president in history to attend the March for Life."
>
> "All of us here today understand an eternal truth: Every child is a precious and sacred gift from God. Together, we must protect, cherish, and defend the dignity and sanctity of every human life."
>
> "And during my first week in office, I reinstated and expanded the Mexico City Policy, and we issued a landmark pro-life rule to govern the use of Title X taxpayer funding."
>
> "I notified Congress that I would veto any legislation that weakens pro-life policies or that encourages the destruction of human life."
>
> "At the United Nations, I made clear that global bureaucrats have no business attacking the sovereignty of nations that protect innocent life."
>
> "Unborn children have never had a stronger defender in the White House."[14]

I couldn't agree more! Do you know when the March for Life started? 1974. In the 46 year history of the march, President Trump is the only president who's ever attended. Can you believe that? He made a profound statement regarding where he stands on abortion.

Do you understand Title X funding and what President Trump did? Title X is a federal grant program for family planning projects. Trump signed legislation that allows states to exclude organizations that perform abortions from their Title X projects. He also issued the Protect Life Rule.

Here's how the March for Life describes that:

> "Last spring, in March of 2018, Congress passed an Omnibus spending bill that continued to fund the nation's

largest abortion provider, despite a pro-life majority in Congress. ... In May 2018, HHS announced the Protect Life Rule, which would disentangle taxpayer dollars from funding abortion, with the money redirected to comprehensive family health and planning centers that don't perform abortions and understand that abortion is not healthcare."[15]

This rule prohibits Title X grantees from providing abortions, referring patients for abortion, and requires them to be both physically and financially separate from abortion operations. As a result of Trumps policies, Planned Parenthood refused to comply and withdrew from the Title X program, a $60 million loss in taxpayer funding for them.[16]

This is what the president of the Susan B. Anthony List, Marjorie Dannenfelser, had to say:

> "President Trump's Title X Protect Life Rule is a huge victory for the majority of taxpayers who reject taxpayer funding of abortion. The Protect Life Rule does not reduce family planning funding by a single dollar; it simply directs taxpayer funding to family planning providers who stay out of the abortion business."[17]

Here's something else President Trump is working on that caught my eye this year. He announced this at the National Sanctity of Human Life day in 2020:

> "My Administration is also building an international coalition to dispel the concept of abortion as a fundamental human right. So far, 24 nations representing more than a billion people have joined this important cause. We oppose any projects that attempt to assert a global right to taxpayer-funded abortion on demand, up to the moment of delivery."[18]

What I find shocking and appalling about the abortion issue is that we've entered a truly dark time in our history because we're seeing people use God's Word to support this practice. People who claim to be Christians who support abortion and state that God does too. I hope you've clearly seen that's absolutely not the case!

It's just as the apostle Paul described to Timothy and as the prophet Isaiah warned:

> For the time will come when they will not listen to the sound doctrine, but having itching ears, will heap up for themselves teachers after their own lusts, and will turn away their ears from the truth, and turn away to fables. (2 Timothy 4:3-4)

> Woe to those who call evil good, and good evil. (Isaiah 5:20)

So, what does the election omen foretell here? **A nation will advance in wickedness until it reaches the polar opposite of God.** We know that God is pro-life. Children are a blessing from God and meant to be celebrated (Psalm 127:3). The polar opposite of that is when we celebrate their death instead. We've unfortunately arrived at this point. As of January 2020, 8 states now allow abortion up until birth.[19] Now that we've reached this point, it's a matter of when do we reach the tipping point when the majority of states or majority of America agree with abortion up until birth, or shockingly after birth. You already know what happens when a nation reaches that point of no return. **When a nation turns completely away from God and reaches the point of no return it will bring judgment upon itself.**

God gives us free will. It's in your hands. Are you going to vote for a candidate like Joe or Bernie who align with the Democrat Party and support abortion up until birth? Or are you going to vote for President Trump, who's very clearly their antithesis, and stem this tide of evil that's advancing across our country?

Abortion must be in your red line because it's certainly an issue God draws the line on. You've learned that God, the author of life, most certainly values life and wants to see everyone saved. There are some issues that can have an impact on another's salvation. This is one of those issues. Christians are called to be separate from the ways of the world for a reason. We're a lamp that leads to Jesus and salvation. Your attitude about saving an unborn baby reveals God's love to a world who doesn't know him. We must vote for the candidate who has a heart like Jesus. He has a heart full of self-sacrificial love. Abortion requires a heart that's the opposite of Jesus's. A heart that loves itself over everything else. We were warned about that type of heart:

> But know this: that in the last days, grievous times will come. For men will be lovers of self, lovers of money, boastful, arrogant, blasphemers, disobedient to parents, unthankful, unholy, without natural affection, unforgiving, slanderers, without self-control, fierce, not lovers of good...... ... But you remain in the things which you have learned and have been assured of, knowing from whom you have learned them. (2 Timothy 3:1-3, 14)

"Remain" in the things you've learned is what Paul the apostle told Timothy to do when faced with these issues that we're seeing now in these last days. It means to stay in one place. Vote pro-life. Stand for life!

CHAPTER 13 – GENDER AND MARRIAGE

The next issue we're going to look at isn't a single issue per se. It's really multiple issues in which gender is at the core. This is about the war on God's definition of gender and marriage. This is a big deal. It's not just about who can use which restroom or who can get spousal benefits. You're going to learn the LGBTQ+ movement is a war on God and religious liberty.

Let's start at the beginning when God created mankind. God created Adam, the first man, after his very own image (Genesis 1:27). Then he created Eve, from Adam's rib, because Adam needed a helper who was suitable and perfect for him (Genesis 2:18). God's creation of mankind culminated in the first marriage between Adam and Eve.

> Therefore a man will leave his father and his mother, and will join with his wife, and they will be one flesh. (Genesis 2:24)

Now, do you recall what happened in the garden right after this marriage? Satan came along and destroyed the relationship that Adam and Eve had with God and had between each other (Genesis 3). I'm going to show you how he did it. Satan's very first words to Eve were, "Has God really said...." He started his attack against God. He questioned what Eve believed about God by twisting what God said to Eve. Then Satan lied to her about what God said. God told them if they ate from the forbidden tree that they would die (Genesis 2:27). Satan told Eve she wouldn't die that instead God was withholding knowledge from her. Eve was deceived and believed Satan over God. Satan successfully broke the relationship Adam and Eve had with God.

Well, you're likely wondering what that has to do with gender issues and marriage. Where was Adam when that conversation between Satan and Eve was taking place? Adam was with her! Yet he failed to protect Eve from Satan's lies. Have you ever considered there's a reason why Satan spoke to Eve instead of Adam? Satan knew that God created a marriage bond between Adam and Eve. He was determined to destroy it along with their relationship to God. You must remember that Satan hates everything that God loves and that God establishes. Satan's goals are to steal, kill, and destroy.

The apostle Paul explained to us that the husband is the head of his wife in the same way that Jesus is the head of his church (Ephesians 5:21-33). A husband is supposed to love his wife like Jesus loves the church. That's a sacrificial love because Jesus gave his life for his church. Satan knew that God created Adam first, that he created Eve from Adam, and that he made Eve as Adam's helper, a role of submission. Satan had a goal in approaching Eve. God created Adam as the leader. Yet Adam didn't take the lead as he should have. He let Eve take over that role. He let Eve talk to Satan, take the forbidden fruit, give him some of it, and then he willingly ate it. Adam let Satan lead Eve astray.

What was the end result to their relationships? Well, when God showed up, Adam and Eve were both hiding from him. This is further evidence that Satan ruined the relationship they had with God. They were now afraid. When God asked what happened, Adam's first words were "The woman whom you gave to be with me...." Wow! Adam immediately blamed Eve for what happened and on top of that, he blamed God too because God gave him Eve after all. Look at the mess that Satan created. Satan successfully broke the relationship that Adam and Eve had with each other as well.

The apostle Paul told us that marriage is a picture of a believer's relationship with Jesus. Satan doesn't want you to have a relationship with Jesus. He doesn't want you to know the truth. Satan is going to do everything in his power to destroy God's truth about gender, gender roles, marriage, and sexual relationships because they all point to Jesus. Satan continues to use the same deceptive tactic that worked on Eve today.

When Satan attacks God's definition of gender and marriage, it opens the door for people to question everything about God. People question God's image. Did God really create mankind male, in his own image, and then create a woman for him? They start to think that perhaps the Bible just doesn't say he created same sex couples. People question God's definition of marriage. Did God really only create marriage between a man and a woman? People question God's love. Would a loving God, who created me as an LGBTQ+ person, really not want me having a loving marriage with someone of the same sex? Now that they have a flawed perspective of God, they also have an incorrect view of sin and their own sin in particular. People then question God's judgment. Does God really consider LGBTQ+ sexual immorality and condemn those who practice it to hell? They start to pick away at God's Word. They say some Scriptures are old and irrelevant, it was written by men, the Bible has errors, the verse wasn't about condemning sin but about ritual purity, and that the Bible isn't really God's truth. People then replace God's truth with Satan's twisted lies that will ultimately lead them through the broad gates of hell.

The Bible is very clear about LGBTQ+ relationships. God says they are a sin. God defining gender and marriage in the beginning was enough for us to understand his truth. But God knew this was going to be a problem for us sinners, so he clarified it in both the Old and New Testaments. Let's look at a couple Scriptures so you can see for yourself:

> You shall not lie with a man as with a woman. That is detestable. (Leviticus 18:22)

> Because knowing God, they didn't glorify him as God, and didn't give thanks, but became vain in their reasoning, and their senseless heart was darkened. ... Therefore God also gave them up in the lusts of their hearts to uncleanness, that their bodies should be dishonored among themselves; who exchanged the truth of God for a lie, and worshiped and served the creature rather than the Creator, who is blessed forever. Amen. For this reason, God gave them up to vile passions. For their women changed the natural function into that which is against nature. Likewise also the men, leaving the natural function of the woman, burned in their lust toward one another, men doing what is inappropriate with men, and receiving in themselves the due penalty of their error. Even as they refused to have God in their knowledge, God gave them up to a reprobate mind, to do those things which are not fitting; being filled with all unrighteousness, sexual immorality, wickedness, covetousness, malice; full of envy, murder, strife, deceit, evil habits, secret slanderers, backbiters, hateful to God, insolent, arrogant, boastful, inventors of evil things, disobedient to parents, without understanding, covenant breakers, without natural affection, unforgiving, unmerciful; who, knowing the ordinance of God, that those who practice such things are worthy of death, not only do the same, but also approve of those who practice them. (Romans 1:21, 24-32)

The LGBTQ+ lifestyle isn't new as some would like you to believe. That first Scripture was a command given by God to Moses and the Israelites way back in the 15th Century BC. Sexual sin has been around since the beginning of time. It's one of the wicked practices that Sodom and Gomorrah were infamously known for and it didn't end well for them (Jude 1:7). Remember, all the men in the city wanted to have to sex with the two angels who appeared (Genesis 19).

Paul the apostle wrote the second Scripture above. God's truth is as plain as day and Paul even explains why they practice these sexual sins. It's just like we discussed. They've become "vain in their reasoning," have a "reprobate mind," and "exchanged the truth of God for a lie." So, they've become foolish, morally corrupt, and listen to Satan's lies instead of God's truth. There are many Scriptures in the Bible that speak to sexual sins and the sinful LGBTQ+ lifestyle. You can refer to 1 Corinthians 6:9-10, 1 Timothy 1:10, 1 Thessalonians 4:3, 1 Timothy 3:2, and Galatians 5:19 for more of God's truth.

That's a key characteristic of today. People no longer want to listen to God's truth. They have a rebellious heart. So, they seek after someone who will tell them what they want to hear.

> For the time will come when they will not listen to the sound doctrine, but having itching ears, will heap up for themselves teachers after their own lusts. (2 Timothy 4:3)

That's what this boils down to. People who are living in sin, any sin, and don't want to repent, don't like it when the Holy Spirit convicts them of their sin. Since believers who have put their faith in Jesus Christ are filled with the Holy Spirit, they don't like it when we tell them what God's Word says regarding their lifestyle. That's because God's Word pierces the soul (Hebrews 4:12).

The LGBTQ+ community tells Christians that Jesus says we're supposed to love our neighbor and that we're not showing love like Jesus when we tell them their behavior is sinful. They call us names like homophobic and tell us our speech is full of hate. Christians don't have an irrational fear of the LGBTQ+ community. We're not homophobic, we simply disagree with the LGBTQ+ lifestyle. We don't hate sinners; we oppose sinful behavior. It's the same with Jesus.

Yes, Jesus said we should love our neighbors. But it's God's definition of love, not ours, someone else's, or the world's, that we should be using. We're to love God with all of our heart, soul, and mind (Matthew 22:37). And how do we do that? By obeying God (John 14:15-31). We replace our hard rebellious heart with an obedient heart. That's how we demonstrate to God that we love. God loves all people. He created every single person after all. But he hates sin and he judges people who don't repent and turn from their sin because he's perfect, holy, and just. Jesus publicly rebuked the religious leaders who failed to see their sin. He even made a whip and drove money changers out of the temple. Jesus expects believers to show his love to a sinful world by illustrating that everyone is a sinner and needs a savior.

Once we've been saved, we cannot continue to identify with the sin that we know Jesus died to save us from. If we do, then we don't really love Jesus because we're not obeying him. God doesn't condone any sin. We are all born sinners. Sin is something we do. It's not who we are. There is no such thing as an adulterating Christian, a murdering Christian, or a gay Christian. Paul the apostle tells us believers not to associate with people who claim to be Christians but indulge in sin (1 Corinthians 5:11-13). It's because their sin is like yeast that will spread throughout all the good dough and corrupt it. If the person is truly saved, then those are sins they used to commit. Sins that they repented of. Those sins no longer define or control them. They are free from their enslavement. They certainly wouldn't be sins they advocate for. No, that's what sinners who aren't saved do. Since they don't have a relationship with Jesus, they encourage and advocate sin, just like Satan does. So, they look for ways to discredit God's Word and twist it to mean what they desire. They look for ways to force their sinful ways upon believers.

That's where the Equality Act comes in. Here's the summary of the Act as it appears on congress.gov:[1]

> This bill prohibits discrimination based on sex, sexual orientation, and gender identity in a wide variety of areas including public accommodations and facilities, education, federal funding, employment, housing, credit, and the jury system. Specifically, the bill defines and includes sex, sexual orientation, and gender identity among the prohibited categories of discrimination or segregation.

The bill expands the definition of public accommodations to include places or establishments that provide (1) exhibitions, recreation, exercise, amusement, gatherings, or displays; (2) goods, services, or programs; and (3) transportation services.

The bill allows the Department of Justice to intervene in equal protection actions in federal court on account of sexual orientation or gender identity.

Protections against discrimination based on race, color, religion, sex, sexual orientation, gender identity, or national origin shall include protections against discrimination based on (1) an association with another person who is a member of such a protected class; or (2) a perception or belief, even if inaccurate, that an individual is a member of such a protected class. The bill prohibits the Religious Freedom Restoration Act of 1993 from providing a claim, defense, or basis for challenging such protections.

The bill prohibits an individual from being denied access to a shared facility, including a restroom, a locker room, and a dressing room, which is in accordance with the individual's gender identity.

Equal rights certainly sounds legitimate, doesn't it? It's a ruse. This Act would replace the word "sex" in the current civil rights legislation with sexual orientation and gender identity. That means a biological male teacher would be allowed to use the same restroom as the biological girls in elementary school if he identified as a female that day. How do you think that's going to turn out? If this became law, we wouldn't be protecting those girls from a potential sexual predator. This would also mean that biological men would be allowed to compete against biological women in all athletics. What happened to the rights of those women? Think of the lost scholarship and Olympic opportunities for them. In a culture that values women's equality, this Act would trample all over that.

That's not the worst of it though. There's a sentence in that summary that reveals what this Act is really all about. It's what Satan's after with the LGBTQ+ movement. "The bill prohibits the Religious Freedom Restoration Act of 1993 from providing a claim, defense, or basis for challenging such protections." Do you understand the gravity of what that means? The US was founded upon liberty. Religious liberty in particular. The Equality Act states that your religious beliefs wouldn't be protected anymore. That the LGBTQ+ agenda overrules them. So, what does this mean? It means a church who allows public events on their premises would be forced to hire LGBTQ+ persons, going directly against their beliefs. It means a faith based adoption agency would be forced to adopt children out to same sex couples, going against their beliefs. It means faith based hospitals would be required to perform sex change operations, going against their beliefs. It means a Christian baker would be forced to bake a cake for a drag queen, going against their beliefs. It means a child could be taken from their parents if the parents refuse them hormone therapy, a sex change operation, or if they want their confused child to have godly gender counseling. It means a faith based school could be forced to teach LGBTQ+ curriculum, just like the public schools.

Here's how Jonathan Cahn describes the Equality Act:

"There is a sword hanging over us - a sword being prepared against religious freedom, against believers, against the Gospel, the likes of which believers in America have never known. And most believers are unaware of it. It wasn't long after the Democratic Party took over the lower house of Congress that it passed what is called The Equality Act. The proposed law has been called the most dangerous law to religious freedom ever proposed on American soil. It legally eradicates the distinction of gender as thus male and female. It codifies homosexuality, pansexuality, and virtually every other sexuality as a federally protected state – against any who might oppose such things or not go along with them."[2]

What do you think the end result is going to be for Christians if the Equality Act becomes law? Persecution. You see, there's a progression with sin and hard hearts. When a rebellious heart is full of anger and hate, that emotion is going to come out, not only in words, but also in deeds. That's when a rebellious heart becomes a hateful murderous heart. Christians will have to compromise their faith or close their businesses because of the fines and legal costs they'll incur from being sued. Christians who preach God's Word and denounce sinful lifestyles, like the LGBTQ+, could find themselves in jail. What's more is the Bible get could get banned because the truth it contains is offensive to the LGBTQ+ community.

The Equality Act and the LGBTQ+ movement have nothing to do with equal rights. Do not let the politicians and media fool you with their propaganda and logical fallacies. Engaging in what God says is sinful isn't a right! We do not have a right to murder, a right to steal, a right to commit adultery, a right to marry the same sex, a right to have sex with children, a right to change the gender God gave us, or a right to commit any other sin whether it's sexual or otherwise. Those are not God-given rights!

God gave us believers clear instructions to make our earthly laws resemble God's laws so that people could come to know him and put their faith in Jesus. The law helps educate people about God's truth. Laws that go against God's Word are in fact condoning and encouraging sin. How is that helpful for a sinner? It's not helpful at all. It's not loving. It's hateful because we're not telling them how to be saved. Instead, we're leading them away from God and toward eternal judgment. The Equality Act doesn't resemble God's laws at all. It's one of Satan's deception tactics to tear people away from God and the truth. Jesus himself said we can't let anyone split apart God's definition of gender and marriage.

> "Haven't you read the Scriptures?" Jesus replied. "They record that from the beginning 'God made them male and female.' And he said, 'This explains why a man leaves his father and mother and is joined to his wife, and the two are united into one.' Since they are no longer two but one, let no one split apart what God has joined together." (Matthew 19:4-6 NLT)

So, let's see where the main 2020 presidential candidates stand on this issue. Once again, we'll continue to look at both Biden and Sanders since Sanders is working with Biden to influence his policies.

Joe Biden is a strong supporter of the Equality Act. Here are some quotes from his website:[3]

> "Biden will make enactment of the Equality Act during his first 100 days as president a top legislative priority. Biden will also direct his Cabinet to ensure immediate and full

enforcement of the Equality Act across all federal departments and agencies."

"On his first day in office, Biden will reinstate the Obama-Biden guidance revoked by the Trump-Pence Administration, which will restore transgender students' access to sports, bathrooms, and locker rooms in accordance with their gender identity."

"Biden will ensure that LGBTQ+ individuals have full access to all appropriate health care treatments and resources. This includes covering care related to transitioning—including gender confirmation surgery."

"The Obama-Biden Administration supported legislative efforts to ban 'conversion therapy' against minors, but today this practice is only fully banned for minors in 19 states. As President, Biden will work to enact the Therapeutic Fraud Prevention Act."

"In 2004 and 2006, Biden voted against a constitutional amendment defining marriage as between one man and one woman."

Bernie Sanders is in the same camp as Biden. These are statements from his website:[4]

"Pass the Equality Act, the Every Child Deserves a Family Act and other bills to prohibit discrimination against LGBTQ+ people."

"Ensure LGBTQ+ people have comprehensive health insurance without discrimination from providers."

"Bernie Sanders' Medicare for All would not only confront the massive health disparities faced by the LGBTQ+ community, it would also cover gender affirming surgeries."

President Trump is against the Equality Act. Here's a quote from the Washington Blade in May of 2019:

"With a vote on the Equality Act in the U.S. House expected on Friday, a senior administration official indicated exclusively to the Washington Blade that President Trump opposes the bill. 'The Trump administration absolutely opposes discrimination of any kind and supports the equal treatment of all; however, this bill in its current form is filled with poison pills that threaten to undermine parental and conscience rights,' the senior administration official said via email."[5]

As for political party support, the bill passed in the US House of Representatives in May 2019. Every Democrat who voted, voted in favor of the Equality Act, 228 of them. On the Republican side, 173 voted against it, while 8 voted for it.[6] It has not yet been voted on in the Senate.

What do you think the election omen foretells about this? We know that **a nation will advance in wickedness until it reaches the polar opposite of God.** Have we reached this point? God defines gender as male and female. God defines marriage as between a man and a woman. God defines sexual sin as anything outside of those definitions. The Republican Party is the only main party which supports marriage between a man and a woman. Even so, all three of the key 2020 presidential candidates—Biden, Sanders, and President Trump—have expressed their support of same sex marriage. Biden and Sanders support the Equality Act. The only reason President Trump doesn't is because it tramples all over religious freedom and the rights of parents. Our culture and national leaders don't agree with God's definition. They think gender is fluid, that you can marry and have sex with whoever you want. It's an anything goes attitude toward gender and sexuality. The polar opposite of a defined gender and marriage is one that's undefined—fluid you could say. Yes, we've certainly reached the polar opposite of God.

Now, you also know what the election omen prophecies about that too. **When a nation turns completely away from God and reaches the point of no return it will bring judgment upon itself.**

If you vote for a candidate who supports the LGBTQ+ movement and the Equality Act, you'll be advancing us one more step toward the Antichrist's regime, the time of judgment, and the time of severe persecution against Christians. Your vote matters more than ever in this coming election because you can help stem the tide of persecution that's been bombarding Christians. I've just illustrated that the Bible teaches the LGBTQ+ lifestyle is sinful. As such, the Bible could very well get deemed hateful to the LGBTQ+ community and banned. We cannot let that happen while we're still here waiting for Jesus to rapture us believers! You can make a difference at your state and local level by voting for representatives that value religious liberty, the very foundation of our government. You can support a presidential candidate who's opposed to the Equality Act. Vote for the candidate who demonstrates an obedient heart that listens to God's Word, not a candidate with a rebellious heart that's inclined their ear toward Satan. Don't let Satan make God's truth illegal.

> But Peter and the apostles answered, "We must obey God rather than men." (Acts 5:29)

> For we cannot oppose the truth, but must always stand for the truth. (2 Corinthians 13:8 NLT)

CHAPTER 14 - DRUGS

The next issue we're going to consider is drug legalization. Marijuana in particular since that's a hot topic right now. As you've read in Chapter 11 when we discussed the government's role in moral laws, we Christians shouldn't have the worldly attitude of do whatever you want if it's not harming me. Any behavior that's contrary to God's laws is harmful for society. So, we shouldn't be advocates for immoral laws. Laws help guide people to live holy lives. That's what God desires for us. He wants everyone to come to know him. We must strive to make our earthly laws reflect God's desires as much as we possibly can. In Jesus's example prayer he did say "May your will be done on earth, as it is in heaven" (Luke 11:2).

Thus, we need to understand what God's Word says about drugs. You might not find the word *drug* in your Bible translation. Instead you'll likely find the word *sorcery*. The original Greek word in the Scriptures that's translated to *sorcery* is *pharmakeia*. As you likely surmised, it's where we get the word *pharmacy* from. It means the use or administering of drugs and it's often in connection with idolatry and witchcraft. So let's see how *pharmakeia* is used in the Bible. It appears three times in the New Testament and two of those times are in the book of Revelation, so this is clearly relevant to the end times that we're now living in:

> Now the deeds of the flesh are obvious, which are: adultery, sexual immorality, uncleanness, lustfulness, idolatry, sorcery, hatred, strife, jealousies, outbursts of anger, rivalries, divisions, heresies, envy, murders, drunkenness, orgies, and things like these; of which I forewarn you, even as I also forewarned you, that those who practice such things will not inherit God's Kingdom. (Galatians 5:19-21)

> They didn't repent of their murders, their sorceries, their sexual immorality, or their thefts. (Revelation 9:21)

> For your merchants were the princes of the earth; for with your sorcery all the nations were deceived. (Revelation 18:23)

The apostle Paul tells us in the first Scripture that "sorcery" or *pharmakeia* is a deed of the flesh. That means it's sinful. He included it right along with sexual sins and murder even. We're supposed to bear fruits of the Spirit not of our sinful human nature. Then we see in the first verse above from Revelation that people who are left behind after the rapture of believers don't repent of their sorceries. They have a hard, unrepentant heart like Satan's. The last verse gives us a clue as to why that is. It's a Scripture about the fall of Babylon and it says through sorcery—drug use—the nations were deceived.

Now, these verses aren't speaking about taking an ibuprofen or drinking caffeine laden coffee. When we consider the definition for *pharmakeia* above, this is about drug use that has idolatry and even witchcraft at the heart of its use. Idolatry is when we worship something other than God. It could be literally anything. However, the Bible tells us that all idolatry is demon worship (1 Corinthians 10:19-20). What do you already know that demons desire most of all? They want to keep you away from God and the truth. Satan and his demonic army of fallen angels will attempt to get you addicted to anything that will pull you away from God and prevent you from understanding God's truth. This is why God tells us to flee from all idol worship and in particular sorcery (Leviticus 12:6; Isaiah 8:19). He's protecting us from demons!

According to WebMD, marijuana has a mind-altering compound, THC, which gets a user "high" because it makes the body release dopamine. This results in feelings of euphoria and relaxation. It also clouds the senses and judgment and makes it difficult for the user to focus, learn, and remember. It can be addictive. They say 1 in 10 users become addicted and the odds are 1 in 6 if the person starts using in their teens. In high doses, it can cause paranoia and hallucinations.[1]

God doesn't want you to look for comfort or joy in anything other than him (Romans 15:13; John 15:11; Psalm 16:11, 37:4). It will leave you empty and won't bring you any happiness. God doesn't want you to have dull senses like someone who is drunk (Romans 13:13; Ephesians 5:15-20). God's will for us is to be sober, watchful, learning about God, and teaching others how to be saved. God doesn't want you addicted, and thus a slave, to anything other than him. The Bible tells us that we're slaves to whatever we obey, whatever controls us (Romans 6:16). If you're a believer, then you aren't a slave to the law anymore and are allowed to do anything. But you must remember that not everything is good for you (1 Corinthians 6:12). If you have Jesus's Holy Spirit living inside of you, your body is now his temple (1 Corinthians 6:19). Sin and drug use defile his temple.

It should be becoming apparent to you that marijuana is certainly a form of idolatry that the demons are backing. The demons don't want you seeking joy from God. They want you to seek joy from the world. They want you in an altered state of consciousness so you can't focus on God's truth, but instead are open to hearing demons speak to you. Satan's goal is to deceive you, just like he did Eve. God has given us a warning about this. In the Scripture above, we learned the nations were deceived through their sorceries, their drug use.

Don't let Satan and his minions deceive you about drug use. We must vote for candidates who oppose legalizing drugs like marijuana. If you're in favor of legalizing marijuana, then you're in favor of idolatry and you're causing others to stumble (1 Corinthians 6:3). We are living in the last of the last days. We must point people to Jesus. Drug use pulls people away from Jesus and into the arms of demons.

Now let's see where the political parties and candidates stand on marijuana legalization. The Democrats, Libertarians, and the Green Party all favor legalizing marijuana. The Republican platform highlights that progress against drug abuse is eroding and cites states legalizing marijuana as an example. As for the 2020 presidential candidates, Bernie Sanders has the most liberal view and is now influencing Biden's stance on this. Sanders is one of the sponsors of the Marijuana Justice Act, which was introduced in the Senate in early 2019, and as such he wants to fully legalize marijuana, remove it from the Controlled Substance Act, and expunge past convictions related to marijuana.[2] Joe Biden wants to decriminalize the use of marijuana, meaning you can't go to jail for that reason alone. He also favors expunging past convictions. He only supports legalizing it for medical purposes.[3] President Trump has no plans to pursue legalizing marijuana at the federal level and has stated the states should make that decision.[4]

This is an issue that is going to come down to each state. So, your specific state and its congressional representatives are going to impact if the federal government legalizes marijuana or not. This is one of those issues where your local vote really does make a big difference.

Let me explain. There are several marijuana related bills that have been introduced in Congress during this legislative cycle. While they could pass the House since it's currently Democrat controlled, they won't pass the Senate because it's Republican controlled. A Politico article from January 2020 highlights that national organizations, like the Marijuana Policy Project, are targeting marijuana legalization campaigns in smaller states because if they can get just a few more senators on their side, marijuana legalization will pass in the federal Senate.[5]

And now, with the damage the coronavirus has done to the US economy and to that of each state, finance analysts are already saying that legalizing marijuana could be the savior.[6] You see, if it was legal, they'd add all sorts of state and local taxes to the sale of marijuana and generate revenue for the government. While this may seem like a good idea, it's not. It reeks of a greedy heart, of someone who desires an ill gotten gain. Don't let Satan trick you into selling out to him.

The election omen states that **a nation will advance in wickedness until it reaches the polar opposite of God.** Well, as a nation, people are in favor of legalizing marijuana. According to a November 2019 Pew Research report, 11 states have legalized marijuana for recreational use, 33 states have legalized it for medical use, and 67% of people polled are in favor of legalization. Back in 1969 only 12% of people polled favored legalization.[7] The year 2010 was the last year the majority of people opposed legalization. This train is moving full steam ahead. We haven't yet reached the polar opposite of God since a majority of states haven't legalized the recreational use of the drug. I have no doubt this is going to pass in a majority of states, it's just a matter of time. As we get closer and closer to the tribulation period and the Antichrist's government, the closer we're going to get to lawlessness. That's when the anything goes attitude will reign supreme.

However, you are not a proponent of anything goes! Vote for your state and local level candidates who oppose legalizing drugs like marijuana. Let's guide people to the path of righteousness. Stand up against Satan's deceptions of sorcery in these last days.

> Stand firm therefore in the liberty by which Christ has made us free, and don't be entangled again with a yoke of bondage. (Galatians 5:1)

CHAPTER 15 - GUN RIGHTS

This next issue we're going to discuss is the second amendment right to bear arms. There's strong opposition against this amendment today, so let's uncover what the Bible says about weapons and see what the candidates say about gun rights.

Even a casual Bible reader will know that weapons come up frequently. God's Word contains many accounts of war. While guns aren't specifically mentioned since they weren't invented when the Scriptures were written, swords, rocks, arrows, and the like certainly are. Since God was directing the Israelites to war against their enemies and conquer them, he clearly sanctions the use of weapons in war. Read the books of Joshua, 1 and 2 Samuel, and 1 Kings if you want to study that. But that's not what the second amendment is about. It's about your personal right to own a weapon and use it. Does the Bible have anything to say about that?

Contrary to what you might think, Jesus wasn't against weapons or self-defense. Jesus made a whip and drove all the money changers out of the temple (John 2:15-16). He wielded a weapon. Recall that his disciples carried swords. There's an infamous account of Peter using his sword to cut the ear off the servant of the high priest when Jesus was being arrested (Luke 22:49-51; Matt 26:51-54; John 18:10-11). Why did Peter have a sword if Jesus was against weapons or self-defense? Don't you think Jesus would have rebuked Peter for having it in that case? Peter had a sword because Jesus told his disciples to carry one with them as they went out to preach the gospel. Jesus is the one speaking in this Scripture:

> He said to them, "When I sent you out without purse, bag, and sandals, did you lack anything?" They said, "Nothing." Then he said to them, "But now, whoever has a purse, let him take it, and likewise a bag. Whoever has none, let him sell his cloak, and buy a sword. (Luke 22:35-36)

It's clear that Jesus doesn't take any issue with someone possessing a weapon. It was so important to Jesus that they have a sword to carry that he even told them to sell their coat in order to buy one if they had to. And when we read a little further in the Scriptures, we learn that

Peter actually had his sword before Jesus told them this because Peter had to point out that he already had one.

So now that we know it's fine by Jesus to possess a weapon, it comes down to how Jesus expects us to behave with one. This is the key. Why did Jesus tell his disciples to carry a sword? Well, it wasn't to use it the way that Peter did when Jesus was being arrested. Jesus told Peter to put his sword away, told him people who lived by the sword would die by it, and then revealed that he was perfectly capable of defending himself (Matthew 26:52-54). Peter got rebuked because he used his sword in error. He was full of fear and unleashed anger and hatred toward those coming for Jesus when the situation didn't warrant that. No one had attacked Jesus. No one had attacked Peter. Sure, they came with clubs and swords, but Peter was the first to make a move.

When Jesus told Peter not to live by the sword it's because he doesn't want any person living in order to kill, seek revenge, or murder. We're not to repay evil with evil (Romans 12:17). People don't get saved that way. We're supposed to strive to live in peace with others. It's too easy for us to confuse justice with revenge. Revenge is for God because his justice is perfect. Ours isn't. Our sinful natures would seek to one-up the injustice that was committed against us. Just consider Jesus's disciples James and John, the Sons of Thunder. When Jesus went to preach in a Samaritan village and the people didn't welcome him, those disciples wanted permission to call down fire from heaven to consume them. Really!? But that's how we are though, isn't it?

Our mission here on earth is to spread the gospel and help people come to know Jesus and be saved. People are drawn to Jesus when we reflect his love. That's why Jesus told us to love our enemies.

> "You have heard that it was said, 'An eye for an eye, and a tooth for a tooth.' But I tell you, don't resist him who is evil; but whoever strikes you on your right cheek, turn to him the other also. ... But I tell you, love your enemies, bless those who curse you, do good to those who hate you, and pray for those who mistreat you and persecute you, that you may be children of your Father who is in heaven." (Matthew 5:38-39, 44-45)

So, if Jesus wants us to turn our cheek, why were the disciples told to carry a sword? After Jesus was arrested, he was slapped by a temple guard when being questioned by the high priest. Did you know that

Jesus in fact did not turn his cheek? Instead he stood up to the high priest, told him to state what he had done wrong, and then questioned why he was being beaten. He verbally rebuked him. Paul the apostle did the same thing the many times he was arrested for preaching the gospel (Acts 23:2-3). Jesus didn't punch the temple guard or the high priest. Paul didn't strike any of his accusers either. The key point here is that they didn't retaliate or seek revenge. They willingly suffered for doing good and left their circumstance in the hands of God (1 Peter 2:20-23). Turning the other cheek isn't about being meek or being unprepared or unwilling to act. It's about giving control of the justice in the matter over to God.

You can carry a weapon and still turn your cheek, because this all comes down to intent and circumstance. It's a matter of your heart. A gun is an object. It can't do anything of its own accord. It requires a user with intent, a purpose. A sword, gun, or any other weapon could be used to hunt, to play a sport, for war, for murder, or to defend. The disciples carried a sword for defense. Jesus sent them out into the world to preach. They didn't have cars back then. They typically walked most places. That sword would be needed to protect against wild animals, bandits, and people bent on committing evil.

Jesus preached about being a good shepherd that defends the flock and is even willing to lay his life down for them (John 10:11-15). He expects the same of us. The apostle Paul tells us to guard ourselves and God's people, to shepherd God's flock (Acts 20:28). Nehemiah is a great example of this. When he and the Israelites returned from Babylonian captivity to rebuild the wall in Jerusalem, their evil enemies were furious and came against them. Nehemiah is the one speaking in these verses.

> Therefore I set guards in the lowest parts of the space behind the wall, in the open places. I set the people by family groups with their swords, their spears, and their bows. I looked, and rose up, and said to the nobles, to the rulers, and to the rest of the people, "Don't be afraid of them! Remember the Lord, who is great and awesome, and fight for your brothers, your sons, your daughters, your wives, and your houses." ... So neither I, nor my brothers, nor my servants, nor the men of the guard who followed me took off our clothes. Everyone took his weapon to the water. (Nehemiah 4:13-14, 23)

Nehemiah made sure everyone had a weapon and could defend themselves, their families, and their houses. None of them went anywhere without a weapon because the evil against them was so intense. It's no different for us. Wicked people who intend to harm others have to be stopped. If we have the ability to prevent someone from being harmed or murdered, we have to act. That's how we guard the flock.

You know, we're in a war right now. You are living in the very last of the last days before Jesus returns. Evil abounds because Satan is still among us. The apostle Paul told us that's who our real enemy is and that we need to be wearing our armor of God every single day. We have a shield to defend ourselves and God's Word as our sword. But you know what? Satan can get a hold of people. He and his fallen angel army can possess people. You've read all the Bible accounts of demon possession, so you know it's real. That's the evil we're up against. You've all seen the mass shootings on the news. If it wasn't for brave people who are being like Nehemiah, carrying a weapon, and are willing to protect all of God's people, many more people would die in those horrible events.

The bottom line is that God supports your right to bear arms and defend yourself and his people against evil. If you choose to have a weapon, when and how you use it is a matter of your heart. Do you have a Holy Spirit filled heart that's brave and loves your fellow man? Then Jesus will help you use that weapon appropriately. However, if you have a heart full of anger and revenge, then Satan could use that weapon to tempt you into sin. Whatever you decide for yourself, you will have to answer to Jesus for everything you do here on earth. So be sure you can explain yourself to him.

So, let's see where the 2020 presidential candidates and the political parties stand on this issue. The Green Party supports the Brady Bill, wants to eliminate the sale of weapons without background checks at gun shows, and wants to extend background checks to all private sales of firearms.[1] The Libertarian Party supports the second amendment and opposes any laws restricting, registering, or monitoring the ownership, manufacture, or transfer of firearms or ammunition.[2]

Joe Biden has a comprehensive list of what he'd do regarding gun rights on his website. Bernie Sanders's website is much briefer on this topic. However, when comparing the two, they support the same initiatives. I want to point out that Biden refers to gun violence as a public health epidemic. You're going to learn in a future chapter that this is a classic propaganda tactic. He's not calling it what it really is. It's a sin problem. They want to hold gun manufacturers civilly liable for their guns, ban the manufacture and sale of assault weapons and high-capacity magazines, ban the importation of assault weapons, restrict the number of weapons you can purchase each month, require background checks for all gun sales, require registration of existing assault weapons, make it illegal to sell guns and ammo online, require people who purchase 3D gun printing kits to pass a background check, prevent federal funds from arming or training teachers, and they support red flag laws. Red flag laws would let family members or law enforcement remove a person's access to firearms when that person is in crisis and poses a danger to themselves or others.[3]

There's one other thing that Biden supports that I want to call out because it's hugely impactful to you as a Christian. He wants to prohibit a person from purchasing or owning a firearm if they've been convicted of a misdemeanor hate crime. Remember in Chapter 13 when we talked about the Equality Act being an assault against religious liberty and in particular against you as a believer? If that act passes, your preaching of the gospel to an LGBTQ+ person and telling them what the Bible says about their sin would be a hate crime! If you're a business owner and you refuse to provide a service to an LGBTQ+ person because it goes against your beliefs, that would be a hate crime too if that act passes. The Democrats would use the Equality Act in conjunction with their gun control legislation to take guns away from Christians. That's exactly what Satan wants.

The Republican Party supports your second amendment right and constitutional carry statutes. They oppose laws that restrict magazine capacity, ban the sale of the modern rifle, require registration, and laws that deprive people of their rights to bear arms without due process of law. That last bit means the party opposes red flag laws.

Now let's see what President Trump has done regarding gun rights since he's been in office. He's been endorsed by the National Rifle Association (NRA).[4] He withdrew the US from the United Nations Arms Trade Treaty which would have surrendered American's second amendment rights to foreign leaders.[5] He's improved school safety with the STOP School Violence Act which is helping schools train teachers to identify and prevent violence.[6] He advocated for teachers to carry guns and now more than 30 states allow teachers who are trained to carry guns in the classroom so they can protect their students. He's also said that "one of the gravest threats to the Second Amendment, and to American freedom itself, are activist judges." He's been appointing conservative judges who interpret the Constitution as it was written.[7] He's a firm supporter of your second amendment right to keep and bear arms.

The election omen for this issue is a bit different than the other issues we've looked at. When a nation takes away gun rights, they take away the people's ability to revolt against that government. So, this issue is about our society and nation advancing toward an oppressive ruler. There's one coming. God foretold it. He's the Antichrist, and he will be the most oppressive ruler ever. The Bible says he forces everyone to worship him and people are unable to war against him (Revelation 13). That sounds like a people who aren't equipped with weapons to rise up, doesn't it?

A time is coming in which gun rights will be trampled on and removed. But now is not that time! Now is your time to vote for our God-given right to carry a weapon so that you can defend yourself and God's people. Vote for your state and local candidates who support the second amendment. Vote for President Trump for reelection because he recognizes your God-given right and the importance of it.

CHAPTER 16 - ISRAEL

If you're a Bible reading Christian, then you know that Israel is the apple of God's eye. As such, it's important for us to understand why that is and how God expects us to behave toward Israel. While we're at it, we're also going to look at Satan's goals regarding Israel. This will help us determine which candidates we should or shouldn't support.

First off, Israel is both a nation and a people group, the Israelites. The Israelites are also referred to as the Jews or Jewish. Now, this can be a bit confusing because you don't have to practice Judaism in order to be Jewish since it's both a nationality and a religion. This is an important point for you to keep in mind; it's going to be important later in the chapter.

God, "Yahweh", created the nation of Israel through Abraham. This took place way back around 2,100 BC.[1] Abraham is referred to as "Abram" in the verse below:

> Now Yahweh said to Abram, "Leave your country, and your relatives, and your father's house, and go to the land that I will show you. I will make of you a great nation." (Genesis 12:1-2)

In addition to creating the nation, God also gave Abraham the land for his nation. Israel has God-defined borders. The covenant is in place for forever (Genesis 17:7-8). God also instructed Israel not to make any peace deals with foreign nations (Exodus 23:32) and not to give any of the land set aside for the Levites—the priestly tribe who served in the temple—away by selling it or exchanging it because it belongs to God and is set apart as holy (Ezekiel 48:8-14). That's Jerusalem.

> In that day Yahweh made a covenant with Abram, saying, "I have given this land to your offspring, from the river of Egypt to the great river, the river Euphrates." (Genesis 15:18)

The Bible describes Israel as God's chosen people, not because he has favorites, but because he created them for a specific purpose (Deuteronomy 7:6-9). God set them apart so that they could be an example for everyone else (1 Corinthians 10:1-11). He displays his power and glory through Israel for the whole world to witness. You can think of them as a lamp.

> Listen, islands, to me. Listen, you peoples, from afar: Yahweh has called me from the womb; from the inside of my mother, he has mentioned my name. ... He said to me, "You are my servant, Israel, in whom I will be glorified." ... Indeed, he says, "It is too light a thing that you should be my servant to raise up the tribes of Jacob, and to restore the preserved of Israel. I will also give you as a light to the nations, that you may be my salvation to the end of the earth." (Isaiah 49:1, 3, 6)

God created Israel and set them apart so they could essentially be a lighthouse for all the other nations and peoples, pointing the way to salvation in Jesus. It's Israel and the city of Jerusalem in particular that Jesus is going to reign from during his millennial kingdom (Isaiah 2:1-4).

Now, Israel is more than a light that points the way. It's also a light that provides and blesses. Another reason God established Israel is so that he can bless everyone through them. This is the rest of the conversation that God had with Abraham:

> "I will make of you a great nation. I will bless you and make your name great. You will be a blessing. I will bless those who bless you, and I will curse him who treats you with contempt. All the families of the earth will be blessed through you." (Genesis 12:2-3)

What kind of blessings and curses is God talking about? To bless means to cause to prosper. The prosperity applies to everything a nation or person does. As you can surmise, a curse is the opposite and entails harm and misfortune. God gives a detailed description of blessings and curses in Deuteronomy 28-30 when he instructs Israel to obey God so that they can reap his blessings.

This promise applies to us. God wants to bless the US and all of us who live here based on how we treat Israel. The Bible is full of examples of nations who came against Israel and who were then punished for that by God. Perhaps you think this is a bit farfetched and that God doesn't directly intervene in mankind's affairs anymore. If so, you should read William Koenig's book *Eye to Eye: Facing The Consequences Of*

Dividing Israel in which he lists 127 catastrophes between 1991 and 2017 that came upon the US when our leaders were pressuring Israel to divide its land.[2] Or read Jonathan Cahn's books, *The Harbinger* and *The Oracle*. This is very much real.

Speaking of coming against Israel, that highlights another reason we must be strong supporters of Israel. It's because Satan is opposed to them. God loves Israel; thus, Satan hates them. Right after Adam and Eve sinned, God told Satan there would be hatred between Satan and Eve's offspring and that one of Eve's offspring would strike Satan's head (Genesis 3). This is a reference to Jesus. Jesus defeated Satan when he was crucified. Throughout history, Satan has attempted to destroy God's people in an attempt to thwart his fate. Satan still thinks he can win. So, he hasn't relented on his attacks against Israel and the Jewish people. Satan's evil scheme will come to a head when the Antichrist reigns. The Antichrist brokers a peace deal with Israel and its neighbors that divides God's land (Joel 3). That act kicks off the tribulation period, a time of God's judgment upon the Antichrist and the entire earth that the Antichrist rules over.

So how are we supposed to treat Israel in order to reap the blessings? God tells us to pray for the peace of Jerusalem (Psalm 122:6), that we should honor Israel because it honors God (Isaiah 60:9), that we should serve them (Isaiah 60:12), and help them financially (Romans 15:27). Think of how much you've been blessed because of Israel. They gave us God's Word, the prophets, the disciples, and Jesus who is King of the Jews. They gave birth to Christianity. If it wasn't for them, we wouldn't know how to be saved. There's a great example of a Gentile, someone who isn't Jewish, blessing the Jewish people in the Bible. It's Cornelius, a Roman centurion. The Bible says he was a devout man who feared God, gave gifts to the needy generously, and always prayed to God (Acts 10). The needy people he was giving to were the people who lived around him, the Jewish people. I imagine he prayed for their healing and welfare too. He had a loving, generous heart. Do you know how God blessed Cornelius? He's the first Gentile believer! God sent an angel to Cornelius who told him his prayers had been noticed and that he was to send for Peter. Peter then preached the gospel to him and Cornelius and his entire household believed. They all received Jesus's Holy Spirit.

You can't be a Holy Spirit filled Christian and despise Israel and the Jewish people. The two are incompatible because Jesus loves them.

Let's see how the 2020 Democrat presidential candidates would treat Israel if they were elected. As we've been doing in all the prior chapters on the issues, we're going to continue looking at both Biden and Sanders since, although Sanders dropped out, he's now influencing Biden's policies. Sanders could very well be Biden's vice president pick. We'll see. Regarding military aid to Israel, Joe Biden said he'd continue to support it. However, Bernie Sanders said aid to Israel would be dependent upon them ending their occupation and moving forward on a peace agreement. The boycott, divest, and sanction (BDS) movement isn't supported by Biden who considers it anti-Semitic. Sanders also says he doesn't support BDS, but believes Americans have a right to do this as a form of protest under the first amendment. Biden doesn't think the US embassy should be moved back to Tel Aviv. Yet, Sanders said it would be considered if Israel continued settlement expansion and the like. Both Biden and Sanders support the establishment of a Palestinian state based on pre-1967 borders.[3] That means Israel wouldn't have Jerusalem because they gained that in their 1967 war. Sanders wrote an article in which he stated:

> "The founding of Israel is understood by another people in the land of Palestine as the cause of their painful displacement. ... Ending that occupation and enabling the Palestinians to have self-determination in an independent, democratic, economically viable state of their own is in the best interests of the United States, Israel, the Palestinians, and the region."[4]

I have to point out that Bernie's actions don't jive with what he's said. He voted against the anti-BDS bill and has Linda Sarsour, an activist for BDS, as one of his campaign surrogates.[5] Seems like he supports BDS to me. I also want to point out that Bernie frequently says he's Jewish. However, he's not referring to his faith. He's talking about his nationality only. I think he does this on purpose to deceive people into thinking he practices Judaism. His parents were Jewish immigrants from Poland. Bernie hasn't professed his faith in God or Jesus. He told a reporter with The Washington Post that he's not actively involved in organized religion.[6] He seems to avoid the question when asked. Here's what he said when Jimmy Kimmel asked him if he believed in God:

> "Well, you know, I am who I am, and what I believe in, what my spirituality is about, is that we're all in this together -- that I think it's not a good thing to believe, as human beings, that we can turn our backs on the suffering of other people."[7]

Someone who's filled with God's Holy Spirit isn't ashamed to talk about God. All indicators illustrate that Bernie is an atheist. I don't think he wants to own up to that because that's not a popular worldview among most Americans.

As for the Green Party, they believe international law and not religious faith should be the basis on which claims to Israel's land are resolved. They also support withholding military and foreign aid to Israel until they withdraw from occupied territories. The Libertarian Party doesn't want to be involved in international affairs. They want to end all foreign intervention including military and economic aid.

As you can see, the Democrat candidates and the Green and Libertarian parties support things regarding Israel that the Bible is against. BDS is Satanic. It harms Israel. It doesn't bless them. The Palestinians don't have a right to Israel's land because God gave it to Israel. Withholding aide to Israel is something Satan would do, not something God wants us to do. Choosing not to participate in foreign matters is the same as sitting on the sidelines and not voting. God has called us to action. We're either for Jesus or against him. It's the same with Israel. Remember that God wants us to bless Israel.

Now let's look at how President Trump has treated Israel since he's been in office. He recognized Jerusalem as Israel's capital and moved the US Embassy there. He withdrew from UNESCO because of their anti-Israel bias. He recognized the Golan Heights as part of Israel.[8] This past December 2019, Trump signed an Executive Order to combat the rise of anti-Semitism. "This action makes clear that Title VI of the Civil Rights Act, which prohibits the federal funding of universities and other institutions that engage in discrimination, applies to institutions that traffic in anti-Semitic hate," Trump said before signing the document.[9] Trump also released a comprehensive peace plan for Israel and the Palestinians which is a two state solution, but does not divide

Jerusalem. In fact, it states:

> "A division of Jerusalem would be inconsistent with the policy statements of the Jerusalem Embassy Act of 1995 of the United States. All former presidents who have been involved in the peace process have agreed that Jerusalem should not be physically divided again. ... Jerusalem will remain the sovereign capital of the State of Israel, and it should remain an undivided city."[10]

As for the election omen, you know that **a nation will advance in wickedness until it reaches the polar opposite of God.** While President Trump, a clear friend of Israel, is in office, I have no doubt that we're going to continue blessing Israel. God will then continue to give us more time to reach those who don't know Jesus yet. The tide of evil that's pressing upon us will continue to be held back. If a Democrat candidate is elected, that person would seek to pressure Israel into giving up or dividing Jerusalem. That's what the Antichrist is going to do. We Christians cannot support that. You must vote for local candidates and state congressmen who oppose BDS and oppose withholding aide to Israel because those local leaders are the ones who allocate the government budgets. If you love the people of Israel, then stand up for them and vote for Trump in 2020.

> Our feet are standing within your gates, Jerusalem! ... Pray for the peace of Jerusalem. Those who love you will prosper. Peace be within your walls, and prosperity within your palaces. For my brothers' and companions' sakes, I will now say, "Peace be within you." For the sake of the house of Yahweh our God, I will seek your good. (Psalm 122:2, 6-9)

CHAPTER 17 - CLIMATE CHANGE

Climate change has been a hot topic for a while now. You may remember that it used to be called global warming. In this chapter, I'm going to show you that God has a name for it too. It's called idolatry.

Climate change advocates and supporters believe that human behavior impacts the environment, thus we have a responsibility to control our behavior so that we can control the climate. It sounds good on the surface and seems to make sense, right? The problem with this belief is that it's missing a key truth. There's a logical fallacy. They forgot to add God to the equation. Doing so changes everything. You see, God created the earth, heavens, wind, rain, snow, sun, tornadoes, earthquakes, volcanoes, cows, oil, coal, and everything else you can think of. God even created the seasons and said they'd exist as long as the earth does (Genesis 8:22). The inconvenient truth of climate change is that God is in complete control of his creation.

> Say this to those who worship other gods: "Your so-called gods, who did not make the heavens and earth, will vanish from the earth and from under the heavens." But God made the earth by his power, and he preserves it by his wisdom. With his own understanding he stretched out the heavens. When he speaks in the thunder, the heavens roar with rain. He causes the clouds to rise over the earth. He sends the lightning with the rain and releases the wind from his storehouses. The whole human race is foolish and has no knowledge! The craftsmen are disgraced by the idols they make, for their carefully shaped works are a fraud. These idols have no breath or power. Idols are worthless; they are ridiculous lies! On the day of reckoning they will all be destroyed. But the God of Israel is no idol! He is the Creator of everything that exists, including Israel, his own special possession. The LORD of Heaven's Armies is his name! (Jeremiah 10:11-16 NLT)

Once you factor in God, it becomes obvious that regardless of what we mere humans do to the environment, God is the one in control. Do you know who the Lord of Heaven's Armies is? It's Jesus. He's God in the flesh. When he returns to the earth at his second coming, he's leading the armies of heaven (Revelation 19). Jesus displayed his power over the climate and weather when he was here on earth the first time.

> Jesus ... got into a boat, his disciples followed him. Behold, a violent storm came up on the sea, so much that the boat was covered with the waves; but he was asleep. The disciples came to him and woke him up, saying, "Save us, Lord! We are dying!" He said to them, "Why are you fearful, O you of little faith?" Then he got up, rebuked the wind and the sea, and there was a great calm. The men marveled, saying, "What kind of man is this, that even the wind and the sea obey him?" (Matthew 8:22-27)

You may wonder why the climate seems so out of control at times when God is in control. Why do we have terrible hurricanes, floods, droughts, and other natural disasters? Well, there are many reasons, but the main one is sin. Before Adam and Eve sinned, they lived in paradise. The weather and nature were perfect. When they sinned, God kicked them out of paradise and cursed all of creation (Genesis 3:17-18). Sin impacted everything.

> Against its will, all creation was subjected to God's curse. But with eager hope, the creation looks forward to the day when it will join God's children in glorious freedom from death and decay. For we know that all creation has been groaning as in the pains of childbirth right up to the present time. (Romans 8:20-22 NLT)

Since we humans are sinners, we cannot earn our own salvation. We also cannot reverse what God has cursed. It's all connected and tied to God's plan of redemption. When Jesus raptures the believers, they're all getting a brand new body that's built to live forever. In a similar fashion, the earth is going to be renewed as well. In fact, God is going to make a new earth and a new heaven after Jesus's second coming and his reign on earth (2 Peter 3:5-13; Revelation 21:1). That new earth will be the utopia the climate change advocates are trying to bring about with all their might.

There's another reason for natural disasters: God uses them as judgment and discipline and ultimately to bring people to him. Consider how God used the weather and nature against Pharaoh when he was judging the Egyptians for enslaving the Israelites. Those same events rescued the Israelites and drew them to him. God sent plagues of hail, darkness, frogs, flies, disease, and even turned the Nile river to blood (Exodus 7-12). Extreme weather is part of God's plan. Jesus himself told us these terrifying and great signs from heaven were going to happen (Matthew 24:7; Luke 21:11). Do you know that God even told us in advance that the planet is going to get hot? The scorching heat of the sun is a hallmark of the tribulation period (Revelation 7:16; 16:8-9). That's the period of time that begins after the rapture of believers. Since we're very near to when that time begins, we shouldn't be in shock that it's getting warmer in some places. What we should be doing is praying. That's what God requires when we see these things come upon us (2 Chronicles 7:13-14).

So, does this mean we can pollute the earth and cut down all the rain forests? Certainly not! Do you recall what job God gave Adam to do when he lived in the garden? Adam was the caretaker of the garden and the animals. We're supposed to be good stewards of everything God has given us (Genesis 1:28, 2:15). He created the planet for us. So that includes everything on the planet. God is speaking with Adam and Eve in this verse:

> God blessed them. God said to them, "Be fruitful, multiply, fill the earth, and subdue it. Have dominion over the fish of the sea, over the birds of the sky, and over every living thing that moves on the earth." (Genesis 1:28)

There's a fine line between being a good custodian of the earth and worshiping the earth. This is where climate change advocates become idolaters. When we idolize and show honor and reverence to something as though it were divine or a god, that's a sin. We place it above the status God gave it. We must only worship God. I want to point out a key truth in the Green New Deal. This is directly from the document on the Green Party's website:

> We reject the belief that our species is the center of creation, and that other life forms exist only for our use and enjoyment.[1]

Yikes! They flat out deny what God's Word says. God did in fact create the planet for humans, and we do have dominion over all of it.

Here's more:

> Climate change is the gravest environmental, social and economic peril that humanity has ever met.
> We have an ambitious plan to make drastic changes quickly to avert global catastrophe.[2]

Climate change supporters believe our lack of intervention is going to bring about the death of the planet. They deny that God created it all, that God is in control, and that God has a plan.

> That which is known of God is revealed in them, for God revealed it to them. For the invisible things of him since the creation of the world are clearly seen, being perceived through the things that are made, even his everlasting power and divinity, that they may be without excuse. ... Professing themselves to be wise, they became fools, and traded the glory of the incorruptible God for the likeness of an image of corruptible man, and of birds, four-footed animals, and creeping things. ... Who exchanged the truth of God for a lie, and worshiped and served the creature rather than the Creator. (Romans 1:19-20, 22-23, 25)

You see, Christians aren't climate change deniers. We have wise and understanding hearts regarding this matter. Instead, climate change supporters are the ones who deny. They deny God's truth. We believers know what God has done, what God has planned, and that he's worthy of our worship. Climate change is nothing but a clever plot by Satan to pull people away from God and toward worshiping themselves and the planet.

Now that we've addressed God's truth regarding climate change, let's see what the political parties and candidates have to say about the matter so that you can determine who you should vote for. Yes, we're going to keep looking at both Biden and Sanders because Sanders is now influencing Biden's policies. I'm going to start with the Green New Deal. The Democrat Party and the Green Party both support it. Here are the key points you need to know:

They want to decarbonize the economy and use only 100% renewable energy, like wind and solar. Bernie Sanders's plan is the most aggressive with a 2030 goal to achieve this because he thinks something catastrophic is going to happen to the planet in 11 years if we don't act.[3] Joe Biden's plan accomplishes this by 2050.[4] This would entail eliminating fossil fuels like oil, coal, and natural gas. Natural gas is one of the cheapest forms of energy by the way. Combustion engines would be eliminated as a result. That means all vehicles would need to be electric. All buildings would be zero carbon. So pretty much every single building, you know your home, your work, the stores, would all have to be gutted and retrofitted with heating and cooling that used a renewable energy source. They'd implement a carbon tax to drive the behavior they want to see. They say nuclear power is dirty, so that would go away too. They want to use high speed rail instead of trucking and airplanes. So, I'm not sure how you'd travel to Europe easily and quickly. Oh, and your lawn is wasteful, so that would be replaced with a vegetable garden because the plan discourages meat consumption because cows produce carbon. The plan doesn't say what happens to all the roads. But they'd have to go away since most of them are asphalt, which is a form of petroleum. Maybe they've got flying electric cars in the works for us.

Next, you need to know that the plan isn't really about the climate. No, it's about a whole new kind of economy. A socialist economy. We're going to dive into that issue in a later chapter. The Green New Deal includes a federal jobs guarantee and a huge amount of public investments. Since a whole slew of jobs and businesses would go away by decarbonizing the economy, the government will give you a new job that pays and has benefits. And your personal property and the property of businesses, well that wouldn't really be yours or your employers anymore. Here's a statement from the Green New Deal:[5]

> Insist that every property right has an implied responsibility to provide for the common good of people, places and the planet.

So, they could force you to turn your front lawn into a community garden for the neighborhood. They could force businesses to stop producing something if they didn't think it was good for everyone. How do you think that's going to impact preachers, churches, independent Christian authors like myself, and publishers who print the Bible? This Green New Deal is about control.[6]

The plan also includes joining the Paris agreement and providing $200 million to the Green Climate Fund to help developing countries go green. These United Nations initiatives would prevent America from producing clean coal, but allow China, India, and even Europe to continue doing so. So, what exactly is that $200 million we'd give them for then? This isn't about climate change at all. Once again, it's economic. It's about wealth distribution and letting other countries have a financial advantage over the US. You know, under President Trump our nation became energy independent. The Green New Deal and Paris Agreement would reverse that and keep America's natural resources in the ground.[7]

The Libertarians are opposed to the Green New Deal because they're against government control of energy.[8] The Republicans support all forms of energy that are marketable in a free economy without subsidies, including coal, oil, natural gas, nuclear power, and hydropower. They believe the United Nations climate change initiatives are political mechanisms and thus they reject the Paris Agreement.

Let's see what President Trump has done regarding the environment since he's been in office. He withdrew the US from the Paris Agreement, approved the Keystone XL and Dakota Access pipelines, expanded offshore drilling, reversed President Obama's suspension of new leases for oil and gas development on federal lands, opened the Arctic National Wildlife Refuge to domestic energy production, and he repealed the Clean Power Plan regulation, saving billions.[9] Oh, and I already mentioned he achieved energy independence for us. For the first time since President Nixon, the US exported more oil than we imported. More than that even, we became the number one producer of oil and gas in the entire world! That's because he promotes energy development.[10]

The election omen tells us that **a nation will advance in wickedness until it reaches the polar opposite of God**. We were created to worship God and give him glory. A polar opposite of that is worshiping the earth that God created instead of God himself. Do the majority of Americans really support this crazy Green New Deal? It's tough to say. Some polls say there's a majority who support it while others don't. We're on the fence. We're at a key turning point. I think this issue won't climax until after the rapture because of the socialist components in the plan. That reeks of an Antichrist government. The tribulation period, when the Antichrist reigns, will be a time in which God uses the climate and weather to display his power. There will be intense hail, fire, earthquakes, locusts, drought, and scorching heat. You know the more we and our leaders try to control the planet, the more God displays his awesome power to show us that he's the one in control.

Don't fret about the climate. God's got this. He's in complete control. Vote for President Trump because he recognizes that the climate change agenda is a farce. Vote for your local and state candidates who recognize that God is the creator of all that exists and that he's in perfect control of his creation.

CHAPTER 18 - WHOSE RESPONSIBILITY IS IT?

There are a number of issues that warrant a conversation regarding whose responsibility is it. Who's responsible for helping someone else? Who should provide health care or education? Is it the government's, yours, churches, non-profit organizations, corporations, or no one's responsibility? These issues include homelessness, taking care of the poor, health care, education, immigration, and many others. Those who believe the government is responsible favor taxes to generate the revenue necessary to support the programs and a bigger government to then operate those programs. Those who believe individuals are responsible believe taxes should be kept low so that people have more disposable income to contribute to the programs they're passionate about. Then there are those who think corporations have a responsibility to help those in their community and thus they should allocate some of their profits to local programs instead of to pocketbooks.

So, which is it? Who does the Bible say is responsible? God has a lot to say about giving and helping others. When God gave the Israelites the law, he gave them many laws regarding tithing, generosity, and lending. They were told not to harvest all their crops but to leave some for the poor to gather (Leviticus 19:9-10). He told them to set aside a tithe of one-tenth of their crops, herds, and flocks that was to provide for the Levites, the priestly tribe who served in the temple and wasn't allotted any land, and for the poor (Deuteronomy 14:22-29, Leviticus 7:36). If a family became poor and had to sell their land, God said a relative should purchase it (Leviticus 25:25). If a fellow Israelite fell into poverty and couldn't support himself, they were told to support him as they would a temporary resident. God instructed them to lend without making a profit (Leviticus 25:35-37). God's law also told them to forgive the debts of their fellow Israelites every seventh year (Deuteronomy 15:1). In this way, God's people were able to recover from poverty. Clearly, God wants his people to take care of each other.

In those Old Testament examples, God demanded his people take care of the poor. They were given laws to compel them to do it. So, one could easily argue that a nation has a responsibility to ensure its people are taking care of its poor. However, we must also consider what the New Testament says. Jesus spoke about how we should be willing to help our fellow man in the parable of the good Samaritan (Luke 10:30-37). You remember the story. A Jewish man was attacked and left for dead along the road. A priest walked by and didn't help him. A temple assistant walked by and didn't help him. But a Samaritan man, whom the Jewish people despised, had compassion and took care of him. Jesus asks us to do the same. Jesus told that story right after he boiled the law down into two commandments we should follow: love God and love your neighbor. It was an illustration of how to love your neighbor. Now, speaking of the law, the apostle Paul tells us in the verses below that things are different now:

> Let each man give according as he has determined in his heart, not grudgingly or under compulsion, for God loves a cheerful giver. And God is able to make all grace abound to you, that you, always having all sufficiency in everything, may abound to every good work. ... Now may he who supplies seed to the sower and bread for food, supply and multiply your seed for sowing, and increase the fruits of your righteousness, you being enriched in everything for all generosity. (2 Corinthians 9:7-8, 10-11)

Jesus made a new covenant with us when he came and died for our sins. He fulfilled the law. So, we're no longer slaves to it. We no longer have to do all that the law required in order to be saved. All we have to do is believe that Jesus is God in the flesh, that he died for our sins, and rose from the grave. With this new covenant, God no longer demands that we give. That Scripture above says he doesn't want anyone giving "grudgingly or under compulsion." Today, God is concerned with the attitude of our heart. If the government, your employer, your family, or anyone else forced you to give, you likely wouldn't be happy about it. I can't think of anyone who enjoys paying a lot of taxes regardless of where they say the money goes.

However, there's another key truth here that we need to look at. There's a reason why God wants individuals to give willingly.

> For this service of giving that you perform not only makes up for lack among the saints, but abounds also through much giving of thanks to God, seeing that through the proof given by this service, they glorify God

for the obedience of your confession to the Good News of Christ and for the generosity of your contribution to them and to all, while they themselves also, with supplication on your behalf, yearn for you by reason of the exceeding grace of God in you. (2 Corinthians 9:12-14)

Paul continues by saying that giving results in several things. First, it "makes up for lack" in other words it provides. Second, it results in "giving of thanks to God." Thirdly, the "generosity of your contribution" demonstrates your "obedience" to God. Those three things then result in the receivers of your generosity giving prayer or "supplication" on your behalf to God. People literally thank God for you and pray for your wellbeing. Then, the best part that we read about first is that God will "increase the fruits of your righteousness" so that you can continue to be generous. It's a matter of the heart. God gives us the ability to produce wealth in order to see what we'll do with it (Deuteronomy 8:17-18).

Just consider the parable of talents in Luke 19. The king gave each of his servants a portion of money and told them to do business with it while he was gone. Some made ten times the amount they were given. Some made five times the amount. They were richly rewarded by the king when he returned. Yet one, didn't do anything with the money except keep it safe by burying it. He was afraid of losing it. That servant was punished instead of blessed.

So now whose responsibility do you think it is? As a Christian, do I want the government to do good things with the tax revenue it gathers from our citizens? Most definitely. However, it's not the government's responsibility to provide for the needy. God wants us as individuals to step up and do it. Consider this: If the government has to force people to provide for others through wealth redistribution, who gets the glory and blessings? Hum, indeed. I don't think anyone does because no one has the opportunity to trust God's promises to those who are generous.

This brings us to an ominous point that describes the current state of affairs. Jesus is the one speaking in the verses below:

"Give, and it will be given to you: good measure, pressed down, shaken together, and running over, will be given to you. For with the same measure you measure it will be measured back to you." (Luke 6:38)

The measure we use in giving is also used upon us. So, what happens if we're a society of a bunch of takers instead of givers? Does that mean God will take from us? Yes, it does. We clearly see it happening today. As a society, we've traded in our heart like Jesus, who gave sacrificially, for a heart like Satan's, who takes and in fact, steals what isn't his. What does the Democrat Party want to do with all your hard earned money today? They want to take it from you and give it to other people. To fund socialist programs that seem like a nice idea on the surface—homes for the homeless, free health care, free education, a living wage for people who aren't working. Except that taking produces more and more taking. It breeds laziness. God warned us that being lazy produces poverty (Proverbs 24:30-34).

Do you remember what happened to Sodom and Gomorrah? God destroyed those cities with fire and brimstone because of their wickedness. Do you recall their specific sins that were so grievous?

> Behold, this was the iniquity of your sister Sodom: pride, fullness of bread, and prosperous ease was in her and in her daughters. She also didn't strengthen the hand of the poor and needy. (Ezekiel 16:49)

Pride, gluttony, and laziness which resulted in them not taking care of the needy. God's Word tells us that in the last days people's hearts will grow cold and only love themselves (Matthew 24:12; 2 Timothy 3:1-2).

The solution isn't the government enforcing wealth distribution. The solution is trading in your stone cold heart for a compassionate heart like Jesus's.

When Jesus was here the first time, did he build homes for all the homeless people? No. Did he build schools? No. Did he provide free health care to everyone? No. Did you know he didn't just heal everyone either? Think about the man at the pool of Bethesda who was sick for 38 years. Jesus asked him if he wanted to get well. You see, his getting well had a consequence. He would be expected to work and provide for himself. He wouldn't be able to sit at the pool all day anymore. Paul the apostle tells us that those who don't work shouldn't eat (2 Thessalonians 3:10). That's referring to people who are quite capable of working but don't want to. People who are lazy. God doesn't want us helping those kinds of people because it doesn't help them. It actually makes their laziness worse, just as Jesus described in Luke 6:38.

This is why programs that are meant to help people often don't work as intended. I think it's difficult for the government or an organization to gauge who's really needy versus who's lazy. But we as individuals can certainly discern that among our family and friends, can't we? That's what Jesus asks us to do. Make a difference one person at a time among those who are closest to us (1 Timothy 5:8).

You see, this points to another problem of relying on the government or an organization to provide for others. The government is a secular institution as are many of the charitable organizations. Do you think they allocate and steward God's resources the way believers do? Do they educate a child the way a believer would? Not a chance. They aren't going to share the gospel or teach a child about God's love. They have an agenda. A politician wants a voter. An organization desires to make money. They will spend your money in such a way that it guarantees their future. That's not how we as believers should give. Jesus told us that every person's heart can be known by their fruit. A good heart will bring forth good. When you as an individual donate, you're doing it from the goodness of your heart. And that's exactly what God desires, a cheerful giver.

Here's an interesting fact for you to consider: Which group do you think accounts for the most charitable giving—individuals, corporations, or foundations? It's individuals by a landslide. In 2018, people gave $292 billion which was 68% of all donations.[1] That's a lot of money that some politicians want to get their hands on. They want to spend the money that God has given you on what matters most to them. They want you to pay more to the government so people you don't know can go to college for free. Wouldn't you prefer to help your own family attend college? They want you to pay more taxes so they can build tiny homes for the homeless. Wouldn't you prefer to help your relatives and friends pay their mortgages and rent instead? Don't let the government have even more of the money God has given you. Vote for candidates who favor lower taxes. Vote for candidates who want to remove roadblocks and promote natural growth in tax revenue, like the creation of jobs. Vote for candidates who don't want to penalize social classes, like the wealthy, with a higher tax burden. All that does is incentivize the wealthy to get out of paying that tax. I'm telling you people don't like the government spending their money. You don't either. So, let God guide you in how he wants you to give. Let

God bless you. Don't let the government steal God's blessing from you.

What we should also be advocating for within the government is better incentives for donating. Yes, God has promised us rewards in heaven based on our actions here on earth (Mark 10:21; 1 Corinthians 3:14). However, it certainly doesn't hurt to encourage giving with some earthly rewards too. It makes a difference. There was a tax change this past year that increased the amount of the standard deduction. Seems like a good thing, less people needing to itemize their deductions, thus making filing taxes easier. Except that it had an unintended consequence. A decrease in the amount of donations. Before the tax change, 30% of taxpayers itemized and in 2018 it was only 10%. It appears the tax change resulted in a charitable giving decline of $15 billion despite the strong economy.[2] I'm sad that the present day Laodicean culture brought us to this point where we're indifferent about donating and only do it for a worldly monetary benefit. Yet, I also know that God wants to bless us through our giving and if incentivizing people now is what it takes to help more people realize that, then I'm all for it.

So how do the political parties stack up regarding who they think is responsible? The Democrats favor big government and increased taxes to support their socialist programs like housing options for the homeless, free tuition at public colleges, universal preschool, and universal health care.[3] The Green Party is very similar to the Democrats.[4] The Libertarian Party is on the complete opposite side. They want to eliminate the income tax, phase out Social Security and replace it with a voluntary system, institute a free market health care system, and they also believe public services should be funded voluntarily.[5] The Republican Party opposes taxes that divide classes, believes any new value add or sales tax should include the elimination of the income tax, believes the best anti-poverty program is a strong family and a good job and wants to help people find work, and instead of free college they favor new systems of learning to compete with traditional four-year schools and private sector participation in student financing.[6]

As for the election omen and what it foretells, we know that **a nation will advance in wickedness until it reaches the polar opposite of God.** God wants us to be cheerful givers and said the measure we use to give will be measured back to us. A government that takes from its citizens instead of relying on its citizens to give incentivizes laziness instead of hard work and penalizes high income wage earners. These are all hallmarks of the polar opposite of God. God blesses people so that they can bless others, not their government. We haven't yet arrived at the antithesis, which would be a socialist or communist government. However, we just took a big leap toward the antithesis with what's happened to our nation because of the coronavirus outbreak. We've seen the Democrat Party try to push more and more of their Green New Deal socialist policies in the relief bills. Regardless of which candidate takes the Democrat Party nomination, socialism is quite popular within that party, and that's what President Trump will be up against in the November 2020 election. We are indeed approaching the point of no return here, which as you know from the election omen, will bring judgment.

Now more than ever, it's important to remember to help your family and friends when they are in need. God has given you that responsibility after all. Don't shirk it or toss it over the wall for the government and taxpayers to deal with. Let your light shine. Vote for candidates who recognize and value God's purpose in having individuals provide for others. In the Scripture below, the "Son of Man" and the "King" are references to Jesus. This is about his second coming. Trust in and stand on God's promises.

> "But when the Son of Man comes in his glory, and all the holy angels with him, then he will sit on the throne of his glory. Before him all the nations will be gathered, and he will separate them one from another, as a shepherd separates the sheep from the goats. He will set the sheep on his right hand, but the goats on the left. Then the King will tell those on his right hand, 'Come, blessed of my Father, inherit the Kingdom prepared for you from the foundation of the world; for I was hungry and you gave me food to eat. I was thirsty and you gave me drink. I was a stranger and you took me in. I was naked and you clothed me. I was sick and you visited me. I was in prison and you came to me.' "Then the righteous will answer him, saying, 'Lord, when did we see you hungry and feed you, or thirsty and give you a drink? When did we see you as a stranger and take you in, or naked and clothe you? When did we see you sick or in prison and come to you?' "The King will answer them, 'Most certainly I tell you, because you did it to one of the least of these my brothers, you did it to me.'" (Matthew 25:31-40)

CHAPTER 19 - THE ISMS

We've come to the last topic that we're going to discuss relating to the key issues of today. This chapter is all about the isms. Communism, socialism, fascism, globalism, nationalism, and capitalism. These are all economic and political systems that are front and center in the news these days. I'm going to start by explaining what each of these are.

Let's start with communism. It was first written about by Karl Marx in his Communist Manifesto published in 1848.[1] The basic principle is that there isn't any private property. Everything is state or government owned and controlled. The government is authoritarian, so there's no constitution in which the leader is responsible to the people, and the power resides in a sole leader. Marx hoped for an eventual withering away of the state so that the people would then own everything. Now, that's never happened and I'm sure you see the obvious fallacy in that logic. An all supreme leader isn't going to give up power. These are some of the policies included in the manifesto. Transfer of property to public purposes, a high income tax, no rights of inheritance, a centralized national bank controlled by the government, centralized communication and transportation controlled by the government, factories and companies owned by the government, government establishment of agricultural jobs, and free public education.[2] I'm sure you noticed these policies have a lot of similarities to the Green New Deal. Communism is in direct opposition to capitalism. The Soviet Union was a former communist nation. Today, China, Cuba, Laos, North Korea, and Vietnam all have communist governments.[3]

Here's an inconvenient, ugly truth about communism directly quoted from the manifesto:

> There are, besides, eternal truths, such as Freedom, Justice, etc., that are common to all states of society. But Communism abolishes eternal truths, it abolishes all religion, and all morality, instead of constituting them on a new basis; it therefore acts in contradiction to all past historical experience.[4]

It abolishes eternal truths, all religion, and all morality! You already know that your enemy, Satan, doesn't want people to seek after

God, who is the eternal truth. I hope you see communism for what it truly is, one of the devil's wicked schemes.

Socialism is a close cousin to communism. Both of them are Marxist ideologies. Communism is in fact a form of socialism. It's a variety of economic and political initiatives that promote government ownership and control of the means of production and distribution of goods. You can think of it as the stage between capitalism and communism. Things like social security, universal health care, and free public education are all socialist in nature.

Now, let's look at capitalism. This is where the means of production and distribution are privately and corporately owned. The government doesn't own companies, and it's not in the business of making or selling products and services. Businesses operate for profit. A competitive market determines prices and levels of production. The US, Canada, Germany, and the United Kingdom are all examples of capitalist countries.

Fascism is coming up a lot lately too. This ideology can be opposed to communism and socialism, or against capitalism and democracy. It essentially places the nation and often a particular race above everything else. The government is in the hands of an autocrat, a sole ruler with unlimited power. Militant nationalism is a key weapon of the government. They use violence to suppress people and the truth. The Nazi regime and Mussolini's rule over Italy were fascist. Today, it's seen in extremist and terrorist groups like the KKK, ISIS, and Antifa. It's interesting that Antifa claims they're anti-fascist, yet they have a logo that's strikingly similar to the 1933 Paramilitary Wing of the Communist Party of Germany, who also claimed they were anti-fascist.[5]

That leaves us with two more isms to discuss: globalism and nationalism. They are polar opposites. Globalism is a one-world, one-government view. It favors open borders, free trade, and rejects a nation's right to autonomy. Thus, nationalism promotes unity within a nation. It respects national culture, borders, localized government, fair trade, and the right of a nation to be self-governed. A global government is coming one day; it's the government the Antichrist will reign from.

Now, consider each of those isms when thinking of important issues today. Freedom of speech would be suppressed in a communist, socialist, and fascist regime because an authoritarian ruler wouldn't have a Constitution or Bill of Rights for the people. Just look at what's going on in China today. They can't open up a web browser and search for anything they want. No, their content is censored. They can't freely speak out against the government or a company because they have a social credit system that penalizes them for dissonance. They also can't freely worship Jesus because their government promotes atheism. The people are oppressed, and truth is suppressed.

How about universal health care? It sounds nice that everyone gets free health care, but does it really work out for your good when there's a monopoly controlling your health? That's what a single payer Medicare for all plan would do, create a monopoly. People assume that the monopoly, which would be the government, is going to deliver the best care possible and operate in your best interest. That's a terribly naive and false assumption. It has no economic incentive to do that. In fact, it has the opposite incentive. Let's look at how a country with universal health care has handled the coronavirus outbreak. People infected with coronavirus often need a critical care bed in a hospital. Forbes recently published an article that displays the number of critical care beds per 100,000 people for several countries. The US leads the world with 34.7 critical care beds per 100,000 Americans. Now, consider Italy. They have a single payer universal health care system. They only have 12.5 critical care beds per 100,000 people.[6] You've seen the news reports about what's happening in Italy. Italy doesn't have enough hospitals, beds, or doctors to handle the epidemic. So, doctors are having to decide who to treat. Who do you think they're going to treat? They're going to prioritize younger, healthier patients over older and sicker patients. How is this considered a model health care system? It's a farce! The politicians advocating this want government control of health care so they can decide who lives and dies. Remember that the Green New Deal and UN Agenda 2030 supporters think we're killing the planet and that we have an unsustainable level of consumption, so depopulation is one of the goals in their plan to save the world.

Think about education under a communist or socialist government. There would be free public school like we have today in the US, but private schools wouldn't exist, and neither would home schooling. You would no longer have a choice regarding what you or your children learn. Many politicians today are promising free college, free child care, and free preschool if they're elected. These are all socialist programs. Free always comes with a price. A government that controls what people learn is quite dangerous. It could easily suppress the truth, teach one sided history, and foster the beliefs the government values. Do you think your children would ever read the Bible and learn about God in a completely socialist education system? Look at what they're teaching in preschool and elementary schools today. States are now requiring students learn LGBTQ+ history.[7] Little children are being told that gender is fluid. The horrifying drag queen story hour has now infiltrated public schools.[8] Remember what you learned above about communism: it abolishes eternal truths, all religion, and all morality. That's what the government would teach.

I think it can be hard for people to grasp the impact socialist policies would have on them specifically. So, let's apply it to a school environment. That's something we should all be familiar with. Campus Reform interviewed college students and asked if they had a favorable or unfavorable opinion of socialism. In the video, each student supported socialism. The interviewer then explained that socialism is about income equality, wealth distribution, and no personal and private property. The interviewer then asked each student to apply socialism to their GPA. When asked if they'd willingly help a struggling student with a low GPA by giving them some of their own higher GPA, incredibly they all balked at the idea. They all acknowledged that they worked really hard for their GPA, so why should they have to give it to someone who didn't. Ah! You see, they don't really support socialism. They just liked the idea of free stuff.[9] Remember that Satan is a thief, and he's behind all the ideologies of taking from people who have and giving it to people who don't.

God has a different policy. Remember back to our conversation in the prior chapter regarding who's responsibility it is. God's policy is for each of us to give willingly, not out of reluctance or because we we're forced to (2 Corinthians 9:7). It's because this is one way in which God tests our heart and our faith. There are rewards and treasure in heaven tied to our behavior here on earth. Satan doesn't want you to have any treasure (Revelation 3:11). If he can steal something from you or force you to give something up, then he's successfully ruined an opportunity for you.

Now, some people think the Bible supports communism because the early believers lived together, shared what they had, and that Sapphira and Ananias died because they wouldn't share (Acts 2:42-47, 4:32-37, 5:1-11). That's only partially true. No one forced the early Christians to give up their property or live together or share everything. They did it of their own accord and free will. God even illustrates with Sapphira and Ananias that personal property was theirs to sell or not as they wished (Acts 5:4). They died because they lied to the Holy Spirit. They said they sold all of their property, but they didn't. Their hearts weren't right with God. You have to consider what these early Christians did as what you would do for your own family. Are you the kind of person who likes to share with your family and friends what God has blessed you with? That's exactly what they did.

You know, when Jesus fed the 5,000 and the 4,000 (John 6; Matthew 14-15), he recognized that many people were following him for the wrong reasons.

> Jesus answered them, "Most certainly I tell you, you seek me, not because you saw signs, but because you ate of the loaves and were filled." ... At this, many of his disciples went back and walked no more with him. (John 6:26, 66)

They just wanted free food. There's a reason Jesus called them out. The apostle Paul gives us some insight:

> For even when we were with you, we commanded you this: "If anyone is not willing to work, don't let him eat." For we hear of some who walk among you in rebellion, who don't work at all, but are busybodies. Now those who are that way, we command and exhort in the Lord Jesus Christ, that they work with quietness and eat their own bread. (2 Thessalonians 3:10-12)

Paul tells us that people refusing to work are walking in rebellion. We're rebelling when we're not obeying God. God has given each of us skills and talents and he expects each of us to use what he's given us. When we do, it rewards us and brings God glory (Matthew 5:16; Colossians 3:23-24). People who refuse to obey and refuse to work are robbing God of the glory he deserves (1 Corinthians 3:13-15).

Jesus communicated this truth in the parable of the talents or minas (Matthew 25:14-30; Luke 19:11-27). A parable depicts life in heaven. This particular parable illustrates that God's kingdom isn't communist or socialist. People aren't treated equally in heaven. In the parable, the master went away and left his servants in charge. That's like Jesus going away and leaving us in charge. He gave each one a portion of talents in proportion to their own ability and told them to invest it while he was gone. One got 5 talents, another 3 talents, and the last got 1 talent. Each servant doubled what they were given, except the servant who only got 1 talent. He buried his talent instead. When the master returned, he called that servant wicked and lazy (Matthew 25:26). Then Jesus said this:

> "He said to those who stood by, 'Take the mina away from him and give it to him who has the ten minas.' "They said to him, 'Lord, he has ten minas!' 'For I tell you that to everyone who has, will more be given; but from him who doesn't have, even that which he has will be taken away from him.'"
> (Luke 19:24-26)

The master, Jesus, took his 1 talent and gave it to the servant who already had 10. He didn't give it to the person who only had 3. Instead he gave it to the person who already had the most. Jesus rewards those who work the hardest and have the most to show for it. Those are the people who are bringing him the most glory.

There's another big reason God doesn't support socialist governments. He wants each of us to depend upon him and not something or someone else. He's the God who provides (Matthew 6:25-33; Philippians 4:19). There's an excellent illustration of this in the Bible. It's the account of the Israelites and their enslavement in Egypt (Genesis 41-47). Now, they didn't start out as slaves. They weren't even conquered and taken into slavery. No, they willingly sold themselves into slavery. It all started when the Egyptian Pharaoh had a dream and Joseph, an Israelite, was brought in to interpret it. God told Joseph that Pharaoh's dream was about a severe drought and famine that was coming. There would be seven years of prosperity followed by seven years of famine. Pharaoh adopted Joseph's plan and had him collect one-fifth of all the crops during the good years. Then they'd be able to sell it to the people during the famine years.

What do you think happened in the famine years when the people's money ran out? They sold their livestock and their land (Genesis 47:13-20). When they had nothing left to sell, they sold themselves (Genesis 47:21-24). So, Pharaoh had all the money, all the land, and everyone worked for Pharaoh. Uh oh! As soon as Joseph and that Pharaoh died, a different Pharaoh came into power who treated the Israelites harshly and forced them to make bricks and work in the fields. Do you think history would have been the same if the people started out by saving grain themselves instead of depending on Pharaoh?

After God rescued the Israelites from their bondage, recall that God gave them manna to eat every day (Exodus 16). They had to go out each day and harvest it. On day six they gathered enough for two days because day seven was the sabbath when they rested. Do you remember what happened to the people who gathered more than they needed on days one through five? It was full of maggots and smelled. Ewe! God was teaching them to depend upon him. To trust that he'd be faithful to provide for them each day. They'd grown accustomed to depending upon a ruler to provide for them. They needed to be broken of that habit.

Another principle that God taught those Israelites after he rescued them is that debt is a bad thing. Don't be fooled by what your financial advisor, tax accountant, or anyone else tells you about all the benefits of debt. That's the worldly way of viewing it. If you're a believer, you are a citizen of heaven and thus, you don't think or behave like the world. Debt leads to slavery. It's a hard lesson the Israelites had to learn. It was for our benefit though. In a socialist and communist government, the people are essentially indebted to the government because the government provides everything for the people. That's exactly what happened to the Israelites in Egypt. Pharaoh rescued them from poverty and gave them food and jobs, but then he made them slaves.

When God gave the Israelites the law, he gave them commands about debt and slavery. Every seven years, they were to forgive the debts of fellow Israelites who owed them money (Deuteronomy 15:1-4). It was God's time of release. A similar law applied to land and any Israelites who had sold themselves into slavery. Every fiftieth year, land returned to its rightful owner and Israelite slaves were freed (Leviticus 25). God commanded that they not take advantage of each other. You see, that's our nature and God knows it. We'll take advantage. That's exactly what a socialist or communist government will do too. Pharaoh proved it. Mao Zedong, Joseph Stalin, Fidel Castro, Kim il-Sung, Ho Chi Minh, Pol Pot, and Adolf Hitler have all proved it.

So, let's see where the political parties and 2020 presidential candidates stand on the isms. In Chapter 17 - Climate Change, you learned that the Democrat Party and the Green Party both support the Green New Deal which is a communist economic policy. The Libertarians and Republicans are against it. The Libertarian Party supports a free and competitive market economy and believes the government should protect property rights. They oppose any redistribution of wealth. However, they do support free trade, which is a form of globalism.[10]

Let's continue understanding Bernie's policies since he's influencing Biden's platform. Bernie Sanders supports Medicare for All, which is a single-payer, national health care program that'll provide everyone free coverage. He also supports tuition-free college, canceling student loan debt, building 10 million housing units for the homeless, free child care, free preschool, and a federal jobs guarantee. He believes the government should set the quality standards for child care and preschool programs. He also wants to ban for-profit charter schools. He also wants to expand "buy American" and "buy local" policies. His website certainly lists a lot of things he plans to provide the people for free. There's one thing I noticed that's missing though. National defense. I didn't see anything that spoke to what he'd do to protect our country and how he'd support our military.[11]

Joe Biden wants to provide two years of community college or the equivalent debt free. However, he also supports tuition-free college for families with incomes below $125,000. He wants to bring back Obamacare and build upon the Affordable Care Act. Like Sanders, he also supports free preschool. He wants to give people $15,000 to buy their first home and plans to develop a strategy to make housing a right for everyone.[12] He does have a good statement about the military:

> "We have the strongest military in the world—and as president, Biden will ensure it stays that way."[13]

Also remember that Sanders and Biden both support the Green New Deal and all of the socialist policies that go with it.

Now, President Trump favors capitalism, nationalism, strong borders, fair trade, a prepared military, low taxes, and less regulations for businesses. He renegotiated the NAFTA trade deal with Mexico and Canada. The new agreement is the USMCA which created 176,000 jobs and $68 billion in economic activity. He withdrew the US from the Trans-Pacific Partnership. He's been building a wall along our southern border and expects to have 450 miles completed by the end of 2020. As for health care, he repealed the Obamacare mandate, expanded access to Association Health plans so small businesses can pool risk across states, and he allowed short-term limited duration plans to be extended up to 12 months. He rebuilt the military and has provided $1.5 trillion to the defense department. He also created a new branch of the military, the United States Space Force. In the education space, he expanded federally funded apprenticeship programs and on-the-job training. Congress passed historic tax cuts which doubled the child tax credit, almost doubled the standard deduction, and reduced small business taxes by 20%. Prior to the coronavirus outbreak, the economy gained 6 million new jobs and the unemployment rate was its lowest in 50 years.[14]

The coronavirus has certainly had a huge impact on economic policy hasn't it? Not just in the US, but all across the globe. President Trump recently signed the CARES Act which provides $2 trillion in relief to Americans and businesses.[15] Congress is still working on additional relief bills. When all is said and done, trillions upon trillions will have been doled out by governments across the world. There is good intent behind the relief; however, it hearkens back to a prior time and to a prior warning. Is this a temporary fire fight, or did we just take one giant leap toward socialism on a global scale?

There's an evil scheme that political parties and candidates who support socialism and communism subscribe to. It's called the Cloward-Piven strategy.[16] It calls for overloading the welfare system in order to spark a crisis that would lead to that system being replaced with a universal income. The steps to create the social state they're after include universal health care, high poverty, unsustainable debt, high taxes, gun control, universal education, pitting the poor against the wealthy, and removing religion.[17] Many of these things are happening today, aren't they?

But here's the thing: we didn't choose the coronavirus. No one elected it. It's a reminder that God is in control. He's allowed this to happen. There's a reason the Marxist ideologies of communism and socialism are front and center today. The election omen holds the key to understanding. Throughout all the other chapters, you've learned that **a nation will advance in wickedness until it reaches the polar opposite of God.** I've shown we've reached that point when looking at several issues. Then, **when a nation turns completely away from God and reaches the point of no return it will bring judgment upon itself.** Once again, we've arrived at this point too. We're at the point in which **God gives a nation the ruler they desire.** That's exactly what's happening right now. We're getting what we as a global society have asked for. For the first time ever, most of the world's population is dissatisfied with democracy, 57.5% of citizens globally. The US has seen the most pronounced increase, from 25% being dissatisfied during post-war decades to 55% dissatisfied today.[18] God is preparing the way for the Antichrist. That's the ruler that the world wants. The Bible tells us that he will be so well liked that people worship him. He's going to establish the one-world communist style government we've talked about (Revelation 13). The global state of affairs due to the coronavirus is a foreshadow of what's to come.

In this truly dark hour for not just our nation but the globe, your voice matters; your vote matters. We don't know when Jesus is coming to rapture his believers. It could happen any minute, any day, or even years from now. Don't vote for the Democrat candidates who desire an Antichrist like economy. You must vote for the state and local candidates who will protect your constitutional rights, your freedom, and who will not take advantage of the situation we're in with the coronavirus and the liberties we've all given up. President Trump wants us and our economy to get back to work. He sees our present situation as temporary. Let your light shine during this dark time and hope that it brings people to God.

> "In the long history of the world, only a few generations have been granted the role of defending freedom in its hour of maximum danger. I do not shrink from this responsibility--I welcome it. I do not believe that any of us would exchange

places with any other people or any other generation. The energy, the faith, the devotion which we bring to this endeavor will light our country and all who serve it--and the glow from that fire can truly light the world.

"And so, my fellow Americans: ask not what your country can do for you--ask what you can do for your country.

"My fellow citizens of the world: ask not what America will do for you, but what together we can do for the freedom of man.

"Finally, whether you are citizens of America or citizens of the world, ask of us here the same high standards of strength and sacrifice which we ask of you. With a good conscience our only sure reward, with history the final judge of our deeds, let us go forth to lead the land we love, asking His blessing and His help, but knowing that here on earth God's work must truly be our own." (President John F. Kennedy's inaugural address, 1961)[19]

PART 6

THE END TIMES OMEN

CHAPTER 20 - THE 2020 ELECTION

The election omen revealed that we're progressing in cycles of polar opposite rulers as we advance on God's last days timeline. It's obvious to a casual observer that President Donald Trump and former President Barack Obama are antithetical rulers. As such, I believe we've come to the end of a cycle with President Trump. I'd label him one of the good kings. That's because he's been a defender of religious liberty, the sanctity of life, and a supporter of Israel. He put an end to a majority of government funded abortion, moved the US embassy to Jerusalem and formally recognized Jerusalem as Israel's capital, and ensured children can pray in public schools. You may recall that during the Obama presidency the biblical definition of marriage was eroded, the government funded abortion both in the US and globally, and Israel's settlements were condemned by the US at the United Nations. Trump was able to roll back some of those anti-Christian policies of the prior administration. That's the same achievement the good kings in the Bible had. They tore down demonic altars.

Sure, Trump has done some things that are sinful, especially in his past. Who hasn't? We're all a bunch of sinners. Look at the good kings in the Bible and the sinful behavior they exhibited at times. King David, not satisfied with the multiple wives he already had, committed adultery again with Bathsheba, got her pregnant, and had her husband murdered to cover it up. If we had a president who did that today people would flip out! Yet, God said he had a heart like his. That's because David was sorrowful and repented of that sin when he was called out for it, and he obeyed God with all his heart. Does Trump have a heart like David's? At the National Prayer Breakfast this year, Vice President Pence said this of Trump:

> "President Trump has made it a practice of opening every Cabinet meeting in prayer. And he's one of only four Presidents in American history who have actually issued multiple proclamations calling the American people to prayer in a single year."[1]

Praying to God on a regular basis, at work, with your colleagues, and asking an entire nation to pray with you requires a reverence for God, a recognition that God is in control, and that you need God's help to succeed. That's a humble heart that respects God. That's a heart that Jesus can occupy and accomplish things through.

Since we've reached the end of a cycle, that also means we're at the beginning of the next cycle. Only time will tell how long this beginning will last. Judah had four good kings in a row when their cycle with King Joash started. Regardless, the cycle will continue, and there will be another ruler who is evil. The election omen will hold true, and the nation will advance in wickedness until it gets a ruler who is the opposite of God. Will that next evil ruler be the Antichrist or someone who advances us toward the Antichrist government?

For the 2020 election, you have the ability to prolong the beginning of this cycle by voting for President Trump. If you'd rather vote for the Democrat candidate, I've made it clear in this book that that party is anti-Christian and pro-atheist, you'd be advancing the nation in the cycle and moving us closer to an ungodly government. The Democrat National Committee even admits they're the party for atheists. They passed a resolution in August 2019 admiring the values of the "religiously unaffiliated" as the "largest religious group within the Democratic Party." In fact, it was unanimously passed. The Secular Coalition of America, who lobbies on behalf of atheists, agnostics, and humanists, celebrated that this was the first time a major political party "embraced American nonbelievers."[2]

If you're a Christian and a registered Democrat, it's time to walk away. Your political party has abandoned you.

Here are some key truths the election omen foretells. If Trump wins reelection, the beginning of the cycle will continue. Depending on what happens with the state and congressional elections, we may just hold our ground, or we might take a step toward God and away from Satan. Today, the control of Congress is split between a Democratic House and a Republican Senate. Even with that split today, Trump has made progress. What we see today could continue.

If Trump wins reelection and the House flips to Republican, I think that would be a clear signal from God that he's not yet ready to intervene and bring the Antichrist on the scene. The people will be choosing to continue living in this phase of the cycle we're in and God will honor that choice. This would be the best scenario for us believers.

The people we care about who don't have a relationship with Jesus yet will have more time to be saved.

Now, if for some reason Trump wins reelection and the Senate flips Democrat, this won't be good. I don't think he'd be president for long. They'd seek to impeach him again and they could have a Senate majority to be successful. I don't think this is a very likely scenario though. If people are choosing Trump for president, I don't think they're going to support his polar opposite at the local level.

As I'm writing this, it looks like the Democrat nominee for president is going to be Joe Biden because Bernie Sanders officially dropped out and endorsed Biden. However, I wouldn't dismiss a contested convention at this point. Biden is 77 years old and is clearly having difficulty articulating and communicating, and he's forgetting things he shouldn't. It doesn't appear that his mental health is optimal. What if he becomes unfit to run? Something interesting could happen at the convention.

We've never been in a situation like the present when most of the nation is shut down because of the coronavirus. What if the states who haven't had primaries yet don't have them? Candidates secure the nomination when they have 1,991 of the 3,979 pledged delegates. That's who votes on the first ballot at the convention. So, if Biden doesn't get to 1,991 delegates prior to the convention, then the super delegates get to vote on the second ballot. There are 771 super delegates. While the pledged delegates aren't legally required to back their candidate, they've pledged to. That's not the case for super delegates. They can vote for whoever they want. This is when the brokering starts happening.[3]

A poll conducted the first week of April 2020 and shared with the New York Post reveals that a majority, 56%, of Democrats prefer Andrew Cuomo, the governor of New York, over Biden for president.[4] Cuomo has been front and center in the news recently because the coronavirus has impacted his state more than others. It's certainly possible that his name could come up at the convention.

Now there's still Bernie. If the super delegates get to vote, would they support Sanders over Biden? Maybe.

Then we should also consider former President Obama in all of this. Biden was his vice president. Yet, Obama didn't endorse him until no one was left in the race and after Bernie already had. Why did he wait so long? Could it be that he didn't like either of the candidates remaining? If Biden doesn't get the delegate count prior to the convention or something happens to his health and he has to drop out, could Obama use his influence to sway the super delegates to vote for someone new? Yes, it could happen. On the "Tucker Carlson Tonight" show, Carlson said, "If you are wondering who the democratic nominee will be, don't bet against Michelle Obama."[5] Well that's interesting, isn't it? Perhaps that's why Obama wasn't eager to endorse anyone; we could see Michelle's name yet surface at the convention. After all, there's still a vice president spot open.

If any Democrat candidate wins the election, the cycle we're in is going to progress toward the Antichrist morality and government. It must, it's what the election omen has shown and foretells. You've seen what's happened to the nation and our economy with the coronavirus shutdown. The loss of liberties we've all experienced and the socialist policies the government is enacting that are all meant to be temporary. Do you think the Democrats will be eager to abandon those policies and go back to what life was like before the virus if they win the November election? Keep in mind that the majority of people will be choosing this course if this is what happens. God will accept this choice as well. If both the House and Senate are Democrat controlled as well, we'll progress in this cycle even more toward wickedness.

Before Bernie had officially dropped out of the race, I had written here that Bernie winning the Democrat presidential nomination and winning the November 2020 election would be the most ominous sign for us believers. Well, that changes now that Bernie dropped out. I think things are actually a bit more ominous now. That's because Bernie is working with Biden to influence Biden's policies. Biden has also indicated that Bernie will be involved in his government. It doesn't matter which Democrat wins the nomination because the most radical candidate, Bernie, is now exerting enormous influence on that party's platform. The far left, progressive junior congresswomen, like Alexandria Ocasio-Cortez, support Sanders. That's because Bernie is an atheist and a supporter of communism and the Green New Deal. What do you think will happen with religious liberty, protecting the sanctity of life, and the support of Israel with a Democrat as president who supports Bernie's policies? In this scenario, we will take a giant leap toward the end of the cycle. The tide of evil will be let loose. There won't be anything to stop it because the voice of unbelievers, people who don't know God, will have risen above the voice of those who do believe.

Could this really happen? The election omen tells us that God gives people the ruler they desire. When a nation turns away from God, they're going to get an ungodly ruler. The apostle Paul tells us what people will be like in the last days:

> But know this: that in the last days, grievous times will come. For men will be lovers of self, lovers of money, boastful, arrogant, blasphemers, disobedient to parents, unthankful, unholy, without natural affection, unforgiving, slanderers, without self-control, fierce, not lovers of good, traitors, headstrong, conceited, lovers of pleasure rather than lovers of God, holding a form of godliness but having denied its power. ... Yes, and all who desire to live godly in Christ Jesus will suffer persecution. But evil men and impostors will grow worse and worse, deceiving and being deceived. (2 Timothy 3:1-5, 12-13)

The last days are definitely upon us! We've been progressing along a path of wickedness for a while now, so it could certainly happen. If it does, we believers should expect persecution. However, we shouldn't be afraid. God is in control and we have his Spirit living inside of us. We have a Spirit of power, not one of fear (1 Timothy 1:7). Everything will work out according to God's plan. There's a wonderful plan ahead for us believers.

Now, I also want to be clear that Bernie isn't the Antichrist. He isn't for a number of reasons, most importantly that ruler can't rise to power until all the people who've put their faith in Jesus have been removed, raptured. Jesus will dish out all sorts of wrath on the Antichrist and believers are not meant for wrath, we'll be in heaven (1 Thessalonians 1:10).

Speaking of the rapture, Jesus could come any minute!

> But we don't want you to be ignorant, brothers, concerning those who have fallen asleep, so that you don't grieve like the rest, who have no hope. For if we believe that Jesus died and rose again, even so God will bring with him those who have fallen asleep in Jesus. For this we tell you by the word of the Lord, that we who are alive, who are left until the coming of the Lord, will

in no way precede those who have fallen asleep. For the Lord himself will descend from heaven with a shout, with the voice of the archangel and with God's trumpet. The dead in Christ will rise first, then we who are alive, who are left, will be caught up together with them in the clouds, to meet the Lord in the air. So we will be with the Lord forever. Therefore comfort one another with these words. (1 Thessalonians 4:13-18)

Yes, we're that close to the Antichrist government. We are living in the absolute last of the last days, people! Every single sign that Jesus gave to signal his return is blaring red.

If God chose to rapture all the believers today, the cycle we're in would immediately advance to the end when the Antichrist reigns.

Have you put your faith in Jesus? If you haven't, you'll be left behind if Jesus comes today. Instead of being in heaven with me and the other believers, you'll be stuck down here with the Antichrist and experience all of God's judgments against wickedness. Don't subject yourself to that. It's likely you won't survive. Instead, know that God loves you. He wants to see you saved. He wants you to live with him forever. But you can only do that if you're perfect because God is perfect and holy. No unclean thing can enter heaven where he lives. That's why Jesus came to save us. You see, he's God in the flesh and he died to save you. Yes, you! If you were the only person alive, he still would have done it. He took all of your sins and gave you his perfect righteousness in return. He rose from the dead since he's God and all-powerful, and he's reigning in heaven.

No one knows when Jesus is coming to rapture his believers. I know it's coming very soon though because of what I've shared with you about the cycles, patterns, and the election omen. While we wait for his return, we must do everything we can to hold our ground. That's what Jesus has asked us to do—stand.

Stand your ground, putting on the belt of truth and the body armor of God's righteousness. (Ephesians 6:14 NLT)

So, what are you going to do to stand with Jesus? How are you going to help hold the ground so more people can be saved?

You're going to participate and vote. That's what you're going to do. Remember that your local and state governments are just as important as the federal government. Choose to participate in every single local election along with the national elections. Vote for candidates who have a heart like Jesus who are pro-life, who value religious freedom, and who support God's definition of sin, marriage, and gender. I realize this isn't always easy to do, especially if a candidate is running unopposed or it doesn't seem like any of the candidates are godly. In this case, God tells us we should look at a person's actions, their "fruit," to determine if they're good.

> By their fruits you will know them. Do you gather grapes from thorns or figs from thistles? Even so, every good tree produces good fruit, but the corrupt tree produces evil fruit. A good tree can't produce evil fruit, neither can a corrupt tree produce good fruit. ... Therefore by their fruits you will know them. (Matthew 7:16-18, 20)

Look at how they've voted on the key issues in the past. If they're a new candidate, look at how they've impacted their family, community, and employer. Is God blessing the person in what they do? Look at who is drawn to them and who supports them. Are they people you respect who have godly values?

You also have to determine what matters most to you. This is critical. What are the one or two issues where you draw the line? Is it abortion? Gun rights? The perfect candidate doesn't exist. If you're looking for that person, it's not going to happen until Jesus returns. Until then, you have to choose someone like yourself, a sinner. The choice isn't going to be black and white. You're not going to find a candidate or political party that you support and agree with on every single issue. I know you don't want to hear this, but you're going to have to compromise. That's why you need to have your own red line. What are the couple things a candidate absolutely must support in order for you to vote for them? Whatever your red line is, make sure you can defend it biblically. Imagine if Jesus asked you to explain why you voted for someone. Be sure you can give him an answer. You don't want to feel ashamed by how you voted or for sticking your head in the ground and not voting at all for that matter.

If you still have a hard time choosing a candidate, perhaps you should consider doing more than just voting. Jesus is still looking for people to stand in the gap.

> I looked for someone who might rebuild the wall of righteousness that guards the land. I searched for someone to stand in the gap in the wall so I wouldn't have to destroy the land, but I found no one. (Ezekiel 22:30 NLT)

It's a truly sad and ominous day when there's no one willing to answer God's call. That's what brings about God's judgment. Think about this: if there's a gap in your local area, maybe you're meant to be that person who fills it. Or perhaps you know someone who'd be perfect for the job and they just need some encouragement and support. Go be that person!

Whatever you do, don't sit. Get up and make a difference!

I'm going to stand for President Trump for reelection because he's on the correct side of my red line. I hope you stand with me.

Vote!

PART 7

END TIMES DECEPTIONS AND COUNTER TACTICS

CHAPTER 21 – SATAN'S DECEPTION TACTICS

I think you'll agree with me when I say it gets harder and harder every day to discern the truth of what's happening in the world. Lies, deception, delusion, and fake news are normal today. This isn't going to get better or go away. It was foretold. The Bible has a lot of information about the tribulation period. That's the period of time after the rapture of the church and before Jesus's second coming. One of the first things that's going to happen after the rapture is strong delusion. In these verses, "the lawless one" is the Antichrist:

> Then the lawless one will be revealed ... whose coming is according to the working of Satan with all power and signs and lying wonders, and with all deception of wickedness for those who are being lost, because they didn't receive the love of the truth, that they might be saved. Because of this, God sends them a powerful delusion, that they should believe a lie, that they all might be judged who didn't believe the truth, but had pleasure in unrighteousness. (2 Thessalonians 2:8-12)

Delusion means a false belief or to mislead. It's an attack on the truth. And who attacks truth? Yes, that's Satan. He's the one behind all the lies because as the Bible says, he's the father of lies (John 8:44). Since we can all readily admit that we now live in a world full of delusion, the tribulation can't be far off. The rapture could happen any minute!

So, what are we to do in these last days? First, we must understand Satan's deception tactics and learn how they surface in the media. That's what we'll discuss in this chapter. Then we must employ counter measures against those tactics, which we'll go over in the next chapter. Let's begin by revealing Satan's true nature.

Satan used his first deception tactic on humans in the garden with Eve. Satan asked Eve, did God really say don't eat fruit from any of the trees (Genesis 3:1)? You know, Satan knew very well what God said, that they could eat from any tree except for one. In fact, he knows God's Word better than any of us do. You need to remember that. Satan isn't dumb. He's a lot smarter than any of us are. He's had thousands of

years to study us and God's Word. Satan twisted Go
meant to deceive Eve. He finished his temptation by fl
her. He told her she wouldn't die if she ate the fruit from
tree. Satan twisted the truth and lied.

Another of Satan's favorite tactics is faking it. As the Scripture
above stated, he uses "lying wonders." Miracles that aren't truthful or
real. They're fake. The Antichrist will seemingly die of a fatal wound
and be resurrected (Revelation 13:3). That won't be a real miracle. But
I know it will be promoted as such. Satan is going to fake a
resurrection. Can't you picture the headlines?

Satan is also a master blasphemer (Revelation 13:6). That's right,
he's a name caller who speaks profane things. And more than that, he's
the accuser. One of his goals is to discredit the truth, so he attacks those
who speak it. You know the Bible says Satan accuses us before God day
and night (Revelation 12:10). Him and his fallen angel minions tell God
about all of the sinful things we each do every single day.

What about when Satan tempted Jesus in the wilderness? What
tactic did Satan use then? Let's look at the three statements Satan, "the
tempter," said to Jesus:

> The tempter came and said to him, "If you are the Son of God, command
> that these stones become bread." ... "If you are the Son of God, throw
> yourself down, for it is written, 'He will command his angels concerning
> you,' and, 'On their hands they will bear you up, so that you don't dash
> your foot against a stone.' " ... Again, the devil took him to an exceedingly
> high mountain, and showed him all the kingdoms of the world and their
> glory. He said to him, "I will give you all of these things, if you will fall
> down and worship me." (Matthew 4:3, 6, 8-9)

Satan did something very different here. He didn't lie. He spoke
God's truth to Jesus. He knew Jesus was the Son of God. He knew
Jesus could make the stones bread. He knew angels would protect
Jesus if he fell. He also knew he had the power to give Jesus all the
kingdoms. Satan is the god of the world right now. We humans lost it
when Adam and Eve sinned in the garden. That's when Satan got it.
Jesus had to die to redeem us and the earth from death that results
from sin. Satan tempted Jesus. He was trying to get Jesus to prove he
was the Son of God, trying to get him to sin, and trying to get him to

andon his mission of saving us. The other thing Satan did was take Scripture out of context. In Jesus's retort to Satan, Jesus always quoted another Scripture back to him. If you don't know God's Word very well, Satan is going to use that against you.

We could go on and on about Satan's schemes. There's a laundry list of adjectives for Satan in the Bible that further describes his nature and thus his tactics. He blinds people from the truth, teaches false doctrine, uses false signs, is disobedient, devours, is full of wrath and rage, instills fear, fights and wages war, is bitter, schemes, is crafty, disguises, chokes faith, murders, oppresses, hinders, delays, sows doubt, deceives, causes division, and distracts. There's even more than that, but that gives us enough detail to understand what he's up to. You can see evidence of Satan in what we see happening with the media, can't you?

Let's have a look at the media's deception tactics. We must keep in mind the purpose of the media has changed from strictly reporting the news and facts. I'm not sure it was ever like that to begin with, but today it's hard for us to distinguish the truth from lies. That's because they're in the business of making money, getting subscribers, and promoting an agenda. Do you know what product they actually produce? It's propaganda. It's when the media pushes a narrative that's meant to sway opinion. Here's how the United States Holocaust Memorial Museum describes it:

> "In contrast to the ideal of an educator, who aims to foster independent judgment and thinking, the practitioner of propaganda does not aim to encourage deliberation by presenting a variety of viewpoints and leaving it up to the audience to determine which perspective is correct. The propagandist transmits only information geared to strengthen his or her case, and consciously omits detrimental information."[1]

Ah, that's interesting. Who wants to suppress the truth? Satan does! I recently finished reading Mark Levin's book, *Unfreedom of the Press*, in which he has a lot to say about propaganda tactics.[2] There are so many of these ploys that books could be written about this topic. Wikipedia lists 89 propaganda techniques, and I counted another 150 logical fallacies on a different Wikipedia page.[3] We're just going to look at a few of these together so you'll be able to discern them for yourself. The news won't be the same for you again.

Here are some of the media's ploys that Mark reveals in his book. They don't give people who disagree with them the right to speak or challenge their opinion. They create what's called an echo chamber. That's when you hear all the news networks and papers saying the exact same thing. Even down to the same phrases or buzz words. It's easy for them to collude because 90% of the US media is controlled by just 4 media conglomerates: Comcast (controls NBC), Disney (controls ABC), ViacomCBS (controls CBS), and AT&T (controls CNN).[4] Since they're only reporting their side, they're suppressing information and self-censoring. They make it difficult for you to discern fact from their opinion because everything is presented like it's an editorial piece. In the war to get viewers and readers, they use deceiving headlines that are like clickbait. What's unfortunate about this is a lot of people don't read past the headlines. They also use offensive language and terms to describe people who disagree with them. You've seen plenty of this name calling: racist, bigot, climate-denier. Who else is a blasphemer? Yes, it's Satan.

Another tactic Mark called out is when the media make assertions in the form of questions. The example he shared is when CNN's chief White House correspondent, Jim Acosta, questioned President Trump about the caravan of people headed toward our southern border. This was back in November 2018.

> ACOSTA: As you know, Mr. President, the caravan was not an invasion. It's a group of migrants moving up from Central America towards the border with the U.S. And...
> TRUMP: Thank you for telling me that. I appreciate it.
> ACOSTA:... why did you characterize it as such?
> TRUMP: Because I consider it an invasion. You and I have a difference of opinion.[5]

Did you see what the reporter did? He didn't just ask a question. He gave his opinion as though it was fact and questioned why the president was lying. Who did you read about earlier that likes to accuse people? That's right, it's Satan!

Now, another thing Mark discussed that we've all seen journalists do is create fake news or what he calls pseudo-events. This is when they speculate, accuse, use anonymous sources, say someone leaked the information and such in order to create a story. The Russian collusion falsehood is the perfect example of this. As you know, Satan is the master of fakery. He's the spirit behind all of these things.

Are you seeing some similarities between Satan's deception tactics and what we're seeing the media do? Of course you are! Let's reveal some more of their tactics. Word play and double speak is when they use language to misconstrue the actual meaning of something. Abortion is a good example here. Politicians in favor of it call it a constitutional right, health care, and contraception. Their word choice is misleading. The Green Party platform has a good example too:

> The concept of a "job" is only a few hundred years old; and the artificial dichotomy between "employment" and "unemployment" has become a tool of social leverage for corporate exploiters.[6]

Do you see what they're doing? They're trying to create a new word to describe someone who doesn't want to have a job, who doesn't want to work. It's called lazy, but that won't fly with their voters or promote their socialist agenda of a universal income, will it?

Another tactic is when a politician creates a straw man. It happens when they state their opponent's position inaccurately, on purpose, and then attack and discredit the inaccurate position. It makes it seem like they easily refuted their opponent's position. But they didn't. They made up a position to refute. This has the master of falsehoods written all over it, doesn't it?

Greenwashing and virtue signaling are favorites of the media and politicians. An example is when someone inaccurately says they are environmentally conscious, have a specific moral trait, or supports a particular cause just to show off and gain supporters when their behavior speaks against the very things they claim to support. Politicians who promote the Green New Deal yet fly around the US in private jets that consume a bunch of fossil fuels, eat hamburgers, and own several mansions, are great examples. A great example of this just happened in March 2020. In the midst of the Coronavirus outbreak, a bunch of celebrities decided to record a cover of John Lennon's anti-Christian song, "Imagine." If you're familiar with the lyrics in that song, it tells you to imagine no heaven, no hell, no religion, no possessions, no countries, and everyone sharing. This communist, atheistic propaganda that's being pushed on the American people is coming from a bunch of millionaires who benefit from the United States economic system, a democratic constitutional republic founded on Christian principles where capitalism flourishes. Really!? Guess who else likes to disguise himself and appear holy when he isn't? You know it's Satan. The Bible tells us that he masquerades around as an angel of the light.

The last tactic I'm going to point out can be difficult to spot. It's a logical fallacy. The media and politicians often use this with an emotional element. The following is a perfect example of one. It's from a transcript of a US Senate hearing regarding the nomination of Russell Vought for deputy director of the office of management and budget. Bernie Sanders is questioning Mr. Vought. This occurred in June 2017.[7]

Senator Sanders: "Let me get to this issue that has bothered me and bothered many other people, and that is in the piece that I referred to that you wrote for a publication called Resurgent. You wrote: 'Muslims do not simply have a deficient theology. They do not know God because they have rejected Jesus Christ, His Son, and they stand condemned.' Do you believe that that statement is Islamophobic?"

Mr. Vought: "Absolutely not, Senator. I am a Christian, and I believe in a Christian set of principles based on my faith. That post, as I stated in the questionnaire to this committee, was to defend my alma mater, Wheaton College, a Christian school that has a statement of faith that includes the centrality of Jesus Christ for salvation, and----"

Senator Sanders: "I understand that. I do not know how many Muslims there are in America. I really do not know, probably a couple million. Are you suggesting that all of those people stand condemned? What about Jews? Do they stand condemned, too?"

Mr. Vought: "Thank you for probing on that question. As a Christian, I believe that all individuals are made in the image of God and are worthy of dignity and respect regardless of their religious beliefs."

Did you spot the logical fallacy that Bernie introduced? What does it mean to be Islamophobic? It means you fear, hate, dislike, or have a prejudice against people of the Islamic faith. Did Mr. Vought show any of those behaviors? No. He said the opposite, that they're worthy of dignity and respect. Mr. Vought simply disagreed with the Muslim faith. And there's the fallacy. Bernie is saying that people who disagree with Muslims are also Islamophobic. Politicians and the media use this fallacy all the time and it drives me nuts because it plays on people's emotions. They make you think the person is the terrible thing they've called them, racist, bigoted, phobic, when they aren't. Just because you disagree with someone doesn't make you racist! The two are unrelated. This is an evil trickery that Satan is at the heart of.

I want to leave you with a quote by Victor Klemperer, a German Jewish writer, that he wrote in 1946 regarding Nazi propaganda:

> "Nazism, permeated the flesh and blood of the people through single words, idioms, and sentence structures which were imposed on them in a million repetitions and taken on board mechanically and unconsciously."[8]

What was a contributing factor that led to the genocide of 6 million Jewish people in World War 2? Propaganda. They used all of the deception tactics you just read about to demonize the Jewish people in the eyes of their neighbors. They were so bombarded with deception that they took it as truth and it became part of them, part of their culture, part of beliefs.

This is why I wanted to expose Satan's deception tactics for you. We can't let what happened in World War 2 to ever happen again! Yet, this is the road we're headed down. It's our fate and also our choice because the people will elect the Antichrist. When the Antichrist rises to power, there will be massive delusion and propaganda. There will be another genocide of God's people (Revelation 6:9, 13:7, 15). But it's not going to happen while I'm still here waiting to get raptured! I hope you agree and stand with me on this. Now let's learn what we can do to overcome these demonic schemes.

CHAPTER 22 - END TIMES ARMOR COUNTER MEASURES

"Let not your heart be troubled." Jesus said this twice to his disciples at the Last Supper (John 14:1, 27). He told them this before he was arrested and crucified. He was preparing them for what was to come. He didn't want them to be afraid, anxious, or distressed. He doesn't want you to be troubled either. Yes, the world is full of evil, wickedness, and deceit. However, the Bible tells us everything we need to know to combat the evil that we're seeing in the world today and how to be at peace.

The first thing you need to do you've already learned about. You need to put on the whole armor of God (Ephesians 6:10-18). This is how you protect yourself in the last days. It's your End Times Armor. If you need a refresher, go back and reread the Introduction to this book where I explain the Scripture and all the components of the armor. Being filled with God's Holy Spirit is a key component of the armor; it's your breastplate of righteousness and helmet of salvation. If you've put your faith in Jesus Christ, then you are filled with his Holy Spirit. This gives you superpowers so to speak because you've got the power of Jesus living inside of you. You see, the Holy Spirit is the Counselor (John 14:26), Spirit of truth (John 16:13), Christ's mind (1 Corinthians 2), and will teach you all things (1 John 2:27).

If you haven't accepted Jesus into your heart and you don't have a personal relationship with him, then now is the time for you to do so. Not only are you not saved and subject to eternity in hell, but you're also at a severe disadvantage regarding discernment. Remember we discussed that Satan blinds people. If you don't have the Holy Spirit, then you don't have God's armor to protect you, and your mind is blinded and veiled by Satan because you don't believe (2 Corinthians 4:3-4). You can't remove this veil yourself. No amount of Bible reading or church attendance is going to do it. The only way to remove this veil is with the power of the Holy Spirit (2 Corinthians 3:14-16).

So now that you're full of the Holy Spirit, you need to be reading the Bible. That's because the Bible is your belt of truth and you combat lies and deceit with the truth (John 17:17), the sword of the Spirit

(Hebrews 4:12). God's Word is a component of your armor that protects you, and it's your weapon. When Jesus was being tempted by Satan in the wilderness, they both used the Bible. Your enemy knows God's Word and will use it against you. When Eve was tempted by Satan in the garden, she incorrectly recalled what God said. That led to her downfall. You must know what the Bible says so that you can spot when someone twists it or uses a verse out of context.

Can you spot the errors in what Pete Buttigieg, a Democrat candidate for president at the time, tweeted on Christmas day 2019?

> "Today I join millions around the world in celebrating the arrival of divinity on earth, who came into this world not in riches but in poverty, not as a citizen but as a refugee."[1]

First off, he refused to name Jesus. Second, the Bible doesn't say Jesus was born into poverty. Joseph was a skilled tradesman, a carpenter. Jesus was born in humble surroundings, a manger, because the inns were full due to the census. Third, Jesus also didn't come into the world as a refugee. A refugee is someone who flees to a foreign country to escape persecution. Jesus was born in Bethlehem, a Roman territory, instead of Nazareth where his parents lived, because they had to go there for the census. His parents fled to Egypt, likely when Jesus was a toddler, to escape the ruler Herod. But guess what, Egypt wasn't a foreign country. It was also under Roman rule. Them moving to Egypt is the equivalent of us moving to a different city within the same country. That wouldn't make us refugees.

Earlier, I discussed that Satan blinds unbelievers. They aren't going to be able to rightly interpret Scripture because they don't have the Holy Spirit living inside of them. You can spot them by their fruit, so things they say and do, and in particular what they say about Jesus. A believer is going to understand who Jesus is, and they aren't going to be ashamed of him or of using his name.

You also need to know the Bible so that you can determine where you stand on a particular issue. You need to consider it under the light of God's Word. Be able to give a reason for why you vote the way that you do. Remember that we're all accountable to God for everything that we say and do (2 Corinthians 5:10). That's why I have a red line of the issues most important to me.

Now, I bet some of you are thinking, "But the Bible was written so long ago, some of it doesn't apply anymore, and it has errors and contradictions because men wrote it after all." Yes, it was written over a 1,600 year period by 40 different authors. However, it was indeed written by God through the power of the Holy Spirit (2 Peter 1:20-21). You must keep in mind that God can literally do anything. He created the earth and the heavens and you and me. Don't you think he can make sure the Bible says what he needs it to say? Seems like a really small task in comparison to creating an entire universe. The authors weren't sharing their own opinions. They were passing along what God told them to say. Everything in the Bible is also applicable to today (2 Timothy 3:15-17). There are no contradictions because God is the author and Jesus himself said he is the Word of God. If you think you've found a contradiction, it's an error in your interpretation. Jesus is perfect and holy. He's God in the flesh. When you think of the Bible, know that Jesus is the author (John 1). It's his personal letter to you about all the wonderful things he's done to save you and everything he has planned for you.

The next thing we can do to combat this barrage of deceit we're constantly attacked with is to use our shield of faith against it. The Bible says if we resist the devil, he will flee from us (James 4:7; 1 Peter 5:9). A key point here is that you have to be prepared and watch for it, otherwise you won't have your shield at the ready. Now, faith is a reflection of your belief in the power of Jesus. Jesus said we just need a tiny bit, just a mustard seed of faith, and we can move mountains (Matthew 17:20). You grow your faith by reading and believing in the Word of God (Romans 10:17). Jesus has overcome the enemy so you can overcome him too.

> You are of God, little children, and have overcome them, because greater is he who is in you than he who is in the world. (1 John 4:4)

If the media labels you homophobic because you obey God's definition of marriage between a biological male and a biological female, your faith will deflect that burning arrow that was meant to hurt you. You know what God's Word says is true. You know that just because you disagree with someone doesn't mean you hate them. You know that no matter what someone says or even what someone does, that you're safe in the hands of Jesus. Remember that Jesus was hated and mocked too (Luke 6:22-23). Whatever lies they throw at us believers, whatever horrible things they threaten us with, and whatever awful things they do to us, stand. Have faith!

> Who shall separate us from the love of Christ? Could oppression, or anguish, or persecution, or famine, or nakedness, or peril, or sword? Even as it is written, "For your sake we are killed all day long. We were accounted as sheep for the slaughter." No, in all these things, we are more than conquerors through him who loved us. For I am persuaded that neither death, nor life, nor angels, nor principalities, nor things present, nor things to come, nor powers, nor height, nor depth, nor any other created thing will be able to separate us from God's love which is in Christ Jesus our Lord. (Romans 8:35-39)

Another thing we can do with our shield of faith is deflect temptation. Much of the propaganda and fake news we see today is meant to incite. You can't let it fill you with rage. That's exactly what the devil wants (Ephesians 4:26-27). Anger will give him a foothold. Remember who the real enemy is in all of this. It's not your neighbor who disagrees with you on who to vote for. It's not the journalist pushing a fabricated story. It's Satan and his fallen angelic cohorts. Unbelievers are essentially his prisoners. Always treat your neighbor with respect and show them Jesus's love. That's how you'll help save them if they don't believe. So, don't go posting hateful inappropriate things on social media, don't call the journalists names in comments on their fake news, and don't use any of the other deceitful tactics we covered in the last chapter. Be respectful and share the truth with people. Remember that if you're filled with the Holy Spirit that you are Jesus's ambassador here on earth.

Now that you're all suited up in your armor and you have your shield and sword at hand, you need to train for war. I'm talking about spiritual warfare. This is about learning and being prepared, not because you're watching, but because you're skilled. In the apostle Paul's description of the armor of God, this is the part about having feet prepared to spread the gospel. Earlier, I mentioned the importance of reading your Bible. You really need to do more than that. You need to study God's Word. You need to be able to put God's Word to use. Can you explain key principles of the faith to someone else? You should be able to tell someone how they can be saved. Can you explain to someone what God's view of abortion is? Yes, you can because you learned about that in Chapter 12. I had an encounter at a secular convention for self-published authors with an unbeliever. When he learned that I wrote Christian Bible prophecy, he asked me when the world was going to end. We had a quick chat about what the Bible says regarding the future. You need to be prepared to answer questions. If you prepare yourself in this way, then it'll be a whole lot easier for you to spot deception tactics coming from the media and politicians.

Jesus's disciple, Luke, gives us a good example of how we should be training:

> The brothers immediately sent Paul and Silas away by night to Beroea. When they arrived, they went into the Jewish synagogue. Now these were more noble than those in Thessalonica, in that they received the word with all readiness of mind, examining the Scriptures daily to see whether these things were so. Many of them therefore believed. (Acts 17:10-12)

The Bereans "examined the Scriptures daily." That means they inspected it closely. They studied it; questioned it. One of the media's deception tactics is the echo chamber. That's where you hear all the news networks telling you the exact same thing. They're using the same argument and same buzz words. Remember that propagandists don't want you to think for yourself. They're going to tell you what to think. You need to counter this group think tactic by doing exactly what the Bereans did. They didn't readily accept what Paul and Silas told them. They verified what Paul and Silas said was actually true. Examine what is being said. Compare it to what the Bible says. Use logic, reasoning, and the Holy Spirit to help you discern the truth. God will help you understand and ascertain the truth. All you need to do is ask him for help (Proverbs 2:1-6).

Another factor in behaving like a Berean is having good source material. They examined God's Word to understand the truth. Of course, we must do that too, but we should also seek reliable sources for news and information. If you're able to, you should watch the presidential candidate debates so that you can see and hear for yourself. Otherwise, find truthful sources that tell you the candidates' views on each issue. You should know what website has information on how a presidential candidate has voted on federal legislation in the past. You should know who is funding a particular candidate's campaign. You should also educate yourself on important facts from history. Know what America's founding documents say—the Constitution, Bill of Rights, and Declaration of Independence. If you know what the constitution says about gun rights, you'll be able to follow along in a debate about that issue better than someone who doesn't.

I know that's a lot to do, and it can be overwhelming. Just take it one day at a time. Focus on the issues that matter the most to you. I have a list of resources to help you in the back of this book and on my website: rapture911.com.

It's also important to know who you're consuming information from. Is the journalist you're listening to a Christian? I'll tell you right now that Sean Hannity quotes the Scripture I started this chapter with on each and every episode of his show, *Hannity*, on Fox News. That's important to me. You really need to be mindful of what you're consuming. You need to be listening to people who are good at exposing these deceptions I've been discussing with you. Stop watching the fake news shows. Stop reading left leaning newspapers owned by liberal billionaires. Stop watching TV shows and movies that promote anti-Christian values. Jesus said our eye is the lamp of our body (Luke 11:34-35). If you're filling your eyes with propaganda all day, it's going to permeate you just like it did the people who lived in Nazi Germany. Instead, start consuming more information from conservative news sources and citizen journalists. I have some suggestions in the Appendix and on my website: rapture911.com.

Stand and pray. These are the last two things I'm going to leave you with regarding the armor of God and protecting yourself from Satan's deception tactics. As I've said throughout this entire book, as a believer, Jesus expects you to stand with him. You need to be brave for this. You need to be bold and vocal when needed. Do what you can to expose the darkness, the lies, the deceit, and the fake news. When you expose something deceitful, share it with your friends and family. If you like social media, then post away. If God is calling you to fill a gap in the wall and report truthful news, then go start a podcast or YouTube channel.

While we've got our armor on, Paul tells us to pray at all times. Praying is just talking to God. It's pouring your heart out to him. Jesus taught his disciples how to pray in Luke 11:1-4. His example had these components: praise to God, prayer for others, prayer for your own needs, and confession of your own sins. There are so many things to pray about in these last days. Pray to God for guidance and wisdom to discern the truth (1 Kings 3:9-10). Pray for God's peace during this time of anxiousness and uncertainty (Philippians 4:6-7). Most importantly, remember what Jesus told us:

> Peace I leave with you, My peace I give to you; not as the world gives do I give to you. Let not your heart be troubled, neither let it be afraid. (John 14:27 NKJV)

PART 8

FUTURE FULFILLMENTS OF THE ELECTION OMEN

CHAPTER 23 - THE FUTURE ELECTION OMEN

There's an election coming in the very near future that will accelerate the election omen to the very end of the very last cycle. When everyone who has put their faith in Jesus Christ is removed from earth and taken to heaven during the rapture, the people left on the planet will not be believers. Sure, some people who were sitting on the fence of indecision will choose to believe in Jesus moments after witnessing the rapture. But the vast majority of people won't. They won't understand what happened and there will be a bombardment of lies and deception to hide the truth.

> Then the lawless one will be revealed, whom the Lord will kill with the breath of his mouth and destroy by the manifestation of his coming; even he whose coming is according to the working of Satan with all power and signs and lying wonders, and with all deception of wickedness for those who are being lost, because they didn't receive the love of the truth, that they might be saved. Because of this, God sends them a powerful delusion, that they should believe a lie, that they all might be judged who didn't believe the truth, but had pleasure in unrighteousness. (2 Thessalonians 2:8-12)

The above Scripture was written by Paul the apostle. It describes what happens after the rapture. We see "the lawless one" is revealed. That's the ruler the people will elect. Then six times Paul mentions lies: "lying wonders," "deception of wickedness," "didn't receive...truth," "powerful delusion," "believe a lie," "didn't believe the truth." This is the culture that's left behind. It'll be an unbelieving, lying culture. The world will be full of people who don't have Jesus's righteous light to guide them. They won't care about God, God's laws, or biblical values. We won't be here to be an influence on them. This is why they'll willingly choose to elect the most evil ruler who will ever live. Remember that the election omen foretells that God gives people the ruler they desire. The people who are left "had pleasure in unrighteousness." So, God gives them a ruler of like mind. That's why the ruler is called the "lawless one." He's unrighteous, ungodly, and disobedient.

Of course, the people won't realize who they're electing because this leader will be a master of deception. The "lawless one" will appear to be the perfect leader. He will say all the right things and seem to have all the answers to moving forward and rebuilding after millions of people have disappeared. We've talked about him before. He's the Antichrist.

Anti means opposite, against, and instead of. This person will be the opposite of Christ and be against everything Jesus is for. It's obviously not the person's name. They aren't going to announce themselves as such. It's a description of their character and intent. I want you to notice in the verses above who this person gets their power and authority from. "Whose coming is according to the working of Satan with all power and signs." This leader is a servant of Satan himself.

Remember that Satan is a fallen angel, a demon, so he can possess people. He will possess the Antichrist leader. Next, think back to Chapter 8 when we talked about who Satan would vote for. All of those qualities that Satan would pick in a heart: wicked, selfish, greedy, rebellious, corrupt, proud, hard, murderous, and ungrateful; this leader will have every one of them. He will have a hate filled heart like Satan.

Why on earth will God allow the Antichrist, who's possessed by Satan, to rule over people? The election omen reveals the reasons. Let's consider each omen.

A nation will advance in wickedness until it reaches the polar opposite of God. Ever since Adam and Eve sinned in the garden we've been moving toward this end. God destroyed the world with the flood when we reached Satan's level of wickedness ages ago. Humanity got a fresh start with Noah after the flood (Genesis 6-8). We were destined to end up here again. It's how God's story of redemption ends. The Antichrist is the antithesis of Jesus Christ. His polar opposite. In these verses, "he opened his mouth" is referring to the Antichrist:

> He opened his mouth for blasphemy against God, to blaspheme his name, his dwelling, and those who dwell in heaven. It was given to him to make war with the saints and to overcome them. Authority over every tribe, people, language, and nation was given to him. (Revelation 13:6-7)

You'll notice that it says he blasphemes God, God's dwelling place which is heaven, and the people who live in heaven, which would be believers who've put their faith in Jesus. That means he'll be disrespectful, profane, and mock. He will hate God and everything and everyone that God loves. Now, it's not just the US that he rules. He will have authority over every single person on the globe. It's the return to a tower of Babel culture with a one world government.

God gives a nation the ruler they desire. This is going to be a difficult pill for some to swallow. The people asked for a ruler who was just like them. The Antichrist is the ruler God gives them because he'll represent their collective attitudes and beliefs. He'll be exactly what the people want. So much so, that the people will worship him as though he's God! In this Scripture, "the beast" is the Antichrist and "the dragon" is Satan:

> The beast which I saw was like a leopard, and his feet were like those of a bear, and his mouth like the mouth of a lion. The dragon gave him his power, his throne, and great authority. One of his heads looked like it had been wounded fatally. His fatal wound was healed, and the whole earth marveled at the beast. They worshiped the dragon because he gave his authority to the beast; and they worshiped the beast, saying, "Who is like the beast? Who is able to make war with him?" (Revelation 13:2-4)

They'll worship the Antichrist because of the signs and wonders he performs and because he appears to rise from the dead, recovering from a fatal wound. What the people won't realize is that he's a liar! He's possessed by the father of lies, Satan himself (John 8:44). All of his signs and wonders are counterfeit. But the people will believe because they want to. Remember from above that the people left behind have no pleasure in the truth. They don't want to have anything to do with God. The same goes for their ruler.

When a nation turns completely away from God and reaches the point of no return it will bring judgment upon itself. *Judgment.* That's an uncomfortable word, isn't it? This is one reason why God allows the Antichrist to rule. You know that God is perfect, holy, and just (Deuteronomy 32:4). Because of that, he has to punish wickedness. We get angry when someone wrongs us. It's the same with God (Psalm 7:11). Every time someone sins, they're committing a wrong against God. Sin eventually gets to a level in which God has to act. Think of a child you've had to discipline, or recall your own childhood and when you were disciplined. We've all experienced a timeout, a slap, a spanking, or a grounding because we were misbehaving. God's discipline is meant to help us see our sin and stop doing it. God's Word is full of warnings regarding what happens if you refuse to obey him. God will use the Antichrist as his instrument to deliver judgment.

> He deceives my own people who dwell on the earth because of the signs he was granted to do in front of the beast, saying to those who dwell on the earth that they should make an image to the beast who had the sword wound and lived. It was given to him to give breath to the image of the beast, that the image of the beast should both speak, and cause as many as wouldn't worship the image of the beast to be killed. He causes all, the small and the great, the rich and the poor, and the free and the slave, to be given marks on their right hands or on their foreheads; and that no one would be able to buy or to sell unless he has that mark. (Revelation 13:14-17)

In the Scripture above, the Antichrist is "the beast." "He deceives" is referring to the False Prophet. He's the right hand man so to speak of the Antichrist. The False Prophet forces everyone to worship the Antichrist. Anyone who refuses will be killed. Let me be clear on this. If you are one of the left behind, worshiping the Antichrist means you've rejected God and chosen Satan. There's no coming back from that. You will have made your choice. Not only will you experience the earthly judgments that come against you during this time period, but you'll seal your eternal fate and condemn yourself to God's final judgment—hell (Revelation 14:9-11).

I'm sure you've heard about the Antichrist's mark. What you might not realize is how he intends to use it. It says no one can buy or sell without the mark. That means you must have the mark in order to buy or sell. You need to understand the immensity of this. You buy and sell things every day. For example, you purchase groceries and you sell your skills and time to your employer. So, you wouldn't be able to do either of those things without the mark. Companies, like the one who employs you, are owned and operated by people who buy and sell things. Companies wouldn't be able to operate if the people who

204 Chapter 23 – The Future Election Omen

worked there didn't have the mark. The Antichrist's mark will literally control the entire global economy and means of production. Everyone and everything with the mark will be government controlled. That's a totalitarian communism government, people!

You may be thinking, "Okay so what's the big deal about getting the mark?" Well, the Antichrist's mark is his weapon of worship. Anyone who gets the mark is choosing to obey the Antichrist and Satan and in turn disobeying God. Getting the mark will seal a person's fate and condemn them to hell right along with Satan (Revelation 14:9-11).

If a person refuses the mark, they'll be refusing to worship the Antichrist, and we read above that those people are killed. There will be the steepest price for loving Jesus during the Antichrist's reign. You could very well be martyred. But it's the same fate Jesus endured for us. Don't be left behind! Put your faith in Jesus today, and you'll escape what's coming.

As if the Antichrist's oppression isn't enough judgment against wickedness, God sends his own judgments against the Antichrist and the inhabitants of earth. The book of Revelation describes them, and they include war, famine, poverty, large hail, widespread fire, scorching heat, water sources turned to blood, boils on people's skin, and a vast amount of death. Millions and millions of people will die.

Judgment and discipline aren't meant to be easy. They are meant to make you realize that you need God. That you need a savior.

> Do you think that I like to see wicked people die? says the Sovereign LORD. Of course not! I want them to turn from their wicked ways and live. (Ezekiel 18:23 NLT)

A nation under an oppressive ruler will remember God and seek him once again. Thus, the final election omen reveals the main reason God allows the Antichrist to reign. It's because God loves everyone he's created. And he's created every single one of us. You are not the result of space sludge that evolved. That's a lie straight from Satan because he wants you blinded to God's truth. God loves you. God made you uniquely and specifically for a purpose. The Antichrist is humanity's final warning from God. It's the last chance to get right with Jesus.

The tribulation period, when the Antichrist reigns, will feature an awesome display of God's power. There will be no mistaking that God exists. No one will be an atheist after God does this.

> The sky was removed like a scroll when it is rolled up. Every mountain and island was moved out of its place. The kings of the earth, the princes, the commanding officers, the rich, the strong, and every slave and free person, hid themselves in the caves and in the rocks of the mountains. They told the mountains and the rocks, "Fall on us, and hide us from the face of him who sits on the throne, and from the wrath of the Lamb, for the great day of his wrath has come; and who is able to stand?" (Revelation 6:14-17)

This makes me sad. The people can't stand and face Jesus. He's the "Lamb" that they see sitting on the throne in heaven. Instead, they hide. What exactly is God expecting people to do as a result of seeing him and experiencing his judgments and miracles?

> People were scorched with great heat, and people blasphemed the name of God who has the power over these plagues. They didn't repent and give him glory. (Revelation 16:9)

Repent! God wants people to turn from their sinful ways and come to him. This is one of the reasons we've had evil rulers like the Antichrist throughout history. They drive people toward God and salvation.

During this election season, make the only decision that truly matters. The one that guards your soul and determines your eternal fate. Walk away from the Antichrist. Choose Jesus and you'll be able to "stand before him without a single fault."

> For God in all his fullness was pleased to live in Christ, and through him God reconciled everything to himself. He made peace with everything in heaven and on earth by means of Christ's blood on the cross. This includes you who were once far away from God. You were his enemies, separated from him by your evil thoughts and actions. Yet now he has reconciled you to himself through the death of Christ in his physical body. As a result, he has brought you into his own presence, and you are holy and blameless as you stand before him without a single fault. But you must continue to believe this truth and stand firmly in it. (Colossians 1:19-23 NLT)

CHAPTER 24 – THE FINAL ELECTION OMEN

A nation under an oppressive ruler will remember God and seek him once again. Just as the election omen foretells, the oppressive rule of the Antichrist and God's judgments will turn people back toward God. God will hear the cry of people who've put their faith in him and intercede. The cycle must end with a ruler who is the polar opposite of the Antichrist. The very last cycle of the election omen will come to an end at Jesus's second coming.

> I saw the heaven opened, and behold, a white horse, and he who sat on it is called Faithful and True. In righteousness he judges and makes war. His eyes are a flame of fire, and on his head are many crowns. ... He is clothed in a garment sprinkled with blood. His name is called "The Word of God." ... He has on his garment and on his thigh a name written, "KING OF KINGS AND LORD OF LORDS." (Revelation 19:11-13, 16)

As you guessed it, the one on the white horse is Jesus. He's the "Word of God" and the "King of Kings."

The tribulation period will only last seven years. The clock begins when the Antichrist brokers a peace treaty with Israel and that nation's enemies (Daniel 9:27). During those seven years, a great many people will come to know Jesus. As you can imagine from what you learned in the prior chapter, many of these believers won't survive the tribulation events. Those who die at the hand of the Antichrist are seen in this Scripture below:

> "For the great day of his wrath has come, and who is able to stand?" ... After these things I looked, and behold, a great multitude which no man could count, out of every nation and of all tribes, peoples, and languages, standing before the throne and before the Lamb, dressed in white robes, with palm branches in their hands. ... And they fell on their faces before his throne, and worshiped God. ... One of the elders answered, saying to me, "These who are arrayed in the white robes, who are they, and where did they come from?" I told him, "My lord, you know." He said to me,

"These are those who came out of the great suffering. They washed their robes and made them white in the Lamb's blood." (Revelation 6:17, 7:9, 11, 13-14)

Notice that an uncountable number of people are present. They come from every nation, tribe, people, and language. Contrary to what you may have heard, God doesn't save a limited number of people during this time or only people from a particular nation. The 144,000 people that many confuse as the number of people saved is actually the number of Jewish people that God calls upon to preach the gospel during the tribulation period (Revelation 7:3-8). This vast amount of people came out of the "great suffering," that's the tribulation period that we discussed in the prior chapter.

You're probably wondering how they came to know Jesus since all the believers got raptured. God ensures every single person on the planet knows how to be saved. There's the 144,000 people that God calls upon to be preachers. There are also 2 witnesses that'll be in Jerusalem during half of the tribulation performing signs and preaching the gospel (Revelation 11). Then there's also an angel who flies around the entire world sharing the good news (Revelation 14:6-7). We must also remember that all of us believers who were raptured will have left a bunch of material behind, like Bibles, devotionals, study books, and commentaries. Some of the people who will be left behind are going to be people who attended church and read the Bible. They just never took that next step of believing in Jesus. Many, many people will be saved.

How about the people who don't die during the Antichrist's rule? What happens to everyone who's still alive when Jesus returns? There are going to be people alive who are believers. They placed their faith in Jesus and miraculously survived. And there will be people who make it through who still don't believe. They haven't repented. They still side with the Antichrist and Satan. So, two things happen. Jesus separates those groups of people and sends them to their next destination. The believers remain alive on earth and get to keep living while Jesus reigns on earth for the next 1,000 years. The unbelievers are cast into hell along with the Antichrist and the False Prophet (Matthew 25:31-41).

Satan doesn't get away unscathed either. He was the one behind the evil Antichrist and False Prophet. So, he's chained up and confined in an abyss for 1,000 years (Revelation 20:1-3). He's not cast into hell just yet. God's not done building his heavenly kingdom, and everyone in God's kingdom makes a choice to be there. So, Satan still has a purpose.

Jesus is going to be the King of kings on earth for a millennium (Revelation 20:4). While the last cycle of the election omen ends here, another cycle also begins. However, it's going to look a lot different than the cycles before it. Jesus is the King of kings which implies there are other kings on earth. So, who are they? Do the people get to elect them?

When Jesus returns at his second coming, he's not alone. He brings a bunch of people with him: all the people who were raptured, everyone who was resurrected at the rapture (the people who put their faith in Jesus but died before the rapture), anyone who believed in Jesus but died during the tribulation period, and all of the Old Testament believers. It's essentially anyone raptured or resurrected. That's because these people are going to be the kings and queens of the millennial period (Revelation 20:4).

Have you put your faith in Jesus? If yes, did you know that you could be a ruler with Jesus in the millennial period?

The millennial period will be ruled by Jesus and completely righteous people. All of the rulers will be righteous because they will all have come from heaven. Only perfect and holy people can live there. When you place your faith in Jesus, he gives you his own righteousness (Hebrews 10). But we still sin while we're on earth because we're not perfect yet. We're just counted as being perfect. When you get to heaven, where there isn't any sin, you won't be a sinner anymore (Philippians 3:12-14; 1 Corinthians 13:9-12; 1 John 3:2).

Jesus will choose all the rulers. This is a key difference in the next cycle that starts with Jesus's reign. There won't be an election by the people who survive the tribulation. Now, only some of the people who return with Jesus will actually be rulers. That's because rulership is a reward. Jesus's parable of the ten servants (Luke 19:11-27) illustrates this. A parable is a story that reveals how things operate in God's kingdom. In this particular parable, a man is called away so he can be crowned king. Before he left, he gave each of his ten servants a portion of money and told them to do business with it while he was gone. After he was crowned king and came back, he called his servants to see what they each did with the money. The servants who invested the money were rewarded with authority over cities. The servant who didn't do anything with the money, had the money they were given taken away and it was given to one of the already rewarded servants. The new king gave rulership as his reward.

The Bible also tells us that only some of Jesus's followers will earn crowns. The Bible mentions five crowns including the incorruptible crown for self-control (1 Corinthians 9:25), the crown of life for believers martyred for their faith (Revelation 2:10), the crown of glory for good leaders (1 Peter 5:2-4), the crown of righteousness for people looking forward to seeing Jesus (2 Timothy 4:8), and the crown of rejoicing for soul winners (1 Thessalonians 2:19-20). There very well could be other crowns, but those are just the ones we know about.

What have you done with the skills, talents, and resources that God has put you in charge of? Will you get rewarded with a crown and rulership during Jesus's reign? Be aware that Satan wants to steal it if you've already earned one (Revelation 3:11). So, finish your life by standing strong for Jesus.

Just because the people living in the millennial period won't be choosing their leaders doesn't mean they won't be free to choose who to worship. While the people who first join the kingdom will all be survivors of the Antichrist and tribulation, those survivors are going to have children. After 1,000 years, you can imagine there's going to be a lot of people. They all will have had Jesus as their king the entire time. But you know what? Some of them won't want to be ruled by Jesus. It's no different than today. Today, a majority of people don't want anything to do with Jesus. It'll be the same when Jesus is actually physically present on the planet too.

God gives a nation the ruler they desire. Because there will be people who would rather have Satan as their ruler, God gives them Satan. You see, God doesn't force anyone to worship him or spend eternity with him. Everyone has a choice. So, Jesus lets Satan loose at the end of the 1,000 years. What's really mind boggling to me is that Satan amasses an army of followers that's numberless (Revelation 20:7-8). The Bible says they are like "the sand of the sea." Wow! People living under the rule of perfect, holy, just, and righteous leaders will still choose Satan.

So, guess what happens to this rebellion? **When a nation turns**

completely away from God and reaches the point of no return it will bring judgment upon itself. That's right. The election omen manifests yet again. But Jesus doesn't let Satan reign. He already did that before, through the Antichrist. No, this time when Satan's army has Jerusalem, where Jesus reigns from, completely surrounded, Jesus rains fire down from heaven and consumes the wicked army. Then Satan is thrown into hell, the lake of fire, where he remains forever (Revelation 20:9-10).

We need to talk about hell for a minute. It's a real place. Satan isn't the ruler of it as you just learned. He's destined to be an occupant. God created hell for Satan and the other fallen angels (Matthew 25:41). It's not meant for you. Heaven is what's meant for you. But you must choose to live there. Hell is your default if you don't choose Jesus. Hell is also not the fun party place that people like to joke about residing in. Hell is opposite of heaven. God lives in heaven. So, hell is the absence of God. God created everything. So, hell is the absence of creation; it's complete and utter darkness (2 Peter 2:4). God is love. So, hell is the torment (Revelation 20:10; Mark 9:43-44). God is peace. So, hell is restless (Revelation 14:11). You do not want to be sent there!

After Satan is dealt with, everyone who's ever lived and hasn't been resurrected yet is resurrected. So, this will be all the people who died during the millennial period and all unbelievers who died throughout history. Jesus will judge each of these people to determine where they'll spend eternity. Those who put their faith in Jesus get to spend eternity with him. Everyone else will go to hell (Revelation 20:11-15).

Then, God creates a brand new heaven and earth for all of the believers. Yes, heaven is a real place too. We'll spend eternity living on a perfect earth, the way God intended it to be. There won't be any pain, sorrow, death, or sadness anymore (Revelation 21). The current earth that you live upon isn't boring, so the new earth won't be either. In fact, God's Word tells us that we can't even imagine all the wonderful things God has in store for us (1 Corinthians 2:9-10). I can think of some pretty fantastic things. I'm sure you can too. Yet none of our wild thoughts compare to what will be revealed. I can hardly wait!

At this point the election omen has come to an end. I hope you've learned a lot through the journey we've taken together. If you were afraid of what was coming during the last days, I hope you aren't any longer. Instead, I hope you've been filled with a desire to act. To vote.

Above all, you must live as citizens of heaven, conducting yourselves in a manner worthy of the Good News about Christ. Then, whether I come and see you again or only hear about you, I will know that you are standing together with one spirit and one purpose, fighting together for the faith, which is the Good News. Don't be intimidated in any way by your enemies. This will be a sign to them that they are going to be destroyed, but that you are going to be saved, even by God himself. (Philippians 1:27-28 NLT)

If you're a believer, you're already a "citizen of heaven." All of God's promises are yours. They will come to pass. As we wait for Jesus, we must do as the apostle Paul says and stand, fight for the faith, and not be intimated by our enemy, Satan. In what may be the last US presidential election before the rapture and the Antichrist, go make your faith be known with your vote!

CHAPTER 25 – TAKE A STAND

Finally, be strong in the Lord and in the strength of his might. Put on the whole armor of God, that you may be able to stand against the wiles of the devil. (Ephesians 6:10-11)

Like the cycles of progression in the election omen, we've come back to where we started, the armor of God. Our End Times Armor. In the introduction, you learned that *stand* is mentioned four times in the description about this armor. It means to rise up, hold your ground, hold your position, endure, and display courage and strength. But it also means pause, stop, halt, and prevail.

That's what's required of you right now. You must rise up and vote for the presidential candidate who most displays the heart that Jesus would vote for. Vote President Trump for reelection. This goes beyond the presidential election though. You must also rise up and vote for your local and state representatives, judges, school board members, etc. who stand for the values that Jesus does.

You know that we're truly living in the last days before Jesus returns. It's never been more evident than it is today. The coronavirus pandemic scared people, awakened people, and they're turning to their Bibles. To God's Word. Maybe that's you. You need to know that God hasn't abandoned us. He hasn't forgotten about you. He loves you. He's coming again very soon. Put your faith in Jesus while you still have the chance. You don't want to be left behind after the rapture. This is why it's so imperative that we stand! There's not much time left, and there are still people to save. We must give people who aren't saved yet every second we can to make a decision for Jesus. The people we care about are depending upon us. Stand for them.

It certainly seems like the world is falling apart at times, especially today. It's actually all coming together! You see, God told us what he was going to do in advance. He's already written the story. That's fate. We can clearly see the signs and warnings he gave us coming to pass. The tribulation events are on the horizon. The rule of the Antichrist and his global government is perhaps just a page away. But we mustn't forget about our free will. We get to choose which path the story takes by voting for president. Who are you going to vote for? Which page in

God's story will we end up turning to next?

Perhaps you've noticed the hatred toward President Trump. The media never says anything good about him, celebrities advocate for his assassination, and the Democrats have tried everything they can to get rid of him. This behavior reminds me of someone. You see, he's treated a tiny nation the same way for thousands of years. That's right. It's Satan! He's been opposed to God's people ever since Adam and Eve were created. He hates everything that God loves, and he opposes everything that God is for. You see, you can tell that God is for President Trump, because Satan is so against him! It's because Trump is a man of prayer, a respecter of God, and a defender of religious liberty.

When the coronavirus pandemic hit our nation, I didn't see any of the Democrat candidates ask the nation to pray. President Trump did. Here's part of what he prayed:

> "As we unite in prayer, we are reminded that there is no burden too heavy for God to lift or for this country to bear with His help. Luke 1:37 promises that 'For with God nothing shall be impossible,' and those words are just as true today as they have ever been. As one Nation under God, we are greater than the hardships we face, and through prayer and acts of compassion and love, we will rise to this challenge and emerge stronger and more united than ever before. May God bless each of you, and may God bless the United States of America."[1]

Prayer is at the heart of our End Times Armor. The apostle Paul instructed us to pray at all times. He also instructed us to pray for our leaders.

> I exhort therefore, first of all, that petitions, prayers, intercessions, and givings of thanks be made for all men, for kings and all who are in high places, that we may lead a tranquil and quiet life in all godliness and reverence. For this is good and acceptable in the sight of God our Savior, who desires all people to be saved and come to full knowledge of the truth. (1 Timothy 2:1-4)

Today, pray for President Trump and give thanks for him. He's stemming the tide of evil so that more people can come to know Jesus and be saved. Ask God to guide your vote and help you choose the candidates that he wills for your city, state, and our nation. Pray for your fellow man, that God shines his light of truth on all of them. Pray for peace between you and your neighbors. We're fighting against Satan, not against each other. Pray for courage to stand with Jesus in this spiritual war.

Of all the Marvel heroes, who do you think is the favorite? The people of America like President Trump and resonate with him for the same reasons we all love Iron Man. He's rich, arrogant, doesn't have any superpowers, is intelligent, has a sinful past, is willing to do what it takes to win, and sacrificed for the benefit of others. He's a flawed hero. He's someone we can root for. I know that God is rooting for him. I'm rooting for him. I hope you will too. Now, go out and Vote!

> "More than 200 years after the patriots fired that first shot heard 'round the world, one revolutionary idea still burns in the hearts of men and women everywhere: A society where man is not beholden to government; government is beholden to man.
> ...
> "Fellow citizens, fellow conservatives, our time has come again. This is our moment. Let us unite, shoulder to shoulder, behind one mighty banner for freedom. And let us go forward from here not with some faint hope that our cause is not yet lost; let us go forward confident that the American people share our values, and that together we will be victorious.
> "And in those moments when we grow tired, when our struggle seems hard, remember what Eric Liddell, Scotland's Olympic champion runner, said in Chariots of Fire: 'So where does the power come from to see the race to its end? From within. God made me for a purpose, and I will run for His pleasure.'
> "If we trust in Him, keep His word, and live our lives for His pleasure, He'll give us the power we need -- power to fight the good fight, to finish the race and to keep the faith.
> "Thank you very much. God bless you and God bless America." (President Ronald Reagan, Our Noble Vision: An Opportunity for All, 1984).[2]

Thanks for taking this journey with me. If you'd like to show your support for my work, please leave a review wherever you purchased this book. It's free to do, and it'll only take you a minute to write a quick sentence expressing your thoughts about the book. Your review is very important to independent, self-published authors like me. Internet and online bookstore algorithms favor books with reviews. They display in search results and at the top of search results more often than books without reviews. I even need a minimum number of reviews before I can purchase certain advertising. So, your review will help more people find this book. That will in turn help me sell more books, which means I can keep writing books for you. Go to rapture911.com/reviews if you need a link to where you can leave a review.

Thanks for your support!

Marsha

APPENDIX

HOW TO BE SAVED

God loves you and wants to spend eternity with you. But there's a problem, and it's called sin. Sin is doing and even thinking anything that isn't perfect and holy. Every single one of us commits sin. We can't help it; it's our nature. It doesn't matter what your sin is or how big or little you perceive your sin to be. It could be lying, lust, pride, or murder. Any sin is sin in God's eyes.

> There is no one who does good, no, not so much as one. (Romans 3:12)

God is perfect and sinless and righteous in every way. Thus, so is where he lives, heaven. Sin is the opposite of God. Sin cannot exist in heaven. Since people are inherently sinful, no one can live with God unless the sin problem is taken care of first.

Case in point: Adam and Eve. They lived in the garden of Eden with God. They saw God every day. Heaven is wherever God is, so they essentially lived in heaven. After they sinned and ate from the forbidden tree, they got kicked out of the garden. They couldn't live with God anymore. This Scripture records that event. God sent "him," which is Adam, out from the garden.

> God sent him out from the garden of Eden, to till the ground from which he was taken. So he drove out the man; and he placed cherubim at the east of the garden of Eden, and a flaming sword which turned every way, to guard the way to the tree of life. (Genesis 3:23-24)

Here's the good news: God has a solution for the sin problem. He demands a perfect and spotless sacrifice to atone for sin. When Adam and Eve first sinned, God killed an animal to clothe them and atone for their sin.

> Yahweh God made garments of animal skins for Adam and for his wife, and clothed them. (Genesis 3:21)

In the Old Testament times before Jesus came, God's people sacrificed animals to atone for their sin.

If anyone of the common people sins unwittingly, in doing any of the things which Yahweh has commanded not to be done, and is guilty, if his sin which he has sinned is made known to him, then he shall bring for his offering a goat, a female without defect, for his sin which he has sinned. He shall lay his hand on the head of the sin offering, and kill the sin offering in the place of burnt offering. (Leviticus 4:27-29)

Under the old system, the high priest brought the blood of animals into the Holy Place as a sacrifice for sin, and the bodies of the animals were burned outside the camp. (Hebrews 13:11 NLT)

Don't run off to find an animal you can sacrifice to atone for your sin. God's already taken care of the sacrifice offering permanently for you. He loves you so much that he sent Jesus, his perfect and sinless and righteous son, down to earth to live as a man. Jesus was then sacrificed for you. He was crucified to atone for your sin. We know this worked because Jesus isn't dead. God raised him from the dead. Then Jesus appeared to hundreds of people in his risen state. All you have to do now is believe.

For God so loved the world, that he gave his one and only Son, that whoever believes in him should not perish, but have eternal life. (John 3:16)

Belief. It seems too simple doesn't it? But that's the irony, it's not simple at all. In fact, belief is really hard. The Bible says the path to God is narrow and most don't find it. That's because we're accustomed to striving for what we want down here on earth. The harder we work, the more we get. We love to boast about our accomplishments. We love to be in control. That's not God's way. God is in control, and it's about what God did, not what you've done. His solution is a gift. He gave his son as a gift to you. You just have to accept it.

But God, being rich in mercy, for his great love with which he loved us, even when we were dead through our trespasses, made us alive together with Christ—by grace you have been saved—... for by grace you have been saved through faith, and that not of yourselves; it is the gift of God. (Ephesians 2:4-5, 8)

> For by grace you have been saved through faith, and that not of yourselves; it is the gift of God, not of works, that no one would boast. (Ephesians 2:8-9)

You see, it's God's grace that saved you. As sinners, we are doomed to an eternal life far removed from God. That's God's rule. Grace is God demonstrating his love for us by pardoning us based on us believing Jesus died for our sins. God treated Jesus the way we deserve to be treated. Jesus was crucified. God did that so he could treat us the way Jesus deserves to be treated. Jesus is now in heaven with God.

A person who believes what they cannot yet see has faith. They believe God and that Jesus died for their sins. Have faith.

> Now faith is assurance of things hoped for, proof of things not seen. (Hebrews 11:1)

Here's what you must come to believe.

You recognize that you are a sinner.
You don't want to be a sinner anymore. You ask God to forgive you.
You want to live with God for eternity in heaven.
You know that you can't save yourself.
You believe that God sent his son Jesus to atone for your sin by dying on the cross.
You believe that God raised Jesus from the dead and that Jesus reigns with God in heaven.
You surrender your salvation to Jesus and ask him to come into your life.

Now, you can't just go through the motions and say these things. You have to actually mean them, deep down from your heart. That's what faith is all about.

This is the good news of the Bible. That Jesus, the son of God, died for your sins, rose from the grave, and reigns from heaven with God.

> Now I declare to you, brothers, the Good News which I preached to you, which also you received, in which you also stand, by which also you are saved, if you hold firmly the word which I preached to you—unless you

believed in vain. For I delivered to you first of all that which I also received: that Christ died for our sins according to the Scriptures, that he was buried, that he was raised on the third day according to the Scriptures. (1 Corinthians 15:1-4)

If you truly believe all those things, then tell God. That's what praying is, just talking to God. Tell him you believe each of those truths and ask him to come into your life. And he will indeed!

It will be that whoever will call on the name of the Lord will be saved. (Acts 2:21)

"For I know the thoughts that I think toward you," says Yahweh, "thoughts of peace, and not of evil, to give you hope and a future. You shall call on me, and you shall go and pray to me, and I will listen to you. You shall seek me, and find me, when you search for me with all your heart." (Jeremiah 29:11-13)

Here's an example prayer you can say to God:

"Lord Jesus, I know that I'm a sinner and that I need your forgiveness so that I can live with you for eternity in heaven. Please forgive me. I believe that you are the son of God and that you died on the cross for my sins. I believe that you rose from the grave! I want to turn from my sins and trust and follow you as Lord and Savior. Please come into my heart and life. In Jesus's name, amen."

Here are some additional Scriptures you can read to learn more about salvation:

Adam, Eve, sin, and Satan - Genesis 2-3

We're all sinners - Romans 3:9-23; 1 John 1:8-10

What is sin - 1 John 3:4; Galatians 5:16-26

Satan is your accuser - Job 1

Sin keeps you separated from God - Isaiah 59:2; Revelation

21:27; Romans 6:23

God's love for you - Romans 8:35-39; John 15:9-13; Ephesians 2:4-6; Romans 5:6-8

Jesus is God in the flesh - Hebrews 1:2-6; Philippians 2:5-11; Colossians 2:9; John 1

Jesus died for your sins - 2 Corinthians 5:21; 1 Corinthians 15:3-4; 1 Peter 2:24; 1 John 2:1-2; 1 Timothy 1:15; Hebrews 2:14-16; Titus 3:4-7; Romans 8

Crucifixion of Jesus - John 19; Luke 23; Mark 15; Matthew 27

Jesus's resurrection - Matthew 28; Mark 16; John 20; Luke 24; Romans 1:2-5; Acts 2:23-24; 1 Corinthians 15:3-8

Saved by grace - Ephesians 2:8-9; John 20:31; 1 Corinthians 15:2-3; Romans 3:25; John 14:6

Sealed by the Holy Spirit - Ephesians 1:12-14; John 16:7-15

VOTER RESOURCES

U.S. Election Assistance Commission
Information on Voter Registration
www.eac.gov/voters/register-and-vote-in-your-state

Donald J. Trump
www.donaldjtrump.com
www.promiseskept.com

Joe Biden - joebiden.com
Bernie Sanders - berniesanders.com

Republican Party - www.gop.com
Democrat Party - democrats.org
Libertarian Party - www.lp.org
Green Party - www.gp.org

My Faith Votes - www.myfaithvotes.org
Christian Voter Guide - www.christianvoterguide.com
Faith & Freedom Coalition - www.ffcoalition.com
Vote Smart - justfacts.votesmart.org
On The Issues - www.ontheissues.org
Center for Responsive Politics - www.opensecrets.org
BallotPedia - ballotpedia.org
Federal Election Commission - www.fec.gov

This list is provided for your convenience to aid you in your own research. Inclusion does not reflect my endorsement of content.

NEWS RESOURCES

The White House - You can subscribe for daily news updates
www.whitehouse.gov

President of the US - twitter.com/potus

The US Senate - www.senate.gov
The US House of Representatives - www.house.gov
C-Span - www.c-span.org
GovTrack.us - www.govtrack.us

Sean Hannity - hannity.com
Tucker Carlson - twitter.com/tuckercarlson
Laura Ingraham - www.lauraingraham.com
Rush Limbaugh - www.rushlimbaugh.com

Citizen Journalists
Amazing Polly - twitter.com/99freemind
RedPill78 - www.youtube.com/c/RedPill78
X22 Report - twitter.com/X22Report
Brandon Tatum - twitter.com/TheOfficerTatum

The Heritage Foundation - www.heritage.org
Judicial Watch - www.judicialwatch.org
National Review - www.nationalreview.com
Townhall - townhall.com
One America News Network - www.oann.com
World News Daily - www.wnd.com
Christian Headlines - www.christianheadlines.com
PragerU - twitter.com/prageru

This list is provided for your convenience to aid you in your own research. Inclusion does not reflect my endorsement of content.

GET FREE BOOKS

BookHip.com/TANMVQ

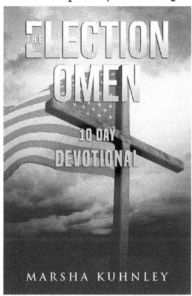

rapture911.com/free

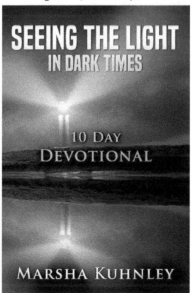

BOOKS BY MARSHA KUHNLEY

Rapture 911 Series
*Rapture 911: What To Do If You're Left Behind
Rapture 911: What To Do If You're Left Behind (Pocket Edition)
Rapture 911: 10 Day Devotional
Rapture 911: Prophecy Reference Bible

End Times Armor Series
The Election Omen: Your Vote Matters
The Election Omen: 10 Day Devotional

Other Works
Seeing The Light In Dark Times: 10 Day Devotional

Visit Marsha's website to find these books
rapture911.com

* - Also available as an audiobook

ABOUT AUTHOR

Marsha Kuhnley is an American author of Christian non-fiction books. She has a passion for Bible prophecy, finance, and economics. She received her MBA in Finance and BA in Economics from the University of New Mexico. Prior to becoming an author, she enjoyed a career at Intel Corporation. She uses her education and career experience to take complex biblical information and present it in easily understandable concepts. You'll benefit from over a decade of her research and study of the Bible, Bible prophecy, and Rapture theology. She lives in Albuquerque, NM with her husband where they attend Calvary Church.

CONNECT WITH MARSHA

rapture911.com/connect

ENDNOTES

Chapter 1

[1] Drew Desilver, "U.S. trails most developed countries in voter turnout," *Pew Research Center*, Mary 21, 2018, https://www.pewresearch.org/fact-tank/2018/05/21/u-s-voter-turnout-trails-most-developed-countries/, accessed April 9, 2020.

[2] "Voting and Registration in the Election of November 2018," United States Census Bureau, https://www.census.gov/data/tables/time-series/demo/voting-and-registration/p20-583.html, accessed April 10, 2020. Table 1, https://www2.census.gov/programs-surveys/cps/tables/p20/583/table01.xlsx, 13% of 153 million registered voters is 20 million.

[3] "Voting and Registration in the Election of November 2018," United States Census Bureau, https://www.census.gov/data/tables/time-series/demo/voting-and-registration/p20-583.html, accessed April 10, 2020. Table 1, https://www2.census.gov/programs-surveys/cps/tables/p20/583/table01.xlsx, 30% of 228 million registered citizens is 68 million.

Chapter 2

[1] Jordan Misra, "Voter Turnout Rates Among All Voting Age and Major Racial and Ethic Groups Were Higher Than in 2014," *United States Census Bureau*, April 23, 2019, https://www.census.gov/library/stories/2019/04/behind-2018-united-states-midterm-election-turnout.html, accessed April 10, 2020.

[2] Thom File, "Voting in America: A Look at the 2016 Presidential Election," *United States Census Bureau*, May 10, 2017, https://www.census.gov/newsroom/blogs/random-samplings/2017/05/voting_in_america.html, accessed April 10, 2020.

[3] Gustavo Lopez and Antonio Flores, "Dislike of candidates or campaign issues was most common reason for not voting in 2016," *Pew Research Center*, June 1, 2017, https://www.pewresearch.org/fact-tank/2017/06/01/dislike-of-candidates-or-campaign-issues-was-most-common-reason-for-not-voting-in-2016/, accessed April 9, 2020.

[4] 100%-61% = 39% didn't vote. 40% of 39% is 15.6%.

[5] "Notional Christians: The Big Election Story in 2016," *Barna*, December 1, 2016, https://www.barna.com/research/notional-christians-big-election-story-2016/, accessed April 9, 2020.

[6] "Notional Christians: The Big Election Story in 2016," *Barna*, December 1, 2016, https://www.barna.com/research/notional-christians-big-election-story-2016/, accessed April 9, 2020.

[7] "Notional Christians: The Big Election Story in 2016," *Barna*, December 1, 2016, https://www.barna.com/research/notional-christians-big-election-story-2016/, accessed April 9, 2020.

[8] "Notional Christians: The Big Election Story in 2016," *Barna*, December 1, 2016, https://www.barna.com/research/notional-christians-big-election-story-2016/, accessed April 9, 2020.

Chapter 3

[1] "Voting Rights In The United States," Wikipedia.org, https://en.wikipedia.org/wiki/Voting_rights_in_the_United_States, accessed April 10, 2020.

[2] "The Constitution: Amendments 11-27," National Archives, https://www.archives.gov/founding-docs/amendments-11-27, accessed April 10, 2020.

[3] "Civil War Facts," *American Battlefield Trust*, https://www.battlefields.org/learn/articles/civil-war-facts, accessed April 10, 2020.

[4] "Selma to Montgomery Marches," Wikipedia.org, https://en.wikipedia.org/wiki/Selma_to_Montgomery_marches, accessed April 10, 2020.

[5] "Address at the Conclusion of the Selma to Montgomery March," Stanford University: The Martin Luther King, Jr. Research and Education Institute, https://kinginstitute.stanford.edu/king-papers/documents/address-conclusion-selma-montgomery-march, accessed April 10, 2020.

[6] "Congress and the Voting Rights Act of 1965," National Archives, https://www.archives.gov/legislative/features/voting-rights-1965, accessed April 10, 2020.

"Voting Rights Act of 1965," Wikipedia.org, https://en.wikipedia.org/wiki/Voting_Rights_Act_of_1965, accessed April 10, 2020.

[7] "Voting Rights for African Americans," Library of Congress, https://www.loc.gov/teachers/classroommaterials/presentationsandactivities/presentations/elections/voting-rights-african-americans.html, accessed April 10, 2020.

[8] "President Johnson's Special Message to the Congress: The American Promise," LBJ Presidential Library, http://www.lbjlibrary.org/lyndon-baines-johnson/speeches-films/president-johnsons-special-message-to-the-congress-the-american-promise/, accessed April 10, 2020.

[9] "Suffrage History," University of Rochester, http://www.rochester.edu/sba/suffrage-history/, accessed April 10, 2020.

[10] "19th Amendment," National Women's History Museum, http://www.crusadeforthevote.org/19-amendment, accessed April 10, 2020.

[11] "Suffrage: Women in the GOP," National Federation of Republican Women, http://www.nfrw.org/women-suffrage, accessed April 10, 2020.

[12] "The Night of Terror: When Suffragists Were Imprisoned and Tortured in 1917," History.com, https://www.history.com/news/night-terror-brutality-suffragists-19th-amendment, accessed April 10, 2020.

[13] "Woodrow Wilson Address to the Senate on the Nineteenth Amendment," The American Presidency Project, https://www.presidency.ucsb.edu/documents/address-the-senate-the-nineteenth-amendment, accessed April 10, 2020.

[14] Tom Wurtz, "In 1920, Republicans Defeated Democrats' War on Women," *The Blaze*, March 31, 2016, https://www.theblaze.com/contributions/in-1920-republicans-defeated-democrats-war-on-women, accessed April 10, 2020.

"Suffrage: Women in the GOP," National Federation of Republican Women, http://www.nfrw.org/women-suffrage, accessed April 10, 2020.

Chapter 4

[1] "Congressional Apportionment," United States Census Bureau, https://www.census.gov/topics/public-sector/congressional-apportionment.html, accessed April 10, 2020.

[2] "The Constitution of the United States: A Transcription," National Archives, https://www.archives.gov/founding-docs/constitution-transcript, accessed April 10, 2020.

[3] "The Constitution: Amendments 11-27," National Archives, https://www.archives.gov/founding-docs/amendments-11-27, accessed April 10, 2020.

[4] Thomas H. Neale, "The Electoral College: How It Works in Contemporary Presidential Elections," *Congressional Research Service*, May 15, 2017, https://fas.org/sgp/crs/misc/RL32611.pdf, accessed April 10, 2020.

[5] "2016 Presidential Election Results," Politico, https://www.politico.com/2016-election/results/map/president/, accessed April 10, 2020.

[6] Varad Mehta, "Nobody Understands What a Popular Vote Presidential Election Would Mean," *National Review*, November 16, 2016, https://www.nationalreview.com/2016/11/popular-vote-hillary-didnt-really-win-it/, accessed April 10, 2020.

[7] "Voting and Registration in the Election of November 2018," United States Census Bureau, https://www.census.gov/data/tables/time-series/demo/voting-and-registration/p20-583.html, accessed April 10, 2020. Table 4a, https://www2.census.gov/programs-surveys/cps/tables/p20/583/table04a.xlsx. 4 states have 30% of the registered voters and the population - California, Texas, Florida, New York. 4 states out of 50 is only 8% of the states. 10 states have 50% of the registered voters and the population - California, Texas, Florida, New York, Pennsylvania, Illinois, Ohio, Michigan, North Carolina, Georgia. 10 states out of 50 is only 20% of the states.

[8] John Merline, "It's Official: Clinton's Popular Vote Win Came Entirely From California," *Investor's Business Daily*, December 16, 2016, https://www.investors.com/politics/commentary/its-official-clintons-popular-vote-win-came-entirely-from-california/, accessed April 10, 2020.

[9] Rusty Weiss, "Ocasio-Cortez Claims Electoral College a Racist Scam to Benefit Middle America," *The Mental Recession*, August 22, 2019, https://menrec.com/ocasio-cortez-claims-electoral-college-a-racist-scam-to-benefit-middle-america/, accessed April 10, 2020.

[10] National Popular Vote, https://www.nationalpopularvote.com/, accessed April 10, 2020.

[11] "The Constitution of the United States: A Transcription," National Archives, https://www.archives.gov/founding-docs/constitution-transcript, accessed April 10, 2020.

[12] "National Mail Voter Registration Form," U.S. Election Assistance Commission, https://www.eac.gov/voters/national-mail-voter-registration-form, accessed April 10, 2020.

[13] "Voter Identification Requirements: Voter ID Laws," National Conference of State Legislatures, https://www.ncsl.org/research/elections-and-campaigns/voter-id.aspx#Laws%20in%20Effect, accessed April 10, 2020.

[14] Deroy Murdock, "Ghost Voters," *National Review*, August 11, 2017, https://www.nationalreview.com/2017/08/election-fraud-registered-voters-outnumber-eligible-voters-462-counties/, accessed April 10, 2020.

[15] "Judicial Watch Sues to Force North Carolina to Clean Its Voter Rolls," *Judicial Watch*, April 9, 2020, https://www.judicialwatch.org/press-releases/judicial-watch-sues-to-force-north-carolina-to-clean-its-voter-rolls/, accessed April 11, 2020.

[16] John Binder, "Federal Data: 16.4M Mail-In Ballots Went Missing in 2016, 2018 Elections," *Breitbart*, April 10, 2020, https://www.breitbart.com/politics/2020/04/10/federal-data-16-4m-mail-in-ballots-went-missing-in-2016-2018-elections/, accessed April 11, 2020.

[17] "A Sampling of Election Fraud Cases From Across the Country," *The Heritage Foundation*, 2020, https://www.whitehouse.gov/sites/whitehouse.gov/files/docs/pacei-voterfraudcases.pdf, accessed April 11, 2020.

[18] John Binder, "Study: Immigration to Redistribute 26 Congressional Seats to Blue States for 2022 Election," *Breitbart*, December 22, 2019, https://www.breitbart.com/politics/2019/12/22/study-immigration-redistribute-26-congressional-seats-blue-states-2020-election/, accessed April 10, 2020.

Chapter 8
[1] Billy Graham, *Angels: God's Secret Agents*, (Nashville, TN: Thomas Nelson, 1975), 99.
[2] "Belshazzar: The second most powerful man in Babylon," Creation.com, https://creation.com/archaeology-belshazzar, accessed April 10, 2020.

Chapter 10
[1] "Washington's Inaugural Address of 1789," National Archives, https://www.archives.gov/exhibits/american_originals/inaugtxt.html, accessed April 10, 2020.
[2] "Notional Christians: The Big Election Story in 2016," *Barna*, December 1, 2016, https://www.barna.com/research/notional-christians-big-election-story-2016/, accessed April 9, 2020.
[3] "How People of Faith Voted in the 2008 Presidential Race," *Barna*, January 28, 2009, https://www.barna.com/research/how-people-of-faith-voted-in-the-2008-presidential-race/, accessed April 9, 2020.
[4] "Countries in the World," Worldometer, https://www.worldometers.info/geography/how-many-countries-are-there-in-the-world/, accessed April 10, 2020.
[5] "Mao Zedong," Wikipedia.org, https://en.wikipedia.org/wiki/Mao_Zedong, accessed April 10, 2020.
[6] Adrian Karatnycky, Freedom in the World: *The Annual Survey of Political Rights & Civil Liberties 1999-2000*, (New York, NY: Freedom House, 2000), 8, https://freedomhouse.org/sites/default/files/2020-02/Freedom_in_the_World_1999-2000_complete_book.pdf, accessed April 9, 2020.
[7] Sarah Repucci, "Freedom in the World 2020: A Leaderless Struggle for Democracy," *Freedom House*, https://freedomhouse.org/report/freedom-world/2020/leaderless-struggle-democracy, accessed April 10, 2020.
[8] Sarah Repucci, "Freedom in the World 2020: A Leaderless Struggle for Democracy," *Freedom House*, https://freedomhouse.org/report/freedom-world/2020/leaderless-struggle-democracy, accessed April 10, 2020. Excel file embedded in the article titled All Data, FIW 2013-2020, https://freedomhouse.org/sites/default/files/2020-02/2020_All_Data_FIW_2013-2020.xlsx.
[9] "U.S. Census Bureau Current Population," United States Census Bureau, https://www.census.gov/popclock/print.php?component=counter, accessed March 4, 2020.
[10] Paul Steinhauser, "Sanders endorses Biden for president, after suspending campaign," *Fox News*, April 13, 2020, https://www.foxnews.com/politics/sanders-endorses-biden-for-president-after-suspending-campaign, accessed April 13, 2020.
[11] Paul Steinhauser, "Sanders endorses Biden for president, after suspending campaign," *Fox News*, April 13, 2020, https://www.foxnews.com/politics/sanders-endorses-biden-for-president-after-suspending-campaign, accessed April 13, 2020.

Chapter 11
[1] "Libertarian Party Platform: As adopted by convention, July 2018," Libertarian Party, July 2018, https://www.lp.org/platform/, accessed April 10, 2020.

[2] Richard Land, "Voting: The Christian's Duty," *Decision*, February 1, 2016, https://decisionmagazine.com/voting-christians-duty/, accessed April 10, 2020.

Chapter 12
[1] Tara C. Jatlaoui, MD et al., "Abortion Surveillance - United States, 2016," *Morbidity and Mortality Weekly Report (MMWR) Surveillance Summaries* 68, no. 11 (November 28, 2019), https://www.cdc.gov/mmwr/volumes/68/ss/pdfs/ss6811a1-H.pdf, accessed April 10, 2020.
[2] "2016 Democratic Party Platform," *Democratic Party*, July 2016, https://democrats.org/where-we-stand/party-platform/, accessed April 10, 2020.
[3] "Libertarian Party Platform: As adopted by convention, July 2018," *Libertarian Party*, July 2018, https://www.lp.org/platform/, accessed April 10, 2020.
[4] "Green Party Platform: Approved by Green National Committee, August 2016," *Green Party*, August 2016, https://www.gp.org/platform, accessed April 10, 2020.
[5] Zack Budryk, "Planned Parenthood launches $45M campaign to back Democrats in 2020," *The Hill*, January 16, 2020, https://thehill.com/policy/healthcare/abortion/478548-planned-parenthood-launches-45m-campaign-to-support-democrats-in, accessed April 10, 2020.
[6] "Republican Platform 2016," *Republican Party*, July 2016, https://www.gop.com/platform/, accessed April 10, 2020.
[7] "Health Care," JoeBiden.com, https://joebiden.com/healthcare/, accessed April 10, 2020.
[8] "Bernie Sanders: No Place for Pro-Life Democrats," *Decision*, February 11, 2020, https://decisionmagazine.com/bernie-sanders-no-place-for-pro-life-democrats/, accessed April 10, 2020.
[9] "Issues: Reproductive Health Care and Justice for All," BernieSanders.com, https://berniesanders.com/issues/reproductive-justice-all/, accessed April 10, 2020.
[10] "Roll Call Vote 108thCongress - 1stSession: Vote Number 402," Senate.Gov, https://www.senate.gov/legislative/LIS/roll_call_lists/roll_call_vote_cfm.cfm?congress=108&session=1&vote=00402, accessed April 10, 2020. A bill to prohibit partial-birth abortion. Vote Date: October 21, 2003.
[11] "Roll Call Vote 116thCongress - 1stSession: Vote Number 27," Senate.Gov, https://www.senate.gov/legislative/LIS/roll_call_lists/roll_call_vote_cfm.cfm?congress=116&session=1&vote=00027, accessed April 10, 2020. A bill to a prohibit a health care practitioner from failing to exercise the proper degree of care in the case of a child who survives an abortion or attempted abortion. Vote Date: February 25, 2019.
[12] "Roll Call Vote 116th Congress - 2nd Session: Vote Number 58," Senate.Gov, https://www.senate.gov/legislative/LIS/roll_call_lists/roll_call_vote_cfm.cfm?congress=116&session=2&vote=00058, accessed April 10, 2020. A bill to prohibit a health care practitioner from failing to exercise the proper degree of care in the case of a child who survives an abortion or attempted abortion. Vote Date: February 25, 2020.
[13] "Death-Loving Democrats Vote Down Bill to Protect Abortion-Surviving Babies," *Pulpit & Pen*, Febuary 13, 2020, https://pulpitandpen.org/2020/02/13/death-loving-democrats-vote-down-bill-to-protect-abortion-surviving-babies/, accessed April 10, 2020.
[14] "Remarks by President Trump at the 47th Annual March for Life," *WhiteHouse.Gov*, January 24, 2020, https://www.whitehouse.gov/briefings-statements/remarks-president-trump-47th-annual-march-life/, accessed April 10, 2020.
[15] "What's The Protect Life Rule All About?," March For Life, https://marchforlife.org/protect-life-rule/, accessed April 10, 2020.

[16] "Abortion Giant Pulls Out of Title X Program," *Decision*, August 20, 2019, https://decisionmagazine.com/abortion-giant-pulls-out-title-x-program/, accessed April 10, 2020.

[17] "Abortion Giant Pulls Out of Title X Program," *Decision*, August 20, 2019, https://decisionmagazine.com/abortion-giant-pulls-out-title-x-program/, accessed April 10, 2020.

[18] "Proclamation on National Sanctity of Human Life Day, 2020," *WhiteHouse.Gov*, January 21, 2020, https://www.whitehouse.gov/presidential-actions/proclamation-national-sanctity-human-life-day-2020/, accessed April 10, 2020.

[19] Amanda Prestigiacomo, "These 8 States Allow Abortion Up To The Moment Of Birth," *The Daily Wire*, January 30, 2019, https://www.dailywire.com/news/these-8-states-allow-abortion-moment-birth-amanda-prestigiacomo, accessed April 10, 2020.

Chapter 13

[1] "H.R.5 - Equality Act: 116th Congress (2019-2020)," Congress.Gov, https://www.congress.gov/bill/116th-congress/house-bill/5, accessed April 10, 2020.

[2] Jonathan Cahn, "A Most Dangerous Sword," *Hope of the World*, February 1, 2020, http://www.hopeoftheworld.org/Sapphires/index.php?op=single&id=2748&title=a-most-dangerous-sword, accessed April 10, 2020.

[3] "The Biden Plan To Advance LGBTQ+ Equality In America And Around The World," JoeBiden.com, https://joebiden.com/lgbtq/, accessed April 10, 2020.

[4] "Issues: Fight for LGBTQ+ Equality," BernieSanders.com, https://berniesanders.com/issues/lgbtq-equality/, accessed April 10, 2020.

[5] Chris Johnson, "EXCLUSIVE: Trump comes out against Equality Act," *Washington Blade*, May 13, 2019, https://www.washingtonblade.com/2019/05/13/exclusive-trump-comes-out-against-equality-act/, accessed April 10, 2020.

[6] "Final Vote Results for Roll Call 217," Clerk.House.Gov, http://clerk.house.gov/evs/2019/roll217.xml#NV, accessed April 10, 2020. HR5 Equality Act vote on May 17, 2019.

Chapter 14

[1] "How Pot Affects Your Mind and Body," WebMD, https://www.webmd.com/mental-health/addiction/marijuana-use-and-its-effects#1, accessed April 10, 2020.

[2] "Issues: Legalizing Marijuana," BernieSanders.com, https://berniesanders.com/issues/legalizing-marijuana/, accessed April 10, 2020. "S.597 - Marijuana Justice Act of 2019: 116th Congress (2019-2020)," Congress.Gov, https://www.congress.gov/bill/116th-congress/senate-bill/597, accessed April 10, 2020.

[3] "Justice," JoeBiden.com, https://joebiden.com/justice/, accessed April 10, 2020.

[4] Sean Williams, "Donald Trump and Marijuana: Everything You Need to Know," *The Motley Fool*, February 16, 2020, https://www.fool.com/investing/2020/02/16/donald-trump-and-marijuana-everything-you-need-to.aspx, accessed April 10, 2020.

[5] Mona Zhang, "Marijuana legalization may hit 40 states. Now what?," *Politico*, January 20, 2020, https://www.politico.com/news/2020/01/20/marijuana-legalization-federal-laws-100688, accessed April 10, 2020.

[6] Ethan Wolff-Mann, "Coronavirus could accelerate US cannabis legalization," *Yahoo Finance*, March 26, 2020, https://finance.yahoo.com/news/coronavirus-could-accelerate-us-cannabis-legalization-153011559.html, accessed April 10, 2020.

[7] Andrew Daniller, "Two-thirds of Americans support marijuana legalization," *Pew Research Center*, November 14, 2019, https://www.pewresearch.org/fact-tank/2019/11/14/americans-support-marijuana-legalization/, accessed April 9, 2020.

Chapter 15

1 "Green Party Platform: Approved by Green National Committee, August 2016," *Green Party*, August 2016, https://www.gp.org/platform, accessed April 10, 2020.
2 "Libertarian Party Platform: As adopted by convention, July 2018," *Libertarian Party*, July 2018, https://www.lp.org/platform/, accessed April 10, 2020.
3 "The Biden Plan To End Our Gun Violence Epidemic," JoeBiden.com, https://joebiden.com/gunsafety/, accessed April 10, 2020.
"Issues: Gun Safety," BernieSanders.com, https://berniesanders.com/issues/gun-safety/, accessed April 10, 2020.
4 "Remarks by President Trump at the National Rifle Association Leadership Forum," *WhiteHouse.Gov*, April 28, 2017, https://www.whitehouse.gov/briefings-statements/remarks-president-trump-national-rifle-association-leadership-forum/, accessed April 10, 2020.
5 David Smith, "Trump withdraws from UN arms treaty as NRA crowd cheers in delight," *The Guardian*, April 26, 2019, https://www.theguardian.com/us-news/2019/apr/26/trump-nra-united-nations-arms-treaty-gun-control, accessed April 10, 2020.
6 "President Donald J. Trump is Taking Immediate Actions to Secure Our Schools," *WhiteHouse.Gov*, March 12, 2018, https://www.whitehouse.gov/briefings-statements/president-donald-j-trump-taking-immediate-actions-secure-schools/, accessed April 10, 2020.
7 "Remarks by President Trump at the NRA-ILA Leadership Forum," *WhiteHouse.Gov*, April 26, 2019, https://www.whitehouse.gov/briefings-statements/remarks-president-trump-nra-ila-leadership-forum-indianapolis/, accessed April 10, 2020.

Chapter 16

1 Tim LaHaye, *Prophecy Study Bible*, King James Version, (AMG Publishers, 2000), 1.
2 William Koenig, *Eye To Eye: Facing The Consequences Of Dividing Israel*, (McLean, VA: Christian Publishers, 2017), 8.
3 Michael Beswetherick, "Israel," *The New York Times*, https://www.nytimes.com/interactive/2020/us/politics/2020-democrats-israel-foreign-policy.html, accessed April 10, 2020.
4 Bernie Sanders, "How to Fight Antisemitism," *Jewish Currents*, November 11, 2019, https://jewishcurrents.org/how-to-fight-antisemitism/, accessed April 10, 2020.
5 JTA, "Where Bernie Sanders stands on issues that matter to Jewish voters in 2020," *The Times of Israel*, December 20, 2019, https://www.timesofisrael.com/where-bernie-sanders-stands-on-issues-that-matter-to-jewish-voters-in-2020/, accessed April 10, 2020.
6 Stoyan Zaimov, "Bernie Sanders Says He's Not an Atheist, Believes in God in His Own Way," *The Christian Post*, January 28, 2016, https://www.christianpost.com/news/bernie-sanders-atheist-believes-god.html, accessed April 10, 2020.
7 Daniel Burke, "The Book of Bernie: Inside Sanders' unorthodox faith," *CNN*, April 15, 2016, https://www.cnn.com/2016/04/14/politics/bernie-sanders-religion/index.html, accessed April 10, 2020.
8 "Trade & Foreign Policy: President Donald J. Trump Achievements," PromisesKept.Com, https://www.promiseskept.com/achievement/overview/foreign-policy/, accessed April 10, 2020.
9 "At Hanukkah party, Trump signs controversial executive order on anti-Semitism," *CUFI*, https://www.cufi.org/at-hanukkah-party-trump-signs-controversial-executive-order-on-anti-semitism/, accessed April 10, 2020.

[10] "Peace to Prosperity: A Vision to Improve the Lives of the Palestinian and Israeli People," *WhiteHouse.Gov*, January 2020, https://www.whitehouse.gov/wp-content/uploads/2020/01/Peace-to-Prosperity-0120.pdf, accessed April 10, 2020.

Chapter 17
[1] "Green Party Platform: Approved by Green National Committee, August 2016," *Green Party*, August 2016, https://www.gp.org/platform, accessed April 10, 2020.
[2] "Green Party Platform: Approved by Green National Committee, August 2016," *Green Party*, August 2016, https://www.gp.org/platform, accessed April 10, 2020.
[3] "Issues: The Green New Deal," BernieSanders.com, https://berniesanders.com/issues/green-new-deal/, accessed April 10, 2020.
[4] "Climate," JoeBiden.com, https://joebiden.com/climate/, accessed April 10, 2020.
[5] "Green Party Platform: Approved by Green National Committee, August 2016," Green Party, August 2016, https://www.gp.org/platform, accessed April 10, 2020.
[6] David Roberts, "The Green New Deal, explained," *Vox*, March 30, 2019, https://www.vox.com/energy-and-environment/2018/12/21/18144138/green-new-deal-alexandria-ocasio-cortez, accessed April 10, 2020.
David Harsanyi, "The 10 Most Insane Requirements Of The Green New Deal," *The Federalist*, February 7, 2019, https://thefederalist.com/2019/02/07/ten-most-insane-requirements-green-new-deal/, accessed April 10, 2020.
"Green Party Platform: Approved by Green National Committee, August 2016," *Green Party*, August 2016, https://www.gp.org/platform, accessed April 10, 2020.
[7] "Statement by President Trump on the Paris Climate Accord," *WhiteHouse.Gov*, June 1, 2017, https://www.whitehouse.gov/briefings-statements/statement-president-trump-paris-climate-accord/, accessed April 10, 2020.
[8] "Libertarian Party Platform: As adopted by convention, July 2018," *Libertarian Party*, July 2018, https://www.lp.org/platform/, accessed April 10, 2020.
[9] "Energy & Environment: President Donald J. Trump Achievements," PromisesKept.Com, https://www.promiseskept.com/achievement/overview/energy-and-environment/, accessed April 10, 2020.
[10] "President Donald J. Trump Is Ending the War on American Energy and Delivering a New Era of Energy Dominance," *WhiteHouse.Gov*, October 23, 2019, https://www.whitehouse.gov/briefings-statements/president-donald-j-trump-ending-war-american-energy-delivering-new-era-energy-dominance/, accessed April 10, 2020.
"Trump Just Achieved What Every President Since Nixon Had Promised: Energy Independence," *Investor's Business Daily*, December 7, 2018, https://www.investors.com/politics/editorials/energy-independence-trump/, accessed April 10, 2020.

Chapter 18
[1] "Giving USA 2019: Americans gave $427.71 billion to charity in 2018 amid complex year for charitable giving," *Giving USA*, June 18, 2019, https://givingusa.org/giving-usa-2019-americans-gave-427-71-billion-to-charity-in-2018-amid-complex-year-for-charitable-giving/, accessed April 10, 2020.
[2] Greg Rosalsky, "Charitable Giving Is Down. It Might Be Time To Reform The Charitable Deduction.," *NPR*, November 12, 2019, https://www.npr.org/sections/money/2019/11/12/778326512/charitable-giving-is-down-it-might-be-time-to-reform-the-charitable-deduction, accessed April 10, 2020.
[3] "2016 Democratic Party Platform," *Democratic Party*, July 2016, https://democrats.org/where-we-stand/party-platform/, accessed April 10, 2020.

4 "Green Party Platform: Approved by Green National Committee, August 2016," *Green Party*, August 2016, https://www.gp.org/platform, accessed April 10, 2020.

5 "Libertarian Party Platform: As adopted by convention, July 2018," *Libertarian Party*, July 2018, https://www.lp.org/platform/, accessed April 10, 2020.

6 "Republican Platform 2016," *Republican Party*, July 2016, https://www.gop.com/platform/, accessed April 10, 2020.

Chapter 19

1 Karl Marx and Frederick Engels, "Manifesto of the Communist Party," February 1848, https://www.marxists.org/archive/marx/works/download/pdf/Manifesto.pdf, accessed April 10, 2020.

2 Karl Marx and Frederick Engels, "Manifesto of the Communist Party," February 1848, https://www.marxists.org/archive/marx/works/download/pdf/Manifesto.pdf, accessed April 10, 2020. Page 26-27.

3 "Communist State," Wikipedia.org, https://en.wikipedia.org/wiki/Communist_state, accessed April 10, 2020.

4 Karl Marx and Frederick Engels, "Manifesto of the Communist Party," February 1848, https://www.marxists.org/archive/marx/works/download/pdf/Manifesto.pdf, accessed April 10, 2020.

5 "Antifaschistische Aktion," Wikipedia.org, https://en.wikipedia.org/wiki/Antifaschistische_Aktion, accessed April 10, 2020.

6 Niall McCarthy, "The Countries With The Most Critical Care Beds Per Capita," *Forbes*, March 12, 2020, https://www.forbes.com/sites/niallmccarthy/2020/03/12/the-countries-with-the-most-critical-care-beds-per-capita-infographic/#367b12507f86, accessed April 10, 2020.

7 Casey Leins, "These States Require Schools to Teach LGBT History," *U.S. News & World Report*, August 14, 2019, https://www.usnews.com/news/best-states/articles/2019-08-14/states-that-require-schools-to-teach-lgbt-history, accessed April 10, 2020.

8 Michael Foust, "'Drag Queen Story Hour' Moves into Public Schools: 'The 1st Graders Loved It'," *Christian Headlines*, January 28, 2020, https://www.christianheadlines.com/contributors/michael-foust/drag-queen-story-hour-moves-into-public-schools-the-1st-graders-loved-it.html, accessed April 10, 2020.

9 Campus Reform, "Students Support Socialism... Until It's Applied To Their GPA," March 29, 2019, Video, https://www.youtube.com/watch?v=yCPcM8GlptM.

10 "Libertarian Party Platform: As adopted by convention, July 2018," *Libertarian Party*, July 2018, https://www.lp.org/platform/, accessed April 10, 2020.

11 "Issues: Bernie Sanders on the issues," BernieSanders.com, https://berniesanders.com/issues/, accessed April 10, 2020.

12 "Joe's Vision for America," JoeBiden.com, https://joebiden.com/joes-vision/, accessed April 10, 2020.

13 "American Leadership," JoeBiden.com, https://joebiden.com/americanleadership/, accessed April 10, 2020.

14 "President Donald J. Trump Has Delivered Record Breaking Results For The American People In His First Three Years In Office," *WhiteHouse.Gov*, December 31, 2019, https://www.whitehouse.gov/briefings-statements/president-donald-j-trump-delivered-record-breaking-results-american-people-first-three-years-office/, accessed April 10, 2020.
"President Donald J. Trump Accomplishments," PromisesKept.Com, https://www.promiseskept.com, accessed April 10, 2020.

[15] "President Donald J. Trump Is Providing Economic Relief to American Workers, Families, and Businesses Impacted by the Coronavirus," *WhiteHouse.Gov*, March 27, 2020, https://www.whitehouse.gov/briefings-statements/president-donald-j-trump-providing-economic-relief-american-workers-families-businesses-impacted-coronavirus/, accessed April 10, 2020.

[16] "Cloward–Piven strategy," Wikipedia.org, https://en.wikipedia.org/wiki/Cloward%E2%80%93Piven_strategy, accessed April 10, 2020.

[17] Geoffrey Grider, "Socialized Medicine Board In Italy Will Mandate That All Italian Citizens Over The Age Of 80 Suffering From The Covid-19 Coronavirus Will Be 'Left To Die'," *Now The End Begins*, March 16, 2020, https://www.nowtheendbegins.com/coronavirus-covid-19-victims-italy-over-age-80-will-be-left-to-die-as-socialized-medicine-board-decrees/, accessed April 10, 2020.

[18] Tyler Durden, "For The First Time Ever, A Majority Of The World's Population Is Dissatisfied With Democracy," *Zero Hedge*, February 2, 2020, https://www.zerohedge.com/markets/first-time-ever-majority-worlds-population-dissatisfied-democracy, accessed April 10, 2020.

[19] John F. Kennedy, "Transcript of President John F. Kennedy's Inaugural Address (1961)," *U.S. National Archives & Records Administration*, 1961, https://www.ourdocuments.gov/doc.php?flash=false&doc=91&page=transcript, accessed April 10, 2020.

Chapter 20

[1] "Remarks by Vice President Pence at the 68th Annual National Prayer Breakfast," *WhiteHouse.Gov*, February 6, 2020, https://www.whitehouse.gov/briefings-statements/remarks-vice-president-pence-68th-annual-national-prayer-breakfast/, accessed April 10, 2020.

[2] Caleb Parke, "Democratic Party embraces nonreligious voters, criticizes 'religious liberty' in new resolution," *Fox News*, August 29, 2019, https://www.foxnews.com/politics/democratic-party-nonreligious-voters, accessed April 10, 2020.

[3] Zach Montellaro, "What's the deal with a contested convention, anyway?," *Politico*, March 1, 2020, https://www.politico.com/news/2020/03/01/contested-democratic-convention-rules-118377, accessed April 11, 2020.

[4] Steven Nelson, "Democrats want to drop Joe Biden for Andrew Cuomo, poll finds," *New York Post*, April 10, 2020, https://nypost.com/2020/04/10/democrats-want-to-drop-joe-biden-for-andrew-cuomo-poll-finds/, accessed April 11, 2020.

[5] David Krayden, "Tucker Carlson: 'Don't Bet Against Michelle Obama' Running For President," *Daily Caller*, November 26, 2019, https://dailycaller.com/2019/11/26/tucker-carlson-michelle-obama-president/, accessed April 11, 2020.

Chapter 21

[1] "What Is Propaganda?," United States Holocaust Memorial Museum, https://www.ushmm.org/propaganda/resources/, accessed April 10, 2020.

[2] Mark R. Levin, *Unfreedom Of The Press*, (New York, NY: Threshold Editions, 2019).

[3] "List Of Fallacies," Wikipedia.org, https://en.wikipedia.org/wiki/List_of_fallacies, accessed April 10, 2020.

"Propaganda Techniques," Wikipedia.org, https://en.wikipedia.org/wiki/Propaganda_techniques, accessed April 10, 2020.

[4] "Media Conglomerate," Wikipedia.org, https://en.wikipedia.org/wiki/Media_conglomerate, accessed April 10, 2020.

[5] Mark R. Levin, *Unfreedom Of The Press*, (New York, NY: Threshold Editions, 2019), 140.
[6] "Green Party Platform: Approved by Green National Committee, August 2016," *Green Party*, August 2016, https://www.gp.org/platform, accessed April 10, 2020.
[7] "Senate Hearing 115-93: Nomination Of Russel T. Vought, Of Virginia, To Be Deputy Director Of The Office Of Management And Budget," Congress.Gov, https://www.congress.gov/115/chrg/CHRG-115shrg26919/CHRG-115shrg26919.htm, accessed April 10, 2020.
[8] "Assessing Guilt: Nazi Crimes and Postwar Trials," United States Holocaust Memorial Museum, https://www.ushmm.org/propaganda/themes/assessing-guilt/, accessed April 10, 2020.

Chapter 22
[1] Sam Dorman, "Pet Buttigieg faces criticism for calling Jesus a refugee," *Fox News*, December 26, 2019, https://www.foxnews.com/politics/pete-buttigieg-backlash-refugee-jesus, accessed April 10, 2020.

Chapter 25
[1] "Proclamation on the National Day of Prayer for all Americans Affected by the Coronavirus Pandemic and for our National Response Efforts," *WhiteHouse.Gov*, March 14, 2020, https://www.whitehouse.gov/presidential-actions/proclamation-national-day-prayer-americans-affected-coronavirus-pandemic-national-response-efforts/, accessed April 10, 2020.
[2] "Ronald Reagan - Our Noble Vision: An Opportunity For All," *The Patriot Post*, March 2, 1984, https://patriotpost.us/pages/444-ronald-reagan-our-noble-vision-an-opportunity-for-all, accessed April 10, 2020.

CPSIA information can be obtained
at www.ICGtesting.com
Printed in the USA
LVHW010211160920
666141LV00016B/1342

9 781947 328402